MW00386911

EXPERIENCE

THE MYSTERY OF

TAROT

About the Author

Katalin Jett Koda (goes by Jett) is a visionary author, tarot reader, Reiki Master teacher, energy healer, and queer mystic. She has been deeply intimate with the natural, non-human, and liminal worlds since she was a child. After a series of health issues, she developed clairvoyant abilities that allow her to see energy fields, guides, and helper spirits. For more than two decades, Jett has studied and worked with the arts of healing, divination, tarot, and ceremony. She has authored several books including *Sacred Path of Reiki*, *Fire of the Goddess: Nine Paths to Ignite the Sacred Feminine*, and *Slade*, a visionary young adult fiction novel.

She has had the fortuitous blessing of receiving wisdom teachings from indigenous elders and lineage masters who hold traditions connected to the lands of India, Tibet, Hawai'i, Mexico, and Costa Rica. While not of these lands, she holds these practices in a sacred and honored way that supports her continued work with the guides and spirits. In July of 2018, Jett was contacted by an Arcturian emissary who gave her access to the wisdom of the Arcturian collective, a group of inter-dimensional star beings who wish to benefit the earth. She continues to receive guidance and inspiration from her ancestors, living teachers, and the Arcturian guides who support her work with clients and students. Find her at jettkoda.com and thetarotmystery.com.

EXPERIENCE
THE MYSTERY OF
TAROT

CEREMONIES, SPREADS, AND MEDITATIONS TO
DEEPEN YOUR CONNECTION TO THE CARDS

KATALIN JETT KODA

Llewellyn Publications
Woodbury, Minnesota

FIRST EDITION
First Printing, 2020

Book design by Samantha Peterson
Cover design by Kevin R. Brown
Editing by Laura Kurtz
Interior art by Llewellyn Art Department

Llewellyn Publications is a registered trademark of Llewellyn Worldwide Ltd.

Library of Congress Cataloging-in-Publication Data
Names: Koda, Katalin, author.
Title: Experience the mystery of tarot : ceremonies, spreads, and
     meditations to deepen your connection to the cards / Katalin Jett Koda.
Description: First edition. | Woodbury, Minnesota : Llewellyn Publications,
     [2020] | Summary: "Examines tarot cards one by one, includes exercises
     and ceremonies to further understand the cards. Includes spreads/layouts
     for reading"—Provided by publisher.
Identifiers: LCCN 2020036751 (print) | LCCN 2020036752 (ebook) | ISBN
     9780738750897 (paperback) | ISBN 9780738755342 (ebook)
Subjects: LCSH: Tarot.
Classification: LCC BF1879.T2 K64 2020 (print) | LCC BF1879.T2 (ebook) |
     DDC 133.3/2424—dc23
LC record available at https://lccn.loc.gov/2020036751
LC ebook record available at https://lccn.loc.gov/2020036752

Llewellyn Worldwide Ltd. does not participate in, endorse, or have any authority or responsibility concerning private business transactions between our authors and the public.

All mail addressed to the author is forwarded but the publisher cannot, unless specifically instructed by the author, give out an address or phone number.

Any internet references contained in this work are current at publication time, but the publisher cannot guarantee that a specific location will continue to be maintained. Please refer to the publisher's website for links to authors' websites and other sources.

Llewellyn Publications
A Division of Llewellyn Worldwide Ltd.
2143 Woodale Drive
Woodbury, MN 55125-2989
www.llewellyn.com

Printed in the United States of America

Other Books by Katalin Jett Koda

Fire of the Goddess: Nine Paths to Ignite the Sacred Feminine (Llewellyn, 2011)

Sacred Path of Reiki: Healing as a Spiritual Discipline (Llewellyn, 2008)

Slade and the Seventh Nuance (Katalin Books, 2011)

Forthcoming Books by Katalin Jett Koda

Conversations with the Arcturians

Passing On: A Poetry Book

This book is dedicated to:
my dad who gave me my first set of cards,
my mom for her support,
Arianna, my first teacher of tarot,
Desiree, my soul star friend in tarot mysteries,
& for my daughter, Yoko Mojave

CONTENTS

ACKNOWLEDGMENTS

This book is a labor of love that took many years, hundreds of readings, and countless lived ceremonies to capture and share the essential qualities of an embodied, ceremonial tarot. Without its predecessors, we would not have access to such a profound way of working our lives. I honor the long lineage of tarot and particularly those who carried the mystery of the tarot forward: Aleister Crowley, Lady Frieda Harris, Pamela Colman Smith, Arthur Waite, and the Order of the Golden Dawn for releasing these important esoteric truths and popularizing them as an essential guide for so many today.

I am profoundly grateful to my very first tarot teachers, Arianna and Rowan Wilson, who laid the groundwork for reading the cards, my ceremonial work, and instilling in me my connection to the earth as a living being. I am eternally grateful for my beloved friend and longtime spiritual sister, Desiree Mwalimu, for the constant creative practice and deep dive into the beauty and wisdom of the tarot. My study of the tarot was deepened by the support and intellectual grace of Mike Bailey which benefitted me enormously and brought me to one of the decks I still use today, Crowley's Thoth Tarot. The ceremonial play and reflective process of the tarot as a journey was undeniably enhanced by my artistic connections with Amber Decelle and Mika Kiburz.

I am humbled to have teachers who have taught me about the art of cultivating a true practice, offering ancient ways to connect with land and spirit, teaching me the value of discipline, and the respect for ceremony in my life development. With a heartfelt bow, I honor Kahuna Ali'i Kumu Ehulani Stephany, H.E. Tai Situ Rinpoche, and H.H. Ogyen Trinley Dorje, the 17th Gyalwang Karmapa, for their gracious gifts. I also wish to thank Leon French, Jill Walton, Samantha Sinclair, Samantha Black, Arianna Terry, Brooke Dabalos,

Skylyn Booth, and Ari Powers for your support and revelatory tarot insights along the way. I am thankful to the owners and staff at New Renaissance, Psychic Sister, and the Wild Unknown for believing in my gifts and providing a space to offer readings. To my editors at Llewellyn, thank you for your patience and clear feedback to bring this book into fruition.

And most importantly, to my beloved family, friends, and clients, and anyone who has ever received a reading from me, I am endlessly grateful for your presence, for showing up, revealing your most intimate and vulnerable selves, and allowing me to peer into your soul with the use of the cards. Without you, a tarot reader is nothing but a lens without a view. My own spiritual growth has been served immeasurably by the use of cards, the living system of tarot; it is my sincere wish that whomever reads this book may receive benefit, insight, and growth on this wonderful, enchanting, and mysterious path.

PREFACE

Experience the Mystery of Tarot evolved from my experience of more than two decades reading tarot and practicing ritual and ceremony. When I was twenty years old, after surviving cancer, I turned to esoteric knowledge to explore alternative energy, healing practices, and mythic arts. I was fortunate to spend a year in deep study of Wicca and tarot with two Pagan teachers, both high priestesses of their coven. Around that time I received my first deck of cards, the Medicine Cards, which introduced me to the method of divination using cards. Soon after, from my father I received my first tarot deck, the Waite-Smith deck. Later, I was gifted the Aleister Crowley Thoth deck and have used that for the last fifteen years, along with several other decks, including The Wild Unknown, The Secret Dakini Oracle, Mana Cards, and the Numinous Tarot. For many years, I mainly read for myself, friends and family and occasionally read for money while traveling throughout India and Asia.

Following my training in earth-based spirituality, my passion for ceremony was fueled by extensive study with impeccable masters of Tibetan Buddhist and Yogic lineages. I lived in India for seven years immersed in a land of ceremonial activity, and six years on the Big Island of Hawai'i where I met my Hawaiian *Kumu* (teacher) who is also a *Kahuna Ali'i* (Master High Priestess). With the opportunity to receive such powerful teachings in relation to my work on earth alongside my trusty cards, I cross-referenced the wisdom of the tarot with the embodiment of ceremony. As I continued to learn about the arts of creating ceremony with the natural world around me, I wove these two arts together as a method for how to embody and use the tarot as a soulful and wholehearted practice. As my work developed, with the help of my guides and helpers, I found myself suggesting ways for my clients to not only assess the situation at hand as presented by the cards, but how to work with it in a way that could help them perhaps let go and dissolve or simply accept difficult situations, come to terms with changes happening on their path, and embrace more joy and love in their lives. This work empowers readers and students of tarot to become more embodied in their earth journey using the mystery of tarot as a guide along the way.

INTRODUCTION

Often called a mirror of the soul, the tarot cards provide a reflective way to look deeper into the issues and problems that we struggle with in life. Tarot cards use symbolism and archetypes to illuminate the human journey as well as color, numerology, and the elements of fire, water, air, and earth. At times, answers to our questions are very specific; other times they indicate a more general approach to an issue. This may rely on the specificity of the question, the trust of the person receiving the reading, and the ability of the reader. Although many people associate being psychic or gifted with tarot reading, I have found that with careful study of the cards, anyone can learn to use the oracle to effectively guide oneself and others.

Similar to dreams or intuition, the tarot works on our subconscious to present insights and awareness about certain aspects of our life that we may be overlooking. For example, I have found that although someone asks a question about his or her career, the cards may show a response to a relationship issue. Finding the interconnection between these different parts of our life is crucial to better understanding our soul's growth and development. We may tend to compartmentalize different parts of our life; however, the reality is that each aspect of our life is connected and dependent to each other.

Tarot helps us to see what is going on below the surface with our relationships and love, money, career, health issues, and spiritual questions. This guidebook explores a fresh perspective on each of the cards and their meanings along with many effective ways to work with each card including exercises, visualizations, and ceremony to help you embody the dynamics of each of the cards. Focusing on the essence of the card using these tools will connect you to the meaning and provide personal insights and growth. You will be able to see more clearly the patterns in your life and make changes as needed.

This work views the tarot as a form of mythic story, a collective dream that appears on our life's journey to teach us about the nature of the world and the universe we inhabit. When we recognize that life is unfolding as our own personal myth, we create a lens that allows us to step back from our current issues and view them as a journey that happening not to us but *through* us and for not only us but for the collective. I hold the view that we are each a unique expression of the Universe desiring to experience each and every possible shade of emotion, creative expression, and learning through our relationships, jobs and careers, family, and soul gifts.

The tarot's symbolic nature provides us with a keen tool to mirror our path and point the direction on our personal mythic storyline. Using the tarot in this way—as a helpful guide to certain outcomes—can prepare us for things in our lives.

When we are able to embody both the positive and negative aspects of our lives and make sense of them through myth, ritual, and ceremony, we have more vivid connection to life's phases. This embodiment enables us to have a better grasp on what is coming up in the future, how to better relate to others, and navigate changes both welcomed and unwelcomed.

Using Ceremony

The word "ceremony" comes from the Medieval Latin *ceremonia* and the Latin *caerimonia,* meaning "holiness, sacredness; awe; reverent rite." "Holiness" in its root sense is to make whole and thus when we create ceremony, we are aligning our body, heart, and mind to create a sense of wholeness in our spirit. In ceremony, which in many ways is spiritually embodied art, we touch into the human sense of awe and reverence that arises in connection to our soul journey. The ceremonies in this book are inspired by the tarot, the elements, and my work with the earth. When you work with these, you will naturally color and embody them in your own unique way.

Experience the Mystery of Tarot is the map to bringing your connection to the ancient oracle of tarot into embodied, practical, and celebratory form. Ceremony, which in this book includes exercises and visualizations, is a creative container to put a specific intention into form. When we create a ceremony, which can be as simple as lighting a candle, we are creating a direct link to our soul through symbol, forms, and elements. Ceremony may include visualization, sounds and music, light and color, and flowers and stones that help us to embody our intention as well as naturally connecting us to the earth and all that we are related to. Included in the book is a guideline to creating ceremony in general as well as many different kinds of ceremonial suggestions to bring your own tarot work to life.

By setting an intention and performing a symbolic action that incorporates the sensory elements, we communicate directly to our soul. For example, if we wish to create more clarity in our lives, manifest a car, let go of a negative relationship, or cultivate gratitude, we can create a ceremony to put this intention more powerfully in motion. This kind of soul "technology" has been used by humans since ancient times as way to find, share, and cultivate gratitude for our resources; connect with the unseen; and honor major life transitions. Using the ancient practice of ceremony with the tarot effectively deepens not only our connection to the oracle but to life itself as ways to find, share, and cultivate gratitude for our resources; celebrate the seasons; connect to the elements and the natural world; build a relationship with the unseen; practice divination and honor major life transitions.

We can also use ceremony to minimize negative implications in our life. When we learn through the tarot that something negative is on the horizon, we can take steps to embody and act out this information before it has to manifest fully in our lives. For example, in a reading about the future, if my client receives the Five of Disks or Pentacles, which often indicates a physical loss or theft, I then suggest doing a ceremonial offering. This gives my client the opportunity to embody that loss and become aware of it before something is actually stolen. This embodiment can prevent the outcome of actually losing something, as we are using the cards or oracle to tune directly into energetic consequences. This is taking destiny into our own hands, accepting responsibility, and using the power of ceremony to change our life.

I also acknowledge that I am a white, queer American person with recent ancestral roots from Hungary, Quebec, and New England (occupied lands of Iroquois, Abenaki, and Wabanaki nations). I have had the fortune and privilege to travel extensively and receive teachings from indigenous elders in India, Tibet, and Hawai'i. Although I have received inspirations from these teachers as well as expressed permissions, much of my sharing still comes from my own direct experience with dreams, spirit guides, helpers and ancestors. My Hungarian grandmother has guided much of my intuitive work through dreams and meditations. I have been clairvoyant and oftentimes clairaudient and clairsentient since I was a very small child, possibly due to overcoming illness both as an infant and later as a teenager. For all intents and purposes except for two specific ceremonies, the rest of this work is inspired by my own spiritually creative experiences. These two are the Bowl of Light and Tonglen which come from Hawaiian and Tibetan tradition respectively, both popularized for Western minds and taught to me by impeccable teachers. Any errors that exist are my own, not those of my teachers.

I also wish to note for the reader, that because these ceremonies come through me and my soul view which is often a wide-angle lens of gratitude, joy and love, they often focus on an individualized and personal perspective of creating change in one's life to bring about more harmony, beauty, and clarity. However, these practices and my view does not discount the truth that those with privilege (myself included) may very well be more resourced and supported to do that kind of work. I recognize, as best I can as I continue doing the work, that we humans are also embedded in complicated and nuanced systems of oppression that affects our day-to-day well-being, particularly for those with fewer privileges regarding race, gender, ability, age, sexual orientation, and the like. I recognize that one small ceremony will likely not transform pain into power, so to speak, or resolve complicated trauma that stems not only from personal and familial issues but also the collective and ancestral trauma calling out with such force to be healed in these times. Many of these ceremonies include work with the land and elements; I encourage you to learn the ancestral history of where you live; acknowledge the original peoples of that place; work on understanding of your own ancestral lineage; and approach this work with a sense of reverence, kindness, humility, and the notion that we are guests here on earth for a short time. I strongly believe in the power of ceremony and ritual. Through this work and the use of tarot, I have a sincere wish that folks will see benefit in their lives by using these as well as creating their own that suit them and their practices with magic, their ancestors, and the land.

HOW TO USE THIS BOOK

Because most standard tarot decks are based upon the Waite-Smith and Thoth or Crowley decks, these two decks are the main inspirations for this book. Though there are hundreds of decks, I feel these two provide a clear cross-section of vivid, readable symbolism that can be used to create ceremony with your own use of tarot in your daily life. These decks have been used by millions of people, thereby creating a collective conscious imprint of the images which enable us to access their meaning more readily through intuition.

To work with the cards, I recommend purchasing the Crowley or Waite-Smith deck or one based on these. You may also want to use an alternative oracle to supplement your work and add your own symbolism, myth, and interpretations to your daily tarot study. The card order in this book is presented as major arcana first and then minor arcana—which includes the suit and court cards in the order of penatcles/disks, cups, swords, and wands.

For the sake of direct connection to the cards, I do not focus on contraindications or reversals for the cards. There are plenty of "negative" cards that afford us the opportunity to work through our challenges using meditation and ceremony. For my own personal method of reading, I view reversals as inward expressions of the card or its energy or essence—not necessarily an opposite meaning.

This book is designed to help you work with a particular card for a set amount of time. You may choose to study a different card each day or each week, whatever feels most comfortable. You may also decide to randomly choose a card from your deck each day and then work with the tools for that card, again over the period of a day, a week, or even longer. Because the major arcana are such powerful cards, I recommend taking at least a week to work with the archetypes, symbolism, and different exercises found for each card.

The major arcana are the twenty-two major life forces crafted as a journey or story, following the path, and unfolding of one archetype to the next. Each card includes a discussion on the archetype and ways to work with them, including various exercises following the cycles of seven. When we take the Fool out of the major arcana, we are left with twenty-one cards that naturally divide into three cycles. Each of these cycles contain seven cards and reflect three major aspects of the human condition: the mundane existence of birth, relations, and worldly interactions; the subconscious of dreams, heart desires, soul growth, fears, and initiations; and the superconscious connected to our divine aspects of self, otherworldly, mystical, and spiritual expressions that aid in fulfillment of the soul.

The first seven cards, one (the Magician) through seven (the Chariot), offer foundational ceremonies to lay the groundwork for your connection to the archetypes and working with the journey overall. The second set of seven cards, numbers eight (Justice) through fourteen (Temperance), include various layouts designed to explore interrelatedness of the archetypes and ways to reflect on various types of questions. The last seven cards, numbers fifteen (the Devil) through twenty-one (the World), include an oracle voice visualization. This voice acts as the ceremonial essence and is a meditative guide that communicates directly from the archetype. I recommend reading aloud and recording the oracle voice so that you can play it back and sink deeply into the experience of the oracle. Often you will discover your own personal insights as you do this and new ways to embody and understand each of the archetypes.

After working through the major arcana, the book provides a look at the tarot's numerology and suits. The numbers apply to both arcana but are primarily relevant here to the minors and their progression through a suit. Each suit is composed of an element and explores these through the exercises, visualizations, and ceremonies. Taking time to work through the ceremonies, using what is offered here, and also perhaps creating your own will allow you to embody the essence of each card and form the tarot in your daily life as a living system. The court cards provide a look at the archetypes and personality characteristics in yourself and your relations and how these are connected to the elements and suits of the minor arcana. Each of these combines the elements of the archetype with the elements of the suit to create a unique way of understanding the process of mastery from page/princess to knight/king. I have also included seven ceremonial layouts found in the second set of major arcana cards for cards Justice through Temperance. There are also layouts provided at the end of the book you can use to give readings to yourself and others.

WORKING WITH YOUR CARDS

Approaching the tarot is an art unto itself. Traditionally, a master or teacher gave tarot cards to a student who was deemed ready, and thus the idea was born that one shouldn't buy their own deck; however, as long as you clean, energize, and set your deck with clear intention, there is no issue with buying your own. That said, I do believe receiving a deck is a powerful part of the path as well, and at times have gifted used decks or bought new ones for people to continue their practice.

Used and new decks carry very different energies; I would advise starting with a new deck. However, receiving an older or used deck from a trusted tarot friend or teacher will also carry with it the wisdom and power of working the cards through time. Either way, you will want to clear a new deck by placing the cards with clear quartz crystals or near a bowl of salt water for a few days during the new moon phase. You can also use a cleansing smoke of your preference to set the cards to a neutral energetic place. Use a special cloth or pouch to wrap your cards in: silk, cotton, or other natural fibers are preferable, but any fabric or cloth you feel a connection to will work to hold and contain your cards. When we wrap our cards each time, we create a sacred boundary between the time of opening the cards or giving the reading and storing them for safe keeping.

Once the cards are cleared and the moon is waxing, you can decide on your intention for your deck. Is this for self-practice only? Will you be giving readings to others? Is this a deck you are learning from? Will you have it out for others to randomly pick up in your home? These are important things to consider as everyone who touches your deck will leave an energetic imprint on the cards. Over the years they become carriers of a living history of all who have

9

contacted their deepest desires, secrets, thoughts, wishes, hopes, and dreams. This is not light stuff! My fifteen-year-old Crowley deck is precious to me and has been touched by hundreds and hundreds of people. However, I never allow anyone to randomly touch that deck—it is only for readings in specific moments. Other decks in my home are out for anyone to pull from, and still others are teaching/learning decks. Once you set your intention around your deck, the cards will hear your intention and begin to read through you.

How to Give a Successful Reading

Like anything, giving readings takes practice. It is helpful to have a partner or tarot friend to work with as you begin your study, especially as practicing on yourself can be very challenging. The mind is tricky and will convince us of a variety of outcomes when we are trying to approach the card ourselves about situations that we have strong feelings or attachments towards. For self-practice, I suggest minimizing readings to one or three cards, so you have the opportunity to carefully track the related events and happenings in your life with the cards you pull. Sometimes the cards are very obvious in their meaning, other times they are more subtle and will take more careful examination.

Once you have established the use of your cards, you will want to create a good space in which to practice your readings. You can read anywhere—just be sure to set up an intentional space before you begin. It's helpful to be in a quiet area free of distractions. Use a cloth over a table or on the floor to place your cards on (separate from the cloth used to wrap your cards). Light a candle, burn some incense, and place crystals or shells you work with in addition to perhaps an offering to the ancestors and/or helper spirits such as a small bowl of water, flowers, or a sweet. Take a moment to tune into your breath and yourself and whomever you are reading for before you begin.

The next step in giving a reading either for yourself or someone else is to think about your intention, focus, and question. This may be something you or your client has thought about long before coming to the reading or it may be something spontaneously arising in the moment. Either way, it is helpful to touch into what is up for you or the person you are reading for. Often when I read in shops, people want me to psychically tune in and "read their mind," but I encourage them to share what is on their heart first as a way to direct the reading. I approach tarot readings as more of a conversation or dialogue between me, the client, and spirit who works through the archetypal energies of the cards. I also firmly believe that in our dialogue, through attentive co-created participation, a client will have deeper discoveries that affect their path more profoundly than me simply telling them what I see. Readers are also fallible and human, so concrete predictions can be less than helpful for a client. At every moment, there are limitless possibilities; while the cards will certainly point out the trend of patterns in your current mythic life story, they are not the *only* influence on your life. The cards are more like arrows or sign posts pointing the way; your feet still have to carry you along the path.

When working to find a good question, it is important to only ask one at a time. You can always do more readings or pull further cards for clarification later. Create an open-ended question, one that leaves room for interpretations. Yes or no questions are closed questions and lead to a kind of dead end that doesn't allow for deeper explorations and reflections on the issue at hand. You could use a yes/no question in a pinch for a fast answer, but you would need to determine fairly clearly what a yes card feels like and what a no card feels like, which is not always as simple as it sounds.

Instead, work on creating an open ended question. For example, instead of asking, "Will I ever fall in love?" perhaps ask, "What is blocking me from falling in love?" or "What do I need to know about being open to partnership?" These questions are more inviting into a place of discovery and also orients you toward potential actions. Open-ended questions start with *how*, *why*, or *what*. Avoid asking questions that start with *will* or *when*, as those lead to more limited answers.

Once you have your question, choose the layout that fits. If the question is about relationships, you can use the relationship layout. For more specific issues, the five-card layout is appropriate. For a general, overarching look at big life issues, the ten- or eight-card Celtic cross layout is helpful to see several different aspects of the question. But don't discount the power of a one-card reading! I have often found these to be immensely helpful in pinpointing the essence of the question in a single image.

Every question can be broken down into follow-up questions that explore the different elements of the original question. For example, a question such as, "How can I live in alignment with my soul's purpose?" can be broken down into the following questions:

- What is coming into my conscious awareness about my soul's purpose?

- How can I discover my soul's purpose?

- What is my soul's purpose?

- How am I presently living in alignment with my soul's purpose?

- What inner work do I need to do to be in alignment with my soul's purpose?

- What resources are available to me that will help me live in alignment with my soul's purpose?

- What will bring me closer to my soul's purpose?

- What may stand in the way of me fulfilling my soul's purpose, and how can I overcome it?

After you have formulated your question and decided on the layout, it is time to pull the cards. I encourage clients to shuffle themselves first so they connect with the cards. I then fan the cards out, have them choose the decided number of cards, and lay them out. Having a client choose lets them embody the process of choice. I encourage clients to take their time and feel into the cards, allowing their hand(s) to be drawn to the specific cards.

Lay the cards out and begin reading. First, note how many major arcana appear in the reading and which cycle(s) of seven they fall into. This observation helps anchor the reading into the querent's spiritual unfolding. Next, notice if there is more than one number in the minor arcana. It is often striking for a reading to contain repeated twos or sevens, for example. Use the numerology reference to determine the energy of what is currently happening. Also take note of which suits appear. Are there mostly cups or wands, for example, or did they receive some of each? Several court cards may indicate a client is doing a lot of learning with and through other people. An absence of court cards can signify a more solitary path.

Take note of what jumps out at you from your own cards. If you are in the beginning phases of reading tarot, it may be helpful to take a few notes on the cards. Allow your intuition to guide you and see which colors, symbols, and qualities are obvious. Ask the querent if anything stands out to them. Begin a dialogue around the cards to dig into the journey's mythic aspects. Try your intuition first—notice what arises in response to the card before turning to a resource, book, or the instructional booklet that accompanies cards. This book provides descriptions for each card as well as ceremonies for many of the cards. If you have never done any ceremony, this following section on creating a ceremony may seem overwhelming at first with so many steps. I encourage those new to ceremony and ritual to take time and also note that many of the ceremonies in the book are quite simple and do not necessarily involve all the steps described below. However, as you begin to work with more complex ceremonies and for those who are adept at this work, you may use the steps to help guide your creations. Once you have determined some qualities, pull a specific "Action to Take" or "Ceremonial" card with the intention of finding a way to embody the reading's essence. Using the steps that follow to create ceremony with guidance of the cards in this book, you can take time to create an inspired ceremony that will help you embody the tarot as a living oracle.

Creating a Ceremony

Creating a ceremony or ritual to connect more deeply to the cards is the essence of this book and bridges the ancient oracle of tarot into an embodied, practical, and celebratory form. When we create a ceremony—which can be as simple as lighting a candle—we are creating a direct link to our soul through symbol, forms, and elements. The Fool's journey is used as an inspiration to discover the progression of archetypes found in the major arcana from one card to the next. The elements of the minor arcana are used to create ceremonies and rituals that connect us to the situations moving through our lives.

By setting an intention and performing a symbolic action that incorporates the sensory elements, we communicate directly to our soul. Since ancient times, humans have used this kind of soul technology to find, share, and cultivate gratitude for our resources; connect with the unseen; honor major life transitions; and connect to the ancestors. Using the ancient practice of ceremony with the tarot effectively deepens not only our connection to the oracle but to life itself. The following steps are a guide to creating your own ceremonies that are found here. The ceremonies are purposely kept simple and accessible but can be developed further in your own practice.

1) Set a Clear Intention

First, decide your intention in creating ceremony. Which card are you creating a ceremony with? Which suit and element are you using as a focus to guide your intention? Setting an intention is akin to pointing an arrow directly at an intended target. The clearer our intention and the more focus we can bring to the purpose of our work, the more powerful the result. Some intentions for creating ceremony could include the following:

- balancing and restoring harmony in relationships, environment, self
- healing for self, family, earth
- manifesting a new job or relationship
- clearing or letting go
- honoring and or celebrating seasons or moon cycles, such as full moon gatherings or solstices

2) Planning and Preparation

The next phase of creating a ceremony is to plan out how you want to put your intention into symbolic form. If you are new to creating ceremony, first look to how you might have done something symbolic in the past. Perhaps you cleared away an old lover's things once? Or made a wish, even on an eyelash? In a simplistic form, these are actually ceremonies. You are setting an intention (or wish) and then putting it into form. Use the guidance from the book to create a ceremony or create your own in alignment with the tarot card you are working with. Once you know your intention, you can design a way to put the intention into form or a symbolic gesture. This communicates directly to your soul that you are committed to your intention. For example, if you are doing a clearing ceremony to let go of something, you may want to make a fire and burn a paper list of negative patterns, ideas, or relationships to clear. Once you have designed your ceremony, gather the items needed and place everything on your altar or a clear space until you are ready to perform the ceremony.

3) Create an Altar

The next step for creating ceremony is to make a central sacred space that functions as the place of power for your sacred work. Using the guidance from the Magician chapter, you can create an altar using images, colors, items from nature, and the tarot cards that you are working with to reflect your intention. For example, if you are doing a cleansing ritual, you could use bowls of salt water, healing crystals, and images that portray clearness or cleansing. If you are going to perform the ceremony outside, consider creating an outdoor altar made of natural items. You can choose a specific direction you feel connects to your intention. For example, the west is often associated with sunset, death, and letting go. If you are creating a letting go ceremony, perhaps you could build an altar in the west. If you have the time and wish to create a more elaborate ceremony, you can build altars in each cardinal directions in addition to sky and/or a central altar. The important part is to be creative without thinking it out too much—just allow the ideas to flow through you into form.

4) Make Offerings

The act of making offerings can be performed throughout the entire ceremony at the altar, for each direction, or during a symbolic ceremonial act. For example, you may wish to burn things to clear in a fire and then give offerings as well to honor the process itself. The act of offering is a symbolic gesture of opening your heart and honoring the guidance, help, and nourishment that comes from our helpers, teachers, and the earth.

5) Cleansing and Purification

Once you are ready to perform your ceremony, it is important to cleanse the space and purify yourself in preparation for sacred work. Just before the ceremony begins, purify the space. This can be done using saltwater, smoke, or smudging with cedar or other herbs; sending healing energy to the space and visualizing it as clear healing light; or any other method. Simply make the intention to cleanse or purify the space. Similarly, you will want to purify your body and aura to prepare for entering ceremonial space. Again, you can use any of the methods mentioned here or another way that feels right to you. This step should be done for every person involved in the ceremony before the directions are called in.

6) Ground and Settle In

Once you have prepared and cleansed the space and yourself, it is helpful to take a moment to ground everyone and/or yourself into the space. This can be as simple as focusing on the breath for a moment or perhaps asking participants to silently call in their helper spirits or guides. You may wish to visualize a cord of light extending into the earth as a way to deepen your awareness of the connection to the earth or hold stones as a symbolic and literal way to ground. Grounding brings awareness into the space and sets a natural container that allows for opening up and readying for the imminent ceremony.

7) Create Sacred Space

Call in the directions and create your sacred space. Inspired by the ceremony of the five directions in the Magician card you can create a personal way of calling in the directions. You may want to give offerings to call in the directions and your helpers. Be sure to give physical or sound/musical offerings as you call in the directions and your helpers. You may choose to also invoke a specific energy or deity to assist in your work. For example, you may wish to honor the earth as a witness and support for your work in helping to heal. It is important to give offerings to the local land spirits when doing healing work to rebalance the earth or waters.

8) Perform the Ceremony

After the preparations, purification and grounding, and creation of sacred space have been completed, you are ready to perform the main part of your ceremony. You will want to go as deeply into this process as possible, which means allowing your doubting self to subside for a while so that you can connect with the multidimensional aspects of your being. When we connect in this manner, we help loosen that smaller sense of self and reconnect in with our expansive self, our relations on earth, the unseen helpers, and in the Dreamtime. There are three components of the ceremony itself:

    a. *Raising energy*: After creating the sacred space, you can raise the energy of the directions, elements, and guides you have called in. You can do this using sound makers, song, movement, dance, and making more offerings. You can continue to add offerings to your fire or the earth, whistle, sing, and make movements to further increase the space's magical power. Try to let go and allow your actions to flow through you without overthinking or worrying about what you look like.

    b. *Sacred gesture or action to symbolize the intention*: This is the act of the ceremony that will symbolize your intention. You might burn a letting-go list here, perform an energy healing on yourself or a friend, cry tears into a bowl of water and flowers, or send an intentional prayer for the earth. You may wish to do a specific dance to honor or celebrate or open up to the ecstatic part of your being.

   c. *Sealing the action*: After you have performed your gesture, you will want to seal in the gesture with final moments of silence, a song, or water blessing.

9) Gratitude and Closing the Space

Before you close the space, be sure to give thanks to all the spirits, helpers, people who have attended, the earth, and the land. After giving thanks, you will want to settle down, rest, and then close the space. This is an important step before moving onto celebration, conversation, eating, and so on. This step can also be the moment to bless the food and drink that will be shared.

10) Celebrate!

After ceremony, it is important to feast and connect. Especially if this is a community gathering that involves many people, this is the opportunity to celebrate, make music and dance, or simply connect. This step helps ground people after a ceremony and enjoy one another's company.

THE MAJOR ARCANA JOURNEY

The major arcana is comprised of twenty-two cards that illuminate the powerful forces that move through our lives. When they show up in a typical tarot reading, they indicate complex insights into our personal lives and how to approach love, relationships, career, jobs, and home. On an even deeper level, the major arcana are a set of evolutionary keys that unlocks hidden aspects of our psyche and reveal our life journey as a spiritual unfolding.

Our birth, life, and death journey is our own personal spiritual quest. Mythologist Joseph Campbell offered the archetypal hero's quest as a way to understand our own lives. As the hero embarks upon the sacred quest, they transform through a series of encounters, dissolving the smaller self into the larger Self of power, wisdom, and love. Similarly, the tarot offers a way to view the major arcana as a journey. Sometimes called the Fool's journey, the Fool travels through the major arcana and passes through a series of gateways, initiations, life challenges, and lessons. On this epic journey, we travel through many landscapes, face and defeat our own inner monsters and demons, and discover that ultimately, we hold the secret elixir within. In our lives, we are continuously called to transform from one way of being into another: transitioning from child to teen to adult, getting a job, becoming a parent, working for an organization, starting our own business, being a partner. These roles require different parts of ourselves and growing beyond the small self of a limited, dependent ego.

As we step into each new role, like the caterpillar transforming into a butterfly, we also must shed our old ways. This may require letting go of attachments, relationships, jobs, or homes. We may face very difficult times such as death, illness, divorce, and trauma which often appears in cards such as the Tower or

Death card. This is the human journey—to move through these times and meet our inner, resilient heart, the part of us that remains ever free and unbroken even beyond the worst situations. At each stage we are given the opportunity to let go of one phase of our journey and open the way for what is new to come in.

In ceremony, we have the opportunity to dissolve our smaller self and enter the greater mythic dream through embodied action. We can draw directly from the well of the collective dream and infuse this energy into our own personal life, thus coloring the mundane tasks with a more powerful meaning through the mythic lens. Tarot is an incredible tool to enrich our lives with mythic symbolism, archetypes, and elements. When we see ourselves as the hero of our own epic life, something curious begins to happen. Although in some ways we become closer to the unfolding story of our life's journey, we also gain a kind of neutral perspective, as if we were watching a film or reading a book. We can pull back and see things from a bird's eye perspective; we are characters in our own living story, our homes and towns are the landscapes of our adventure, and challenges are our monsters to slay and puzzles to solve. We can practice this kind of embodiment by looking back at a difficult time in our life and view ourselves from afar. If we use the mythic lens, we can cast each person as an archetypal theme or character. Our grumpy boss may be a wounded prince. Our raging daughter may be a warrior who has not yet received her initiation. Our divorce may be the destruction of a mighty fortress, freeing the queen and her people.

Humans are woven with stories as naturally as trees are with water and air; they are part of us and have been a way to understand, survive, and thrive in our natural world. Dreams, art, story, poetry, myth, and ceremony all offer ways of communication between the heart, mind, body, and soul. Similarly, tarot offers us this mirrorlike role of reflection, neutrality, and disengaged but compassionate guidance. Using the cards as signposts within the adventure story, we discover where we are in the plot and are shown ways to deal with a particular type of "monster" or challenge we are facing.

Like many before me, I view the major arcana card progression as a mythic adventure moving from one phase of development to the next. The Fool, number zero, and the first (or last) card of the major arcana is akin to the hero in many classic tales. In the hero's journey, they set off to defeat a monster, slay the dragon, or find the secret elixir. In all stories, the Fool returns triumphant, which indeed makes them the hero, but not before facing a great many trials and challenges which symbolically represent the inner monsters, dragons, and ultimately discovering the elixir of the true Self. When we view the major arcana as a journey, we develop deeper relationships to the cards. The Emperor is the father figure in the Fool's life; the Tower is the mid-life crisis that comes in the form of divorce or a sudden loss each of us will encounter at some point in our lives; the Star is eternal guidance that shows up in the right moment to assist us along the way. In this way, the tarot cards are universal and apply to all humans on the journey of life.

In the major arcana journey, each phase of life is symbolized by the major arcana archetypes, and each card holds within it all the lessons learned from the previous cards. When major arcana cards show up in a reading, they indicate not only major turning points in life but also a depth of wisdom in the layers of cards and cycles of seven that will be explored further as we enter the major arcana journey. Viewing the unfolding has profound connections not only in each of the major arcana themselves, but also *in relation* to the cards that come before and after it. Understanding the majors as markers on a path, we can then also look at what has come before and what will follow. This perspective will dramatically influence readings and orientation in any work with the cards.

The first card of the major arcana is the Fool, the zero card, who represents the beginning and the end. The path of the cards follows the journey of the Fool through each card as a step on the journey. As each card turns from one into the next, it includes all the previous cards. Working with each card on its own in the next section while also anchoring it in the awareness of the card as a progression helps provide more in-depth readings and insights into your own spiritual journey. Each section includes an explanation of the card, symbolic interpretations of the popular Waite-Smith and Crowley decks, and divinatory meanings.

To deepen your perspective, you may want to dedicate a certain amount of time getting to know just the majors. I recommend purchasing a "teaching" or "working" deck, one that you don't use for readings for self and others but just for your study. It is helpful to lay out the cards in their full story progressively on a wall in your home or on the floor, starting with the Fool and ending with the World card. Perhaps you want to group them loosely in the cycles of seven to begin to understand the movement from one set of cards to the next. Seeing the entire major arcana as a visual journey on your wall helps you to get a sense of the majors as a journey or storyline. I also recommend giving yourself dedicated time for each card, perhaps a week or a month to connect deeply to the archetype. When we set intentional practices around these keys, naturally reflections, teachings, and growing opportunities will appear in our life to assist us in opening to deeper understanding of the card.

Cycles of Seven

The major arcana is naturally divided into cycles of seven. Seven is a powerful number in many alchemical or initiatory systems symbolizing spiritual truth and intelligence. There are seven main chakras in the Yogic system, seven lower stations of the Tree of Life in the Kabbalah, seven days of the week, and so on. Inspired by Rachel Pollack's version of the cycles of seven, we see a distinct path emerge that the Fool takes on their epic quest.

The first seven major arcana, cards one through seven, are the outer influences of our lives and are associated with external consciousness and the outer concerns of society, including the general world of stories, culture, body, parents, teachers, religious doctrine, and imprints on the early parts of our lives. Each major arcana in the first set of seven include foundational ceremonies to direct you on your path.

The very first cards on the journey are the Magician and High Priestess, symbolizing our spiritual entry into the life journey at conception, birth, and the early dreaming stages of infancy and childhood. The Empress and the Emperor symbolize our parents, family, and upbringing. The Hierophant represents moral, religious, and social constructs and the imprints of authority and culture. The Lovers symbolizes our first experiences of love through family, friends, and teachers. How we move through the transition from this set of cards to the next set is represented by the Chariot.

The second set of seven cards represent our search inward, delving into the subconscious and inner workings of our multidimensional selves to include modern depth psychology, self-awareness, awakening, and heart-mind development. In this section, each major arcana card includes a uniquely designed ceremonial layout to investigate the inner aspects of our heart growth in relation to the second set of seven cards. These layouts are reflective of the archetype of that particular card and include ceremonial elements to inspire a more embodied reading.

The first card we meet in this second set is paradoxical—Waite switched the traditional Justice, card number eight, with Strength, card number eleven. We will work with this further in the book, but I personally follow Crowley's restoration to the traditional path in which Justice is number eight—where we meet our inner equilibrium and balance and the transition from outer influences into inner depths of moral being. Next, the Hermit symbolizes the reservoir of our unconscious self and connection to nature. The Wheel of Fortune is the card of destiny and forces of karma, soul contracts, and the appearance of things that we cannot always control. The Strength card indicates our personal power and the appearance of an inward fire that begins to manifest outwardly. The Hanged Man symbolizes a time when things come to a standstill and life is viewed from a completely different perspective. The Death card symbolizes a metaphorical death, representing a deep transformation, the movement from one way of being to a completely new way. Lastly, the Temperance card transitions us into the final set of seven cards bearing the gifts of the inner seeking through the alchemical process of inward initiation, creativity, and mixing of opposites.

The last set of seven cards shows our interrelation with the huge forces at work connected to our superconscious, development of spiritual awareness, and evolution. Here the Fool experiences a confrontation and unity with great forces of life itself. There is a potential for spiritual liberation, and a deeper understanding of the mythical, quantum reality, that is essence-level soul development. On the one hand, we are small human forms seemingly at the whims of nature and culture; on the other, we hold the power to effect great change. This is the part of the quest in which the Fool's ego has gone through a death and transformation and emerges as the larger self in concert with mythos of the collective. This section includes visualizations and oracle visions for each card to connect to the overarching spiritual aspects of the cards. Oracle visions are the voice of the cards themselves offering direct insights into their wisdom.

On the path, the Fool encounters the Devil, who brings up the dark residue remaining not only within ourselves but also as reflected by society. Following this is the Tower, which shakes any foundations in our world that no longer resonate with truth and authenticity. The card that follows, the Star, indicates the clear light after the storm and the presence of spiritual guidance. The Moon reminds us to take notice of relations, connections, or actions that still bear imprints of our old, clinging self before we are warmed by the Sun card which brings about the manifestation of dreams, beauty, and activation. The Judgement card heralds powerful guidance and an almost otherworldly view of the path, a reckoning and appreciation for the long journey that is almost finished. Lastly, the World offers us the potential for bringing all that has transpired to the collective as a final offering ... before the adventure begins again!

The major arcana's path gives us a sense of how you might use them to understand the depths of the Fool's journey. As each card turns from one into the next, it includes all the previous cards. Working with each card on its own in the next section while also anchoring it in the awareness of the card as a progression will help to provide more in-depth readings and insights into your own spiritual journey.

0: THE FOOL

As in many stories and epic myths, the major arcana journey begins with a single traveler—in this case, the Fool. Our hero may be unsure or reluctant to step onto the path...or perhaps they are willing to go, excited about the adventure. Often the Fool is portrayed as somewhat naive and ignorant to what lies ahead. Many stories begin with someone either arriving or departing, which is the mark of a change, a turning in the story, or the beginning of a new adventure.

In the tarot, the Fool is the number zero, the only number that is at both the beginning and the end. The zero symbolizes the potential of all things. This is a state of liberation to be in a place that is beyond the Beyond. And yet, society views the fool in an often negative and condescending light. The fool is a person who acts unwisely or imprudently; a silly person. A foolish person is someone who lacks sense or judgment and instead relies completely on intuition. Fools spend time idly or aimlessly. How do we make sense of folly or foolishness in relation to the Fool card?

Curiously, the Fool is the only major arcana card that appears in a regular deck of playing cards in the form of the classic joker. Historically, the joker or court jester was not only a performer but also held the role of reflecting and commenting on political or social issues. We find that today in the role of comedians and certain clown traditions wherein the performers use the medium of humor, and bizarre and confrontational acts to evoke a response in the audience, present an alternative perspective on social issues, and offer transformation within the experience of the performance itself.

In some indigenous traditions, the clown was considered sacred. They performed a specific role during ceremonies to open people's hearts and ready them to receive the transformative qualities of ceremony. Clowns use the power of humor to help remember humility, vulnerability, and standing in the pure essence of the heart. Similarly, other aspects of the Fool archetype can be found in indigenous stories featuring the Trickster, Heyoka, Coyote, or Raven. These characters trick us out of our ego, surrendering our pride and arrogance. In the spiritual exploration of the tarot in *Wisdom of the Tarot* by Elisabeth Haich, the Fool is situated at the end of the major arcana journey, just before the final card of the World. Instead of appearing at the beginning, here the Fool is the culminating enlightened soul, the one who has worked their way through each trial and tribulation of this life journey as symbolized by the major arcana.

In the classical Rider-Waite-Smith deck, the Fool, a gender neutral figure, is poised on the edge of a cliff. Their face is upturned toward a bright yellow vast sky. They carry very little with them, indicating a life free of burdens and the ability to move unencumbered into the next part of the journey. Their left hand, the hand closest to the heart, is open and holding up a white flower toward the sun, a symbol of truth, beauty, and innocence. In the background loom craggy mountains indicating the potential obstacles and difficulties of the journey. Yet the Fool's face shows no fear or concern. Is this ignorance, naivete, or total trust? Perhaps it is a combination of all three. Nipping at the Fool's heels is a small white dog, symbolizing the instinctual or intuitive nature that accompanies us on our journey through life. This is the aspect of our nature that relies on inner knowing and wise guidance. We can view the dog as a compassionate spirit helper, our unseen guide who accompanies us on the journey even if we are not aware of them.

In the Crowley deck, we see an image of a horned green man, his legs spread like the opening of a jumping jack. The Green Man in ancient Pagan tradition is the wild, earth-loving aspect of the masculine worshipped alongside the Goddess. He symbolizes growth, vital life force, and the quickening of the spring energies. Many symbols adorn the Fool here: grapes represent the fullness of life, the butterfly symbolizes the transformational energy, the tiger is akin to the small dog nipping at the Fool's thigh, reminding us of our own pure instinct and intuition.

At the base of the card is an alligator, a symbol of sexual energy and our lower emotional body or base desires that arise from greed, anger, and ignorance. Through spiritual practices, following the journey of the Fool through the major arcana, there is the potential to transform the emotional qualities of raw desire, aggression, dominance, and victimhood into power, compassionate love, spiritual gifts, and insights. Along the cord of light that loops around the card we see the ancient medical symbol, the caduceus. Historically, the caduceus is related to Hermes (Mercury in Roman mythology) and is a magical symbol that bestows blessings upon travel, commerce, and philanthropy. In esoteric views, this symbol of two snakes indicates a unification of opposites, balance of duality. This symbol is also connected to the two major nadis (yogic nerve pathways) in Ayurveda and the two strands of our DNA that coil around one another, symbolizing the balance and interplay of opposite energies. Anchoring this cord of light along the heart center is the dove, an ancient symbol of grace and the transformation of the heart. Many spiritual practices begin with work to scour away at the energetic crust over the heart center, allowing us to open more fully, become more trusting, and more vulnerable.

Although traditionally written as male, the Fool holds qualities we may associate with femininity, masculinity, and beyond. This figure is not bound to any gender—within the potentiated energy of the Fool is the capacity to transcend gender completely. Our culture tends to hold people to specific, rigid qualities and behaviors starting in childhood, e.g., giving pink, flowery, "feminine" gifts to girls and blue, mechanistic, "masculine" gifts to boys. In the spiritual expressions based on Jung's work, we find a sharp divide between the passive "feminine" and active "masculine." In contrast, Yogic texts associate feminine divinity as active while the sacred masculine is passive. The Fool offers us a chance to explore our own inner qualities and deconstruct our associations with male/female and masculine/feminine. In several ancient myths we find alternative genders, asexual beings, hermaphrodites, and beings with feminine and masculine characteristics. The potentiated energy of going beyond limiting binary structures such as gender is symbolized by the Fool's number, zero. Zero contains everything yet symbolizes nothing. It is both the alpha and the omega, the end which meets the beginning, the ouroboros or snake devouring its own tail.

The arrival of the Fool in a reading indicates you are moving in a new direction. This is the time to trust and open to a new beginning. The word "fool" is connected to folly and foolishness but also to playfulness, joy, openness, and vulnerability. This figure may also indicate an unusual or unlikely solution to a current problem. The Fool, as number zero, is full with infinite possibilities;

there are likely millions of ways to solve a problem you have never thought of. The Fool is pure instinct and leaps in total trust that the wings will appear.

The Fool in the major arcana journey indicates that something new and unlikely is about to enter your life. Perhaps a chance meeting, a series of synchronicities, or more specifically a journey to a new place or new venture on the horizon. The key to embodying this card is to trust your intuition. The Fool reminds us that it is okay to take risks, that we can't know what is coming our way, but it is okay to open our hearts and leap!

> *Essential Qualities:* play, innocence, trust, open heart, wander, wonder, living in the moment, intuition, instinct, vulnerable
>
> *Suggestions:* Take an aimless wander around your neighborhood. Don't choose any destination—just wander. Play! Practice juggling, prance, dance, get into your body and out of the house. Do something foolish, trick your ego out of yourself. Go get a tattoo. Say hello to someone new. Smile at people randomly. Give money to the homeless on the street. Wear a chicken suit to work.

Ceremony: Welcome the Dawn

This simple ceremony inspires us to step onto the next phase of our life's journey. Get up before dawn and go to a place where you can watch the sun rise. Choose a place on a cliff, hill, mountain, or any spot in nature that overlooks a view to inspire the sense of possibility and openness. Once there, close your eyes and ask yourself "Who am I?" with no expectation. Allow answers to rise within. Open your eyes and watch the sun rise over the horizon and witness this majesty with the fresh eyes of innocence and newness. Imagine it is the very first and last sunrise you will ever see in your life. In fact, it is…no sunrise will ever be the same. Make a vow to treasure the entire day as if it were your first and last day on earth. Be open to the miracle. Accept your life fully as it is now, in its full, potentiated state of beauty and trust.

1: THE MAGICIAN

In the major arcana journey, our Fool has now fully stepped onto the transformative path. They have willingly (or perhaps unwillingly) leapt off the cliff into the wild unknown. At this moment on the journey, we often encounter a clear sign of our inner power, our gifts that we came to earth to share. This sign is the Magician card. When the young and unlikely hero of *Star Wars*, Luke Skywalker, first heeds the call to leave his home, he meets Ben Kenobi, or Obi Wan Kenobi. Similarly, in the movie *Black Panther*, T'Challa must begin his journey as king the moment his father dies. He ingests the magical heart-shaped herb and travels to the realm of the ancestors to meet his recently deceased father. Both of these figures meet a symbolic Magician. In our lives, this is a person or event which reminds us all that our power and abilities lie within us. We have everything we need! This seems impossible at times, for we look to the outer world to meet our basic needs, find love, and experience pleasure and happiness.

When we view the Magician from the cycle of seven in the major arcana journey, the Magician is the very beginning of the cycle of consciousness. In this view, the Fool is on the journey and the first set of seven cards is their movement into the outer world, the conscious step onto an external manifestation of the soul's journey. The Magician is the moment we separate from the womb all primordial potential into our own singular being. This is the spark of life, conception, the "a-ha" idea, the start of something new.

The Magician is the number one, the seed. Within the seed is the entire oak tree, a little and wonderful dream. Hold a seed in your hand and think about the magic of that! One tiny seed can become a huge tree that will produce hundreds of seeds that could potentially grow thousands of trees and so on. That one seed holds infinity. Cards number 10 (Wheel of Fortune) through 19 (The Sun) all contain the power and energy of the Magician's intention. When we look back (or forward) at the journey, we can see how the power of intention, the seed, has a dramatic effect on later aspects of our path.

The Magician is very creative, takes initiative, and cultivates the skill of clear speech and precise communication. He may seem unemotional at times and can appear fast, clever, curious, slippery, and slick. Magicians use their efforts and skills to their advantage. In an ultimate sense, there is no morality, no wrong or right, no good or bad, only energy. Yet in the human realm, we operate within agreed upon moral rules and karmic consequences that affect each decision we make. However, when we use the energy of the Magician, we are able to slip past the ordinary and access the clear magical energy that transcends time and space.

The Magician is beautiful, illusory, solitary, and charismatic. He has everything he needs and is in contact with raw power and energy that allow him to draw what he needs directly to himself. The Magician is connected to enchantments and magic. The power of magic is rooted in both our intention and careful craft of the words. The word "enchantment" is derived from the Latin *incantare*, the root of which is of *cantare*, "to sing." The Magician is the essence or seed reminder of our own personal soul song. To sing or call out through chanting is as old as human history itself and many of us have forgotten the power of sound moving through us.

The Magician reminds us to be clear in our words and intentions. What are we crafting with our words? What are we committing to out loud? Track your words and take note of when you are speaking well or ill of others, when you are putting yourself down or blocking your way forward with your own statements, or when you are putting out something positive and powerful through word or sound.

In the Waite-Smith deck, the Magician stands behind an altar of magic. On it are four symbols that correspond to the four suits, or minor arcana of the tarot deck. We see carefully laid out: the pentacle, the cup, the sword, and the wand. Each represents four aspects of the human expression: body, emotion, mind, and spirit; and each is associated with the four elements: earth, water, air, and fire. One of the Magician's hands is lifted high into the air, holding the wand, receiving the power; the other is pointed down to the earth, grounding it in. The wand is a magical tool used for divination, manifestation, destruction, and directing one's will. Above his head is the infinity symbol, reminding us of our limitless potential.

In the Crowley deck, the Magician appears to be rising up into the air, transcending form and working directly with the energies that surround him. He is nude, showing his effortless power, and is surrounded by the tools of the minor arcana, able to access them as needed. Even his wand floats above him signifying his masterful skill that is well grounded in non-attachment or clinging. Above his head are two entwined serpents, symbolic of eternity, potential, and creative transformation.

When the Magician appears in a reading, it symbolizes a new beginning, setting intentions, and becoming disciplined in our work using our tools. Potentials come into focus and there is a clear crystallization of the vision and what is to be done. The Magician card appears as a bid for power in our lives. This may be a job offer, new relationship, creative vision, or a new concept. It is up to us to grasp this wand and begin to use it to increase our own potential and power and wield the magic, or not. We always have a choice.

The Magician may also indicate the arrival of a mercurial kind of person or energy in our lives, someone or something distinctly connected to communication, magic, creation, and potential. We may feel a strong attraction or pull toward this person and can recognize it as the start of a brilliant new energetic stream within our soul's evolution. The Fool then carries the brilliant seed of the Magician, planting it into the dark and mysterious soils of the High Priestess. There the seed is nourished by the mystery of intuition and dreaming, preparing the magical soul seed for growth and spiritual evolution.

Essential Qualities: magic, intention, incantation, spell, tools, value, seed, one, elemental, intuition, beginning, spark

Suggestions: Plant a seed or contemplate a seed. Write down an intention for the new year. Meditate on your intentions for the next several days. Connect to the elements of earth, water, air, and fire. Create an altar! Place symbols of the elements there along with images or symbols of what you are calling into your life. Cook something up from scratch! Find magic in the everyday beauty of the world.

Ceremony: Establishing the Five Directions

This ceremony is a beautiful way to create a center for yourself wherever you go in the world. Most earth-based cultures have certain associations and spiritual connections to the four directions that often relate to seasons, elements, animals, spirit guides, geographical features, and so on. This way of relating to the earth and oneself is central to cosmology and orients them to the earth in profound ways. Many of us have lost this connection and can reclaim it in a simple way by connecting with our sense of the four directions.

This practice is done outside on a lawn, meadow, or field where you can walk ten steps in each direction. For this practice, disregard other associations you already have with the four directions and ask the land of the place you are in to show you what your personal connection to each direction looks like. Bring a small bundle of offerings to leave in each of the directions such as grains, flowers, or water. Find a stone to place at the center of your circle and figure out where the four cardinal directions are: east, south, west, and north. Starting with the east, stand at the center of the circle and walk ten steps in that direction. Place your offering and then open yourself up to sensing the east. You may wish to breathe intentionally for a moment to bring your awareness more fully to the present moment.

Use all of your senses to carefully observe your environment. Notice the sky, the wind, the trees, and plants growing here, the feel of the earth. Be open to seeing any signs, animals, or hearing sounds or an inner spirit song in that direction. After a few moments or several minutes (as long as you feel), return to the center and repeat the exercise in the remaining directions.

Take a moment at the center to thank the directions and put into your memory any information you received. This can be done on different lands where you live or visit as a way to connect to place, honor the land and spirits of that place, and receive information and guidance about the creatures, plants, rocks, and water there.

Exercise: Creating an Altar

Using what you have learned in the five directions practice, you can embody the work in a foundational way by creating an altar. This is a powerful step in setting the intention to begin soul working. When you set aside a space in your room, or home, or on your land to honor your journey on earth, you open up the conversation between soul and body which helps to connect to your higher self, intuition, and wise guidance.

To create an altar, first find a place in your home or yard where you will be able to place items or images that you connect with and that inspire you. This can be a small shelf, table, an entire room, or a part of your yard or the land outside. This is a sacred space that you will cultivate over a period of time, so choose an area that won't be disturbed by pets, children, or others.

Spend time choosing images that inspire you such as particular deities, pictures, your teachers, and things from nature. If you are new to creating altars, I encourage experimenting on your own, simply placing whatever feels right, and not thinking about it too much. As time goes on, you may wish to create your altar as a reflection of the immediate seasons and earth changes as well, adding and taking away as these change, reminding you to connect in with the earth.

Inspired by the Magician card, choose four items that represent the elements and suits of the tarot: a stone or a coin for earth or pentacles; a feather for air or swords; a stick or candle for fire or wands; a cup or bowl of water for water or cups. You may also take time to choose a card each morning at your altar space, opening up to guidance and receiving clarity on the intention you are putting into your day. You may wish to add other magical items for specific intentions around clearing, manifestation, or calling in a guide. The possibilities are endless and the space is a creative portal for you to work with your own soul manifest as a human creator.

2: THE HIGH PRIESTESS

As we continue on our major arcana journey, the Fool's next encounter is with the mystical and mysterious High Priestess. While the Magician holds the ability to outwardly manifest potential vision, the High Priestess governs the inner worlds of imagination, dreams, omens, signs, and synchronicities. She sits on her throne as fully realized gatekeeper into the Great Mystery, the void, or the unknown. Here the Fool encounters themselves in the looking glass; it is the universe eyeing itself, the eye or gaze, the peering into a crystal ball or mirror to divine the path and where it leads.

As a representative of the point of division, the High Priestess indicates the moment of reflection. This is the point in the journey where the Fool looks back upon ourselves as symbolized by the High Priestess's crystal ball of insight above her head. This is resting upon the crescent moon, an ancient symbol of the Goddess. As the number two, the High Priestess is like a seed that has sprouted its first two leaves. The new sprout is anchored in the dark, enriching soil and is tender, full of life and potential and growth. On many tarot cards, the High Priestess stands between two pillars, one black, one white, which later appear as sphinxes in the Chariot card. She is a bridge between the worlds of conscious and unconscious; dark and light; above and below; earth and sky; seen and unseen worlds.

As the Fool progresses through the first cycle of seven, where the Magician offers us the brilliant visionary perspective, the High Priestess is the wise, shadow counterpart that may help us in the more troubling times of our own soul's journey on the path. Oftentimes we seek out help during times of transition, pain, trouble, or fear. Intuitive readers, diviners, mediums, and seers rest at the crossroads comfortably offering wise counsel only because they themselves have delved deep into the subterranean of pain, darkness, and sorrow, and transformed it into wisdom, light, and compassion. They are imbued with the gift of seeing into the non-ordinary or unseen worlds. In modern culture, the High Priestess appears as our contemporary therapists, healers, energy workers, and readers.

The High Priestess remains in consort with the divine as her primary work, hovering at the edge of the precipice, about to descend into the dark to retrieve necessary information for healing, creativity, growth, and soul transformation. The High Priestess, as ruler of the skies and mysteries, is also known as the queen of heaven, a manifestation or emanation of the goddesses Isis and Inanna. Both of these deities carry many qualities of the sacred feminine including beauty, truth, power, love, and wisdom. While Isis embodies qualities of the divine mother, Inanna is the powerful archetype of the initiate.

In the ancient Sumerian myth, Inanna willingly descends into the dark underworld to meet with her sister Ereshkigal, the dark goddess who represents the aspects of the sacred feminine that have been repressed, traumatized, and hidden away deep in the darkness. After passing through seven gates where Inanna is stripped of her clothing, her jewelry, her pride, her gifts, nothing is left, and she is hung on a hook for three days where she dies. Through a witnessing that helps heal Ereshkigal's pain, Inanna is restored to life and allowed to return to the upper world. Her return marks the passage of time into rebirth, carrying with her the wisdom of transformation, the power of witnessing pain and trauma, and the love of the dark shadows that offers us so much on our path.

When the Fool encounters the High Priestess, they receive wisdom from someone who has already passed the tests of initiation and returned, full of wisdom and clarity. The High Priestess reminds us to return to the place that is beyond words or concepts and reconnect with our deepest and wildest selves, the intuitive heart that carries the spark of our spirit's truth. We can seek guidance from others *and* we can also seek it within. The High Priestess acts as a guide toward our higher self, connection to the divine, and our pathway to the subconscious that shows us the way deep into the intuitive heart and back out again. She may require a sacrifice along the way, a relinquishing of the old self. Meeting the dark and wild feminine may be difficult, requiring us to see our pain and wounds; however, the mysterious surrender of the unknown is also where our gifts reside.

In the Waite-Smith deck, we see a female figure clothed in blue robes that flow into water, symbolizing the use of intuition and feeling to navigate the path. She sits between two pillars, between the gateway of the worlds connecting us to both the seen and unseen, offering her truth and wisdom as the embodied initiate. At her feet rests a crescent moon; on her head sits the horned crown with a seer's crystal orb, reminding us of her connection to ancient Goddess wisdom. The background is a curtain of pomegranates, a fruit historically connected to women's mysteries and wisdom.

In the Crowley deck, the High Priestess is akin to Isis, the goddess of wisdom, mothering, power, and love. She raises her hands in the air and is surrounded by vibrating lines of energy that symbolize the energy fields that surround and interpenetrate our world, whether we acknowledge them or not. This depiction suggests that we are affected by the emotions of others as well as guides, unseen helpers, elementals, and nature's many forms. This netlike imagery reminds us that everything in all dimensions is happening simultaneously in the vast mysterious here and now, which ultimately points us to the non-dual nature of the universe.

When the High Priestess appears in a reading, she encourages the seeker to pay close attention to dreams, synchronicities, omens, and intuition. This may be a time to seek guidance, healing, and assistance from a wise person who has walked the path before us. We may need to find a mentor for our work; conversely, we may be called to step into a leadership or mentor role. The High Priestess rules over the arts of ceremony and ritual in ancient times, and she is a figure of power and guidance in contemporary times as well. She may take the form as an officiant for a wedding, a facilitator for a creative group, or the leader of a conference. Stepping into power guided by the High Priestess is always infused with love and intuitive guidance so that the most people may benefit from a situation.

Essential Qualities: intuition, omens, liminal, threshold, leadership, power, subliminal, guidance, unseen realms, water, beauty, grace

Suggestions: Spend a whole week following your intuition—one whole week, even if it goes against logic, rationalization, or shoulds and should-nots.

Note when things flow and when they don't! We can only learn to trust our intuition fully when we carefully track our thoughts and perceptions and notice when we have affirmations and when we do not. Pay attention to your dreams. Take time to journal and write things down.

Exercise: Moon Divination Ceremony

The art of divination is as old as humans themselves. Used primarily to assist in finding water, resources, tracking animals, and to connect with non-humans and the unseen world, this craft still has its place in many indigenous cultures as well as modern day issues around money, relationships, career, and love. One natural method in which people performed divination was to scry, or gaze into water or a crystal ball, to determine the future. When we take time to do this, we activate our intuitive centers and open ourselves to nonordinary reality.

For this practice, look at the moon reflected in water. Go out into nature to a lake, river, or pool on a full moon night and practice gazing into the water. If this is inaccessible, simply set up a bowl of water on a moonlit night and sit outside with your bowl. You may wish to create an altar and tune into the five directions as you did in the Magician card, as well as access the guardian helpers which are established in the Emperor ceremony (on page 46). Visualize a bright, vivid sphere of light surrounding and protecting you before you begin.

Before you begin, it is helpful to set an intention or ask a question about something troubling you. Take a few moments to close your eyes, focus on the breath, and feel into your question. Then slowly open your eyes and gaze into the water before you. You can repeat the process of closing your eyes, slowly opening them, and looking into the water several times. Allow impressions, images, thoughts to move across your mind's eye opening you up to your more intuitive self. Do not be concerned with receiving a direct, immediate answer right away—simply allow yourself to have this experience.

When you are finished, thank the waters and the moon for their presence and guidance. Perhaps make an offering at the water's edge or pour your bowl of water with intention before closing this simply divination ceremony. Before you go to sleep, ask to receive further guidance in your dream state as a continuation of the process of connecting to your intuitive and wise self.

3: THE EMPRESS

The Fool travels from their meeting with the High Priestess, emerging from the depths of the liminal space of the initiatory, up and outward into the glowing realm of the Empress. The Empress's world is one of beauty, abundance, and nurturing. While the High Priestess is the magical aspect of the sacred feminine, the Empress is the more earthly and external manifestations of power and love. She is the queen who must make decisions that benefit not only herself but also her family, the land, and those in her care. The Empress rests in divine counterpart to her partner, the Emperor. Together they rule the lands of the Fool's youth, the ever-present and deeply imprinted qualities of our parental and ancestral lines.

After journeying into our shadow self of the High Priestess, facing the rich, darker aspects and learning to navigate between dark and light, the Fool is ready to bring the seed of potential that has sprouted out into day. The Empress fertilizes this seed with her beauty, confidence, grace, and wisdom. She is the manifestation of light in daylight, the bright and brilliant aspects of the divine feminine as progressed from the darker High Priestess before her. While the High Priestess navigates between dark and light, the Empress holds the seed of growing light within the darkness of her womb readying it for birth into the fullness of day.

We shift from the number two of balance and duality into the three, a trine of interdependence between three aspects. When two join together they form a third—such as in the obvious way, of creating a child—but also in other ways such as growing a business or project, planting a garden, or nurturing an idea into form. The Empress takes the Magician's conception that was nourished by the High Priestess's powerful dreaming and begins to grow and birth it into physical reality encouraged by deep attention and care.

The Empress indicates a woman as a leader in contemporary times. This card encourages both men and women to lead with the wisdom of the Empress, one that takes the earth into consideration when making choices. She is a voice that reminds us of not only our connection to earth but to our parents, and also to methods more sustainable. Not all women are mothers and neither are men; however, we all have the potential to create and carry life in other forms. Tapping into womb consciousness and the primordial creatrix is a powerful way to connect to our inner wisdom and strength.

The Empress is the feminine as a ruler or leader. In the Waite-Smith deck she is figured with a scepter, a solid staff with an orb that signifies the power of the feminine. This power can be a grounded presence that indicates wisdom, truth, and divine knowing. Spheres symbolize reflective seeing, the power of circles, and having a pulse on the future. Moons and stars in broad daylight on the card indicate lights as a form of divine radiance.

In the Crowley deck, the Empress holds a blue lotus at her heart center, a symbols of compassionate wisdom and the effortless quality of natural growth and opening. At her feet are a swan and a shield, indicating grace, beauty, protection, endurance, and longevity. The fluid and watery qualities around her remind us of the gentle, clear, nourishing qualities of water.

In both the Waite and Crowley decks, the Empress is seated, draped in flowing cloths over her body. Perhaps she is pregnant, awaiting the birth of her growing child, gardens, projects, and dreams. "Mother," connected to the Latin word *mater* or "matter," indicates the power of the Empress residing in the earthly realms of manifestation. She is concerned with our physical lives and our direct kinship relations with our own mothers, with ourselves as mothers and with the earth as matter.

When this card appears in a reading, it may signify pregnancy; becoming a parent; or the inception of an idea, project, garden, dream, or plan in its growth stages. The guidance is to be patient with the growth to allow it to fully come to fruition. The Empress encourages us to surrender to the process of growing while nurturing the gestation through good nutrition or nourishing the project or idea with positive thoughts and people who support its unfolding.

This card can also indicate a need to examine our relationship with our mother or mother lineage to look more deeply at the patterns stored there. Inevitably, our mother is our first connection to the world. Even if we were adopted, went into foster care, or never had the opportunity to meet our birth mother, she carried us from seed and conception to birth. At that moment of birth, a great rush of spiritual energies and support are available for both mother and child.

Many of us may have had a traumatic or painful birth—doing healing work around this time is a powerful way to reconnect with our inherent birthrights of joy, love, and beauty. This type of healing work can release the feelings of anger, shame, and sorrow that may lie in our birth. These negative feelings can be the result of trauma, abuse, our mother's wishing they weren't pregnant, feeling overwhelmed by a coming child, or simply the intense process of birth itself.

The Empress reminds us of our own inner grace and strength as well as our interconnectedness with all of the matter of this wide and diverse planet. She is that which is so abundant in our lives, overflowing with plenty, pregnant with possibility of more to come. The Empress is infinitely creative and growing in new ways, pushing up and outward into the skies. Her appearance in a reading may indicate a time of flowering and gratitude, of connection and delight.

Essential Qualities: patience, abundance, pregnancy, mother, mother lineage, harvest, fertile, nurturing, embrace, love, warmth, golden

Suggestions: Track items in your life and notice the complexity of materials that surround you. Start a gratitude journal and write down something you are grateful for every day. Count your blessings…literally, count them! They are endless like seeds and they have the potential to grow. Get a plant and put it in the earth or a houseplant for your home. Fertilize a creative dream, project, or plan. Did you set an intention with the Magician card? Time to add some juice, some love, and a little beauty to coax along your manifestations into abundant, potent things that may be shared with the world.

Exercise: Journey into Dreamtime Garden Sanctuary

The dreamtime is the place of extraordinary reality, the place beyond our ordinary senses where we have access to our soul language, unseen helpers, and guides. In this exercise, we will visit the dreamtime to establish our own personal garden sanctuary which can be visited as much as we want to do safe, energetic, healing and magical work. This is a nourishing place that provides rest and healing for our inner psyche. You may want to connect to the earth in real time first, using the exercise from the pentacles or disks introduction to touch into the element of earth.

For this practice, it is helpful to either record the visualization and/or use a rhythmic drum beat or binaural beats to establish a relaxed brain pattern. To do this practice, you may want to lay down or sit in a relaxed upright position while using headphones for the sound. Set your intention to visit your personal garden sanctuary. Imagine you are walking down a set of ten steps, counting down from ten to one. At the bottom of the steps is a doorway. Pass through the door into your healing garden sanctuary. Notice what is there and simply explore. Be open to experiencing your garden through all your senses: sight, sound, touch, smell, feelings in your body. Notice the plants, trees, flowers, and other things growing in the garden. Is there a body of water? Animals? Stones or crystals? Take note and make an intention to remember this place and feel the connection embodied in your heart-mind.

Perhaps you meet a creature or guide. Perhaps you are taken to a specific place. Perhaps you just feel a sense of knowing something. There is no wrong way to explore your garden in dreamtime. When you are finished, thank the garden sanctuary and make a commitment to keep connected if you wish. You can return to this healing garden sanctuary any time to rest, heal, connect, or ask for guidance. Leave the garden and go back through the door. Return to present state awareness by counting up one to ten, slowly moving back up the steps into where you are laying or sitting. Write down any experiences as a way to anchor in the creating of the healing garden sanctuary.

4: THE EMPEROR

Once the Fool has become acquainted with the deep nurturing and abundance of the Empress, they move into the realms of manifestation and creative impulses, the form and container of the Emperor. Moving from creative generation, the Fool now has the opportunity to manifest things more fully into form before bringing them to the level of spiritual truths found in the Hierophant. Here, the Fool encounters the concepts of structure, formats, and the work of building a firm foundation on the path.

The Emperor is a regal ruler, king of his own domain. In balanced authority, he is in sovereign control of his land, a just and fair leader who holds a firm view of those who contribute to his domain. He surveys his creations with a measuring eye, weighing the options. As the number four, the Emperor indicates the quality of foundation. Most buildings and rooms have four corners, there are four directions, four seasons, four basic elements, four suits in the tarot that correspond with our four primary bodies: physical, emotional, mental, and spiritual. This is the number of solidity and completion, foundational and firm. From the strength and secure base of four we can build up to our next levels of development.

In the Waite-Smith deck, the Emperor appears to be looking to the left at the Empress for guidance. Although portrayed as a fierce ruler, he is also seeking the natural world as support. He is draped in red, the color of grounding, vitality, foundation, and protection. He is clad in iron, symbolizing the forceful quality of his focus and firmly holding a staff of power and authority. The rams on his throne indicate strength, action, and initiative.

In the Crowley deck, we see a figure in red and gold looking even more firmly to the left. When you lay the Empress next to the Emperor, we clearly see the two figures gazing into one another's eyes. They are in direct communication; one does not exist without the other, just as our own father line cannot exist without our mother line. Regardless of personal relationship, we carry the DNA from these ancestral lines in our embodied self and have an opportunity to look at how these manifest in our lives through personal relationships, health, and career.

In this image, the Emperor's right leg is crossed over his left to form the number four, the value of foundation and structure as mentioned above. The other card that carries this imagery in the deck is the Hanged Man, the most esoteric figure of the entire deck. Although the Empress may be the Emperor's counterpart, the Hanged Man may actually be his opposing force. Crowley's inspiration to link the formation of the legs implies a deeper connection to the masculine energies, one active and primordial, the other of sacrifice and surrender. We all know the story of Jesus hanging on the cross as the ultimate surrender to love on the behalf of all beings. Which archetype is truly more powerful?

In the progression of seven, this card is related to our father and the deep imprints left by the main male figure in our lives who informs us as men and/ or our masculine side. His presence in a reading may signify the need for discipline or to make peace with our father or inner masculinity. In the tarot and in many spiritual traditions, the feminine is often portrayed as the receptive and intuitive aspect while the masculine is the active and manifest aspect. However, we each contain different aspects of these qualities and carry within us both mother and father lines.

In a world that has been primarily ruled by a white patriarchy for thousands of years, it is important to examine this effect on our own psyche and what we carry in terms of masculine influence and likely need to clear away negative imprints and reframe our ways of acting and manifesting in the world. We are in the midst of reexamining our personal, societal, and global reflections of the systemic issues of patriarchy and questioning the dominant leader archetypes. In a rising tide of fierce grace, the sacred feminine is returning to the forefront of our human destiny. There is a call to redefine the sacred masculine alongside this feminine voice rising in the tide as a roar. We are being summoned to clear out the old ways, the outdated systems that work purely on profit at the expenditure of human life and the health of the earth.

In a balanced state, the Emperor is the part of us that extends outward to activate a just and peaceful world. In his fully aligned self, he asks us to contribute to the creation of a sovereign nation that operates from accessing our gifts and sharing them to cocreate social, economic, and political systems that seek to benefit others, not destroy. Perhaps this is idealistic, but change is gnashing at our heels and the time to take any steps we can to activate these ideals into motion is now. The Emperor is grounded in his decisions. He is the authority figure of his life and indicates the need for us to take full accountability for everything in our lives. He encourages us to ground into our own personal truths and find what resonates with social and global truths; to activate the heart and move from the foundation of justice for all.

When the Emperor appears in a reading he asks us to explore our creations, work with money, and career or job choices. Although the Emperor may feel heavy and cumbersome in comparison to the previous enchanting cards, his appearance is the necessary grounding force to materialize our dreams. It is time for the Fool to take his vision (Magician), empowered by intuition (High Priestess) and creativity (The Empress), and ground this into form. This may be taking steps to buying a new home, remodeling, starting your business or bringing it to the next level of operations, investing, or participating in more worldly matters. This certainly indicates form and matter and is further augmented by the appearance of disks or pentacles in a reading.

The Emperor is concerned with social matters such as law, marketplace, homes, and businesses. How do these affect you in your daily life? What interactions are you regularly a part of? What is your personal domain like in your home or personal business compared to others such as working for someone, your family home, or community spaces. The appearance of the Emperor in a reading may also signify the need to set stronger boundaries and reinforce your foundations emotionally, physically, mentally, or spiritually depending on the other cards in the reading. The indication can be the importance of committing to a practice, discipline, or creative endeavor. The Emperor can remind us to pay attention to our health and physical self. Although the Emperor is not afraid of conflict, this is primarily because he is able to channel anger into clarity and even compassion. He reminds us that often anger is a protective guardian of our inner being acting as the gatekeeper to the sensitive realms of our developing psyche.

Conversely, this card may suggest being too rigid, forceful, active, or controlling in a situation. Notice in your life where you can soften and open and where you can be more firm and clear. Using the ceremony from the Four of Disks card can help you explore this further. The Emperor encourages us to take a clear look at our relationship to money and how we may or may not save for the future. Building foundation skills helps us to learn about our human path as an embodied form. Exercise, eating good foods, and nourishing our bodies are ways to feel more connected to the physicality of our existence and assist in the process of manifestation.

> *Essential Qualities:* firm, authority, groundedness, stability, authority, masculine, father, boundaries, empire, building, land, foundation
>
> *Suggestions:* Examine the following questions and do a free write from one as a prompt to explore your own connection to money. Do you have shame around money? What is your dream empire? What prevents you from dreaming big? Make a commitment for a week to discipline yourself with healthy food choices, exercise, or meditation.

Ceremony: Establishing Your Guardians

This ceremony connects directly with the unseen helpers, directions and elements, benevolent ancestors, and helpers in your tarot work. The Emperor carries protective energy and invites us to establish those energetic boundaries and guardians to assist us in our work. In this practice you will journey to your dreamtime garden established in the Empress with the intention of meeting a guide, helper, or ancestor who will specifically assist you in your tarot reading.

Set your intention to meet your helper or guide. Then, as you practiced with the Empress, play soft drumming or binaural beats, visualize descending the ten steps, and passing through the door and into your garden sanctuary. Wander around the garden until you come to a clearing. Perhaps there is a tree at the center of the clearing. Ask to meet a guide who will assist you on your tarot journey and be a protector in your work. Perhaps you see an animal, an ancestor, a colored light, or you simply sense a presence of well-being. If a guide presents itself, ask them if they have a message for you or if they can show you a way to work with them.

When you have finished, thank the guide and travel back up the ten steps into present awareness. You may journey to this realm as many times as you want to work directly with this helper. You can call them into your space as a protective guide when doing your tarot work and giving readings.

Exercise: Grounding Cord

This exercise is useful for grounding your energy field into the earth and helping to stabilize your form. We often become ungrounded through stress, overwhelming life situations, or trauma; practicing a basic grounding exercise can help us to reconnect to our body and breath awareness. And over time, grounding helps us feel more focused, clear, and present in our lives. We are naturally led to healing and connection in this way. It may be helpful to record the following visualization and play it back until you remember the steps on your own.

Sit in a cross-legged position. Keep the spine straight and focus on a few breaths. Concentrate on where you are sitting. Focus on your buttocks, legs, and feet pressing into the floor or ground beneath you. Concentrate on where you are sitting; if you wish, also focus on the root chakra and visualize a clear, bright, red cord or any clear color. Imagine the cord as a root growing downward into the floor below. Allow the cord to continue downward, into the rooms or ground below. The cord sinks further into the rock, water, and soil below, into the very core of the earth. Notice your grounding cord's qualities: size, color, and whether it goes straight down to the core or extends in another direction. Allow the energy of the earth to intermingle with your cord, cleansing any dark or muddled spots.

Observe as the cord grows further down into the rock and soil. Notice plant roots, creatures in the soil, and the qualities of earth. Visualize the grounding cord extending downward through the water that is below the rock and through crystal and mineral ores. Continue to notice the color of the cord, if it changes or stays red. Observe any feelings that arise as you ground. Eventually tap the grounding cord into the central, fiery, molten core at the center of the earth. Acknowledge your connection between the ground of your body with the central inner ground of the earth. Keep the grounding cord in place, then slowly come back into awareness of your body. Touch the floor with your hands and open your eyes.

5: THE HIEROPHANT

As the Fool continues the sacred journey along the path of the major arcana, they leave behind their childhood innocence and the magic and mystery of the Magician and the High Priestess. The Fool now carries the awareness of the innate wisdom and gifts within along with the parental imprints of the Empress (mother) and Emperor (father).

Arriving at the temple of the Hierophant, the Fool meets spiritual teachings that begin to manifest outwardly in the form of rituals, sacred words, religious texts, and doctrines. In more contemporary terms, these are our beliefs (or lack of beliefs) connected to the sacred or divine as well as our personal religion. It is also related to how we connect to community through what we consider sacred—God, Goddess, nature, our own path, friends and family.

The Hierophant is a curious archetype for our modern day world. The word itself has an archaic and mystical quality to it and is derived from the Greek *hierophantēs* from *hieros* "sacred" + *phainein* "to show, reveal." The Hierophant is sometimes depicted as a High Priest or Pope. Some decks have used the archetypes of medicine person or mystic to symbolize the spiritual gatekeeper and healer of soul issues. In the Star Wars deck, the Hierophant is Yoda, the classic contemporary wise being who holds the secrets to understanding and using the Force or cosmic energy to battle evil to restore what is good and true.

On the major arcana journey, the Hierophant marks the moment on the journey when our emotional, mental, and psychological selves shift to the next level through an act of initiation. He symbolizes the higher wisdom and teachings that spiritual bodies of knowledge offer us. Distilling our life experiences into this potent moment, we recognize the deep and powerful truths of Self that outlive us. The Hierophant maintains his own inner spiritual authority through the practice of self-worth. This is not worth derived from our parents, our own lives, or society but worth that comes from our higher self, connection to the divine, or the eternal spirit that lives within.

The number five in tarot symbolizes adjustment, change, dissolution, and opening. This number can challenge us, particularly as it follows the sedentary, formal, and comfortable place of the Emperor at number four. Yet grow we must on this path; the Hierophant appears to help us begin the process of examining our own connection to spirituality, authority, and conditioning. In this way, the Hierophant is the Fool's deepest encounter thus far with something that shakes up the soul path. Meeting with spiritual knowledge and authority brings up questions and may indicate a time of questioning inner truths in relation to our previously held or family's beliefs. We may align more deeply with these or reject them altogether.

As our awareness grows on the path, we begin to touch into the part of us that is beyond this very limited human form and experience compassion for self and others. In the pure form, the Hierophant embodies this, holding a state of clear-sighted compassion. This may be a sense of profound connection with the collective or a personal awareness of our own self-love and autonomy, both qualities that often precede moving into the vivid dance of the Lovers. This level of awareness, however, may also require the intense process of purification and burning away of attachments to old stories, relationships, and belief systems. While the pure aspect of the Hierophant invites us to embody a spiritual awareness, it also asks us to surrender outmoded beliefs, family imprints and societal conditioning. We may be pulled into work more deeply to heal ancestral trauma and negative perspectives that limit our access to love.

In the Waite-Smith deck we see two people bowing low receiving a blessing or prayer at the foot of the seated figure. This is the first time in the journey that other figures appear in the cards. The two people supplicate themselves to higher spiritual truths and symbolize the willingness to make sacrifices of the earthly body to move into the higher realms. This can indicate our own recognition of the need to release an addiction or negative pattern to make room for more vital life growth and deepen our connection to spirit.

In the Crowley deck, we see a figure standing erect with a figure of justice or balance in front of him and a child in a pentacle at his heart center. Instead of two figures supplicating themselves, they are shown as integrated parts of the human consciousness and development. The figure holds a staff with three rings indicating the merging of body, mind, and spirit—a symbol for the new age coming to earth. Surrounding the card are four masks connected to the four elements and quadrants of the astrological wheel that may govern destiny. However, these masks may also indicate the outdated conditioned parts of us that need to be discarded. While often a guide of spiritual discovery, the Hierophant may also be an authoritative figure or conditioning that no longer serves our path. Discovering our own personal growth in relation to our spirit's path and how it reflects out into the world is the Hierophant's teaching.

The appearance of the Hierophant in a reading may indicate higher learning, going back to school or getting a higher degree. Perhaps you feel a call to join a community, cause, or organization to become a part of something that benefits others or is your great work. This may be a time to invest your energy in social or spiritual activism. The Hierophant may also indicate a time to challenge communities, groups, leaders, or authority that feel heavy, burdensome, or even traumatic. This card encourages us to look at the deeply embedded conditioning we have undergone to become "productive" members of society. Perhaps these rules and expectations feel constraining or overwhelming for us and there is a call to throw off the old masks of the past and look for new forms of expression and truth. Use the ceremony below to release the traumatic imprints of your ancestral lines to illuminate or reveal your own personal sacred Hierophant truths.

Essential Qualities: adjustment, guidance, masks, authority, learning, warrior, teacher, teaching, student, transformation, reflection, rank, hierarchy, beliefs, conditioning

Suggestions: Meditate for five minutes every morning and evening. Seek classes, community, or a spiritual group that interests or excites you. Join a social network with common interests. Spend time examining your beliefs around money, religion, partnerships, and community—contemplate where these beliefs come from. Are they from your parents, family, social circles, society, or yourself? Notice how beliefs make you feel and challenge yourself to turn them upside down and work on dissolving them.

Ceremony: Ancestral Fire

I have used this fire ceremony to help clients release and let go of painful trauma associated specifically with their parents, ancestral lineage, and intergenerational trauma in addition to other imprints that are connected to social systems, religious beliefs, and other deep social conditioning. The fire ceremony helps to release you, your parents, and your ancestors from limited roles and patterning. It also honors them in a respectful manner free of attachments and the heavy or toxic burdens that may be felt about parents and ancestors.

When we bring our parents to the fire, we have the opportunity to speak about our lineage in a positive way, make offerings to release them, and heal the past. In some cultures, it is tradition at the time of puberty for the child who is becoming an adult to go through an initiation ceremony to release their parents and step into the path where the earth, sky, ancestors, unseen helpers, and others in their social group all become guides. When we "fire" our parents, we relinquish them from being the only ones who can support us. Many people today have experienced so much loss and trauma from their parents and ancestral lineages; this ceremony is one way to both honor and release them and step onto the path more fully. In ceremonial work, linear time does not exist; as you heal your ancestral lines, you also heal yourself and your descendants (whether actual children or the people who will continue on when you leave).

To prepare for this ceremony, plan the timing of the fire to be around the new moon, a time of releasing and letting go. Plan a month or more in advance so you have time to do preparatory work. You will create two bundles that will be burned in the fire, one for each parent and their lineage. You may wish to choose a color for each bundle that you feel represents that parent. Use colored cloth to wrap burnable offerings such as dried cedar, lavender, or other plants. You can add salt for cleansing. Write down on paper the aspects of your parent you are clearing away, such as addictions, traumas, or obstacles. Put this paper in the bundle as well. On another paper, write down the gifts you have received from your parents, attributes that you honor and are cultivating. This will be kept separate from the bundle.

Around the new moon time, find a safe place to make your ceremonial fire with a friend or witness to assist and hear you during the ceremony. Call in the protective sphere of light and your helpers including any guardians, spirit guides, and/or benevolent ancestors. Bring to mind each parent and see them in their humanness with as much compassion as you can. Take a moment to honor and respect that you are here in this life because of your parents, regardless of the situation. When you are ready, burn the bundle associated with the parent you are visualizing with the intention of clearing and releasing them. After you have burned the bundle, read the list of values you walk with that you have received from that parent. You can do the same for the other parent. It is important to speak about them in a good way, if possible, as there is potential for ancestral healing to happen through you back to your parents and their lineage when you do this.

When finished, release the protective circle, thank the helpers, and close the ceremony. If you can, allow the fire to burn down; smother with sand or dirt if you have to leave it. Unless you have no choice, it is recommended not put out ceremonial fires with water, as this can lessen the energetic power the ceremony created. However, please observe safety first: be sure there no coals are left behind when you close your ceremonial work.

6: THE LOVERS

Emerging from the profound spiritual realizations of the Hierophant, the Fool travels along and encounters others at their level for the first time, the Lovers. Here the Fool meets others who reflect the true essence of their truth and beauty, feeling the opening of the heart as they move into the depths of loving. In a spiritual sense, this is a moment of choice to open to the next level of growth as their heart awakens.

The number six is the energy of balance, harmony, and the potent mixing to form something completely new. Six is the number of the heart, connection, balance, and beauty. The union of two threes, six indicates growth and beauty. After the five, we experience a blossoming and richness that stabilizes in the number six and enables us to experience a sense of wholeness on the path. When two sixes come together, we have twelve, the number of petals on the heart chakra mandala.

Love is the opener, the amazing joy of being, the alchemical process that encourages us to stretch our hearts. When we fall in love, we often feel an incredible rush of potential, possibility, and new growth. Many people describe this experience as heady, intoxicating, a rush, or high like no other. Although on a physiological level our brain is being flooded with chemicals when we feel love, there is still such mystery to this immense beauty of experiencing life anew. It is as if we are born again. With this wondrous opening comes the truth of not only beginnings but also endings. Some part of us knows this rush will pass and the glimpse into the Beloved is simply reflected by the lover who sits beside us.

Lovers are known to abandon reason, following the potentially orgiastic madness that is love and pleasure and bliss. Perhaps we need to revisit this wild nourishment in different ways, for to have life without it leads to repression and stagnancy. Learning through intimacy and relationships is some of the most important work on our path as human beings.

Unlike the Two of Cups, where love between two people is rooted in exchange and signifies a more grounded commitment such as marriage, the Lovers is provocative and inherently contains the mystery of the unknown. There is almost an element of danger or the seed of loss—on some level, we all know that a low follows the high of such ecstatic growth. In the spiritual aspects of the Lovers, we learn how to integrate the experience in a grounded way and be open to the inherent pain of loss of love when the breakup or dissolution inevitably happens.

The key of the Lovers' truth is the discovery that the wellspring of love lives in our own heart. We do not need to rely on others or the world to satisfy this demand. Recognizing that our beloved is simply a reflection may require us to traverse the wounds and conditioning that have prevented or traumatized us from that full experience. When the Fool meets the Lovers, they dive deep to discover that ultimately, love is our only goal here on earth—to learn to accept and give love.

In the Waite-Smith deck, we see two figures, naked and free in the shining imagery of the sun symbolizing the illumined beauty of love. Above them is an angel making the gesture of divine guidance and blessings that accompanies an experience of deep loving, passion, growth, and beauty. Behind the lovers are fruiting trees and a mountain peak symbolizing growth that is upward, reaching new heights through an impassioned experience.

In the Crowley deck, the two figures face one another—one dark, one light, one male, one female. In this way we see a coming together of two different energies that allow us to grow and dissolve limiting boundaries. At the bottom of the card are two children, symbols of the innocence and playfulness that accompanies the experience of love. The children are a reminder to delight in our life and find the beauty and miracles in small things. When we fall in love our senses are often heightened and we attune to the magic and mystery continuously alive and permeated with love.

Above the Lovers is Cupid, pointing his arrow of pleasure and passion. Cupid is a diminutive version of the more ancient power of Eros, the mystical force of the creative wild that moves through all things. Being shot with an arrow of love is an often erratic and unexpected experience. The appearance of the Lovers card may indicate that a passionate love is on its way that will be wild, untamed, and won't happen in a convenient or orderly way. In this way, the Lovers shakes the Fool's plans in preparation for the next phase of the journey on the Chariot.

When the Lovers card appears in a reading, we ask ourselves, who do we love? How do we love? Why do we love? Sometimes it indicates the appearance of new lover or deepening of passion with a current beloved. Other times it is a call to make a choice to take the higher path of love and follow an inner passion or take a leap of courage. The Lovers indicates a time when we must make a choice, and in doing so, leave behind others or paths in order to take the new one. The Fool has deepened their understanding of gifts, skills, and parental imprints and has reflected on the spiritual truths. They are ready to choose something guided by love, courage, beauty, and the deepening journey into the unknown.

> *Essential Qualities:* love, connection, wildness, danger, excitement, union, play, sensuality, reflection, choice, passion, energy, compassion, creativity
>
> *Suggestions:* Pay attention to everything occurring in your life right now. Is it harmonious or filled with drama? Are you suffering or do you feel content with the world? Notice the way you express and experience love in your life. Do you focus on family, romantic relationships, parenting, work, or nature? Do you allow love in or do you shut it out? Can you feel some kind of love moving through you each day? Fall in love! Fall in love with the fleeting world. Although there are terrible things and frightening scenarios being played out, there is also immense beauty surrounding us all the time. No matter who we are or what state our lives are in, each of us is a unique and brilliant soul briefly transiting an earthly body. Allow yourself to feel love for that journey and embody the truth of the Lovers more fully each day.

Ceremony: Self-Marriage

Although the Lovers card is often associated with passion or sharing love with another person, it can also symbolize the connection to our own self-love. One of the most potent ceremonies I did for myself was to travel to far eastern India and create a self-marriage ceremony. This act arose out of a need to recommit to my own path and clear vision of my offering to the world; I was married at the time yet needed to find my center once again. The ceremony acted as a catalyst to my next phase of work with the sacred feminine and the Fire of the Goddess. The first vow I spoke was to call back all parts of myself, which is the quintessential component of the Lovers card: reunion with all of who we are. When I spoke those words aloud in the witness of the temple priest and surrounded by ancient Dakini goddess images of the divine feminine, I felt a deep shift. My self-marriage acted as a powerful initiation; after this ceremony, I felt a profound sense of joy and purpose. We often lack direction in Western culture; this ceremony was a way for me to anchor it into my own life and path.

The two most important elements of the self-marriage ceremony are stating vows to oneself and having a witness. Crafting a set of intentional vows or promises is a powerful statement for both the seen and unseen worlds. Having someone witness this seals the healing and offers us the needed reflection in your ceremonial work. Your self-marriage ceremony can be as intricate and complex or as simple as you want. I have assisted many friends and clients with creating elaborate ceremonies where they invited friends and families, held a party, and shared their vows in a dramatic way. Others have simply lit a candle and spoken their vows with one other person present as a witness.

Suggestions for creating your self-marriage ceremony: find a beautiful place in nature; incorporate candles, flowers, bowls of water, or other elements you associate with love, connection, beauty, and grace. If you want, wear something special that embodies your inner beloved in celebration of your true Self. Spend time contemplating and writing your vows beforehand and then state them aloud with one or more witnesses. You may offer flowers to the water as a way to invoke beauty and love. Include songs, prayers, and blessings just as you might in a conventional wedding. This is a creative, intentional initiation that connects you deeply to your inner Self and aligns you more fully on your soul journey.

7: THE CHARIOT

As our Fool emerges from an encounter with the beloved, they are empowered, ready to meet the world and blaze forward. The Chariot energy is full of active energy and moving ahead, whether we are ready for it or not. Like a fire running behind him, the Fool is propelled to the next phase of life, leaving behind what is no longer needed and headed into activity, growth, creativity and expansion of the Chariot. In the spiritual evolutionary aspect of the Lovers, the Fool makes a clear choice to go one way. This may be a commitment to a relationship or the choice to leave one. It may be accepting a promotion or quitting altogether. Once a choice or decision is reached, the Chariot is the rush of energy that follows the choice. It is like the arrow, gathering speed as it moves through the air in search of its target. There is no stopping the arrow once it is in motion.

The Chariot is the number seven, which integrates many aspects of the human experience: the seven chakras, seven planets of classical astrology, the seven day week, the seven souls of God and the seven creative powers. There are seven colors in the rainbow, seven intervals in an octave, and seven vertebral bones in our neck. Sevens indicate magic, growth, research, and expansion.

The Chariot marks the end of the first cycle of the major arcana journey. In the first stage, the Fool is developing awareness of the world and learning the will to be. They discover the feminine and masculine qualities, the gifts that we bring in our soul's journey, and they begin the process of integration. The Chariot bridges the Fool on the journey into the next set of seven cards, where psychological development and the deeper work of spiritual evolution is found in the ways the individual relates to the world.

The Chariot illuminates full-fledged emergence from the previous cards into action and will. We learn to navigate and balance the art of surrender and control; when to follow and when to lead. The Chariot symbolizes victory, maturity, and wisdom that has been gained by facing the challenges and conflicts of life. What are you moving on from, letting go of? What intentional seeds were planted during the Magician that are now beginning to take root? Look back at the last month and year of your life and notice what you have consciously or unconsciously set into motion. Before setting intentions for the next phase of your life, it is helpful to reflect on what has already manifested.

In the Waite-Smith deck, we see a chariot guided by an armored figure with a tapestry of stars above him. The armor symbolizes protection and the container for vital life force to be guided into a powerful, intentional direction. Unlike the wild openness of the Fool or the Magician, this energy is now purposeful and focused. The Chariot is on a clear and distinct path, guided by unseen forces. The Chariot is led by two sphinxes, black and white, indicating the merging of duality, finding the flow, and expression between and beyond male/female, the seen/unseen, the unconscious/conscious minds.

The sphinx symbolism found in the Chariot card shows a deeper connection to the High Priestess card, the archetypal force that sits between the worlds. While the High Priestess guards and provides access to the unseen realms of the subconscious, dreamtime, spirits, and magical reality, the Chariot moves through the external world guided and assisted by these unseen helpers. We see symbolic interpretations of this throughout the tarot such as angels, helpers, and guardians and are reminded that we are not alone. Whether you tune into this energy as your higher self or as specific spirit helpers, acknowledging the unseen forces, both mundane and spiritual, are a way to connect more deeply with the energy of the Chariot card.

In the Crowley deck, we see a figure clad in gold holding a red and blue disk. There is a palpable energy in the card symbolizing movement, clarity, focus, and brilliance. The disk represents the raw forces of manifestation and creation held into a focused intention that moves along with the energy of the Chariot. It is the seeded destination or arrow of intention gathering momentum and speed. The gold armor indicates a connection to divine will and purpose on the path.

When the Chariot appears in a reading, it is signifying that everything is moving forward and we have no choice but to follow the momentum as it pulls us along. In this moment, it is up to us whether we want to be dragged along or take the reins. We have within us the potential to guide the energy of the Chariot towards our intended destination. You may ask yourself, what is my destination? Am I working on a project that needs to be finished? Is there some discipline you wish to put into place?

Essential Qualities: will, illumination, grace, movement, action, guidance, direction, bold, energetic, activity, forward, golden, clarity, purpose

Suggestions: Build a fire. Do an interpretive dance. Go on a trip, short or long, to visit a beautiful place. Seek out and make connections to develop your art/business/dream plan! Stay focused on completing a project. Set a twenty-one-day discipline in motion.

Ceremony: Full Moon Activation Fire

This ceremony is the final one in the major arcana section and marks the transition of the first cycle of seven into the next. These ceremonies set a solid foundation for practicing the elemental ceremonies of the minor arcana. The energy of the Chariot is a bright, strong powerful push to bring things from the dreaming or subconscious reality into conscious manifestation. Activating intentions and dreams set during the Magician will help your projects, relationships, and health have a chance to come into form. The moon is fully illuminated by the sun during the full moon, which energizes rituals and ceremony. Using the previous foundational ceremonies, you can create an activated full moon fire ritual to honor and celebrate your spiritual journey.

In the work with the Hierophant card, you had the opportunity to release your parents and ancestral burdens to clear the way for healing conditional love, trauma, and negative imprinting. In the Chariot ceremony, we now invite the guardians of earth and sky to step in as support for the unfolding path. Some traditions view the sky as father and earth as mother; others view the sky as a celestial goddess and the earth as god. Perhaps you relate to these views, or you can drop the gendered view entirely and simply call in the qualities or essences of sky and earth along with the directional elements. Using elements from the previous ceremonies combined together can help you to create a very rich environment for soul work.

For this ceremony, you will want to set aside time when the moon is full and find a space where you can make a fire or, at least, a space to light seven candles. Gather one stone to create a simple talisman or charged ceremonial object along with seven candles, one for each of the four directions, one for above, one for below, and a personal candle for the center. Set up a small table as an altar and decorate it with a few items to make the space personal such as flowers, a mirror, incense, a bowl of water, tarot cards—in particular the Chariot card—as well as other images that mean something to you and enable you to connect in with the earth and sky. The full moon is also an excellent time to charge items with the moonlight's energy and brilliance such as crystals, stones, healing wands, and your tarot decks.

Light the fire and call to each direction, welcoming it in with an elemental offering such as incense for the east, ash for the south, water for the west, and salt for the north. Then light one candle for each direction and invite any spirit helpers or guides you already work with. Take time to honor the elements and spirits of the land and waters, feeling gratitude for plants, trees, animals, stones, and so on. Then, visualize a clear gold or silver sphere surrounding you, your space, your altar, the candles, and your fire. You may wish to do the grounding cord exercise established in the Emperor card. Next, imagine connecting yourself to the full moon and asking for the illuminated power to guide you in the coming days and weeks.

To amplify the energy of the space, you can visualize the moonlight streaming into your sacred circle and filling it up. Chant or sing, use instruments, or move your body to fill the power of the space. Make that space potent and charged with energy. Imagine the moonlight coming down into your body, through the top of your head and spreading out through the rest of you, filling you with light, love, and power. Imagine the moon reflecting the sun shining down and filling you up with healing light that can be used to focus your intentions of healing, abundance, and joy as made manifest by the energy of the Chariot. Visualize your magical items also filling up with moonlight, becoming fully charged by the energy in the sacred space under the moon.

Once your space is illumined, charged, and amplified, light your fifth candle to honor the sacred self at the center of your four directions. You may wish to say a vow from your self-marriage work in the Lovers card ceremony to help activate the inner union. This is also a good time to use the practice of the High Priestess card and scry or reflect in a bowl of water. If you wish, you may want to draw cards from a deck for guidance or simply allow yourself to receive intuitive heart wisdom on how to manifest or bring more activated energy into a particular goal, intention, or dream.

When you are ready, call upon the sky for guidance and support and as a reminder of the long view of the life journey. Light your sky candle and invite the essence of the stars, celestial bodies, the infinite grace of night, and illumined darkness as offered by the vast space above us. Then, call upon the earth for guidance, support, and a ground for your journey in this body or human vessel while on earth. Light your earth candle and invite the essence of earth; all who dwell here; and your relations of humans, plants, trees, elements, stones, and so on.

When all seven candles are lit, feel into the energized power of the space and the movement the Chariot characterizes. Take a moment to call out loud what you wish to activate and bring more fully into your life. This may be just one word such as grace, joy, or surrender, or it may be something specific and concrete such as a partnership, new job, guidance on a conflict, more community, et cetera. Blow the activated breath of the moon, sun, firelight, sky, and earth into your stone creating a simple talisman you can carry with you for the next seven days or beyond. You may simply carry it or find a way to wear it.

To close the ceremony, imagine the sphere of light surrounding you dissolving into a drop of nectar and entering the space between your solar plexus and the heart center. As the illumined energy of the moon and the sun enters you, it aligns your higher will with your personal will as carried by the Chariot card's energy. Then, release each direction and element and blow out the candles. Sit in quiet moonlit contemplation, feeling full of renewed energy and power. If possible, allow the fire to burn down on its own, or extinguish it safely with dirt or sand. Thank the energies and contemplate your journey thus far as you prepare to move into the next cycle of seven on the major arcana path.

8: JUSTICE (STRENGTH)

The first seven cards of the major arcana represent the outer aspects of life including our parents and caregivers, our teachers, falling in love with our lovers, our community, and perhaps an introduction or exposure to religious or spiritual teachings. As we enter the next phase of the major arcana journey, we begin to work from our emotional and relational selves. The next seven cards encourage us to dive more deeply into the language of the heart and the emotive interpersonal expressions that connect us to our life journey. In this next part of our journey, we allow truths to emerge that teach us about our soul's purpose and growth on earth.

After the energy of the Chariot, the Fool finds themselves facing deeper clarity in the revelations of Justice, card number eight (number eleven in the Waite-Smith deck). This card marks the arrival of becoming more aware of the larger picture of life and the deeper realization on our Fool's path of awakening of how our journey is not only ours—each and every thought, word, and action affect others in our lives. We are not really isolated, independent beings but interconnected to many others for survival, resourced support, emotional growth, and spiritual development.

Originally, the eighth card of the major arcana was Justice, but Arthur Edward Waite changed it, effectively switching the eighth and eleventh cards. Because Waite's deck grew to be so popular that it became the standard for tarot, the switched progression stuck and most decks still follow Waite's perspective. Although it is open to speculation, many believe he switched the cards so that they would be more in alignment with the cards' astrological progression. In this way, the number eight mirrors the eight month of August, associated with Leo, strength, power, light, and illumination as depicted in the classical image of a woman with a lion on the Strength card.

Later, Crowley switched the cards again, restoring Justice to number eight and Strength at number eleven. For the sake of original tradition, we follow Crowley's progression, however I encourage you to contemplate the order in your own tarot study and decide which makes more sense to you. Interestingly, both numbers have a parallel quality, with eight resembling a turned infinity symbol and the eleven symbolized by two pillared lines. Because of the switch, the two cards are inextricably linked, creating a pairing that deepens the significance of both cards. In this kind of relationship, we cannot have Strength without the neutrality of Justice, nor can we have Justice without the power and presence of Strength. The Strength card is one of inner power and resourcefulness that reminds us of our own center and place in the universe.

On the personal level, justice is our sense of morality and what is right or wrong. We often judge others who are different from us and condemn actions that we perceive to be unaligned with our values. Where does this judgment come from? Are we actually projecting aspects of ourselves or attempting to distance our own self from someone so that our ego may feel better or superior? How can we see ourselves together as one without judgment? Is there a way to move toward radical acceptance?

With this card we begin to examine more social justice issues and patterns of conditioning in our world. What is actually just in our culture? Who receives fair justice and who does not? How does our privilege and status in the world affect our decisions, life opportunities, and outcomes? As we move into this second cycle of seven, more profound life questions arise. Here, we may deeply question free will as opposed to fate and how both play out in our beliefs and lives. Many religions deem certain choices as immoral or wrong, and it is helpful to examine whether we have internalized these views and, if so, how they affect our lives. As we progress on the spiritual path, we become aware of our own social conditioning, programming, and truths which have been taught to us but may not necessarily be our truth. Society seems to hold us to expectations around having a partner, creating a family, moving forward in a career, buying a house, and so on. So often, the soul longs for a different experience, or we may find inspirations beyond the apparent truths we are told. We are required to look inward for answers.

When challenges arise in our lives, we likewise have the opportunity to meet them with heaviness or lightness. Change, chaos, endings, disharmony, death, disease, and suffering occur in everyone's life; it is up to us whether we meet these moments with fear and denial or grace and love … no easy task! We can be inspired by the height of high flying birds such as hawks, eagles, or osprey who circle above the situation taking in the larger picture without getting overwhelmed by heavier emotions.

In the Waite-Smith deck, we see a solemn figure draped in red robes who holds a set of scales in the left hand and an upright sword in the right. Swords are extremely heavy; the effortless manner in which Justice holds the sword reminds us of the strength it requires to stay balanced, focused, and dedicated. The scales indicate the measured balance of emotions and mental states. Similar to the High Priestess, the figure sits between two pillars offering the awareness of resting between right and wrong and finding the way between binary thinking. The right foot is extended, symbolizing movements or actions toward making the "right step."

In the Crowley deck, the neutralizing colors of green and blue fill the card, reminding us of water and plants, creating a healing and tranquil atmosphere. The figure holds a large sword, resting it almost delicately on the ground, finding the perfect point of balance that holds more than one perspective in awareness. The cooling colors in the card encourage neutral communication, clear thinking, rest, and nourishment.

Traditionally, Justice is associated with the law. When this card appears in a reading, it may indicate dealing with legal matters in one's life, contracts, and agreements. We may need to create, resolve, or amend a contract in order to move into right balance with people in our lives, work, and home. The Justice card asks us to examine areas in our life that need a more neutral perspective in order to progress, such as a witness or mediator in a personal or legal problem, or taking time and space from something that seems unworkable. Often when we give space and breath and time to something, an unforeseen solution may arise that we had not previously thought of.

This card may indicate working with social justice issues and becoming aware of societal imbalances in our personal lives. Justice is a reminder to unpack privileges we experience and how this affects those around us, encouraging us to take actions that are grounded in right view. Justice may also indicate a general need to balance our lives and find clear insight. This card reveals the need to cut through our fear, denial, and pain to get to the heart of the matter. This is a time for discernment from a neutral space, to move away from the heaviness of wallowing emotion and into the clarity of the all-seeing view.

Essential Qualities: balance, alignment, threshold, healing, two sides of the coin, neutrality, calm, quiet, introspective, speaking one's truth, law, legal matters, boundaries

Suggestions: Take a day for self-care and nourishing your body. Meditate. Notice where things feel out of alignment with friends or at work and make a decision to say something with compassion. Set clear boundaries. Look at an area of your life that feels out of balance and make a commitment to work on this issue for twenty-one days, for example quitting a toxic substance or food, budgeting time or money better, setting clearer priorities, or waking up early each day.

Justice Layout: Balancing

This is the first of the layouts offered in the second cycle of seven of the tarot. These layouts can be done as basic tarot readings in addition to ceremonial suggestions to deepen the experience, wisdom, and discovery that can happen during a reading. You may want to revisit how to do a reading in the introduction to refresh yourself on the process of creating questions and laying out cards.

This seven-card layout looks at two different sides of an issue, relationship, job situation, or spiritual question. As a call for a more neutral perspective, Justice asks us to look at two sides of an issue. Sometimes we struggle with binary thinking and need guidance to allow our minds to move more into a neutral view, the language of the heart. This reading helps us to see what is hidden from view in assessing a situation and moving forward. Refer to "How to Give a Successful Reading" on page 11 if you need help determining a question, but it is important to choose an issue that requires you to make a decision, has two possible outcomes, or you don't understand the other side or perspective.

Gather a few items to create a ceremonial space for this reading, including a small branch that extends outward in two directions, a dark blue candle, a yellow candle, a larger tarot candle to invoke the helpers, and a bowl of salt water for cleansing. Create a simple altar and call in your guardian helpers as established in the Emperor ceremony. Place the dark blue candle on the left, symbolizing what is hidden or mysterious, and the yellow candle on the right, symbolizing what is clear and obvious. Put your small Y-shaped branch in the center with the guardian tarot candle. Light the candles and then decide on your question or intention. Shuffle the cards and then lay them out as follows:

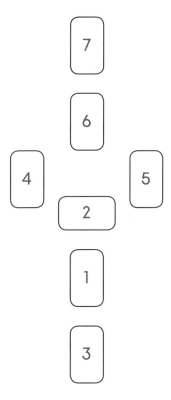

- Card 1: Querent or self
- Card 2: Issue at hand
- Card 3: Past Influences
- Card 4: Left branch—the hidden, mysterious, subconscious aspects of the question

- Card 5: Right branch—the conscious, direct, and external conscious aspects of the question
- Card 6: What is guiding the situation
- Card 7: Outcome

Once you have completed your reading and looked at the perspectives, allow for time to contemplate both sides. Perhaps journal in response to the ideas. When finished, blow out the candles and put away the cards.

9: THE HERMIT

The Fool continues along their journey of the major arcana from the Justice (or Strength) card to meet the quiet, contemplative energy of the Hermit. After the healing and neutralizing energy of the Justice card, the Fool is empowered to move inward and illuminate the shadows. They encounter the mysterious, nocturnal, and curious Hermit. In most decks we see the Hermit as a hooded figure, holding a lamp to light his way in an otherwise dark and wintry background.

The Hermit card encourages a time to take a step back from the busyness of life and perhaps rediscover a sense of purpose and understanding that comes about in the quiet hours, sitting in nature, when we are alone, or at night. The Hermit may ask us to look more deeply within and process any raw emotions that have not had a chance to fully express themselves.

The Hermit is the number, nine, is a coming together of three threes, symbolizing completion, integration, and understanding. It is helpful to remember that each card on the major arcana journey includes every card that has come before it. Thus the Hermit includes the wisdom and truths found in all the cards from the Magician to Justice (or Strength). We can take a moment here to reflect on the journey through the majors cards and how we have worked with various aspects on the path to cultivate our understanding. At this point in our work, I encourage you to layout the first nine major arcana, from the Fool to the Hermit. This will help you to get a sense of the journey thus far, remembering that each major arcana contains within it all the lessons that have come before.

The Hermit encourages us to take time to reflect on our inner self and discover authentic power. He reminds us that discovery is possible in silence, contemplation, meditation, or prayer. He is often depicted in a cave in nature, encouraging us to retreat to a quiet place, a wild place, or an undisturbed area of the forest. The Hermit is akin to the yogis and yoginis who live in caves high in the Himalayan mountains. He is the monk who dwells in the forest retreat; he is Artemis, the huntress goddess of the wild who chooses to never marry and remain firm in her commitment to protect women, children, and virgin forests. To retreat into the wild is to drop the trappings of culture and expectations, familial obligations, and the illusion that we are important. Often it is only when we are alone and profoundly still that deep insights rise to the surface. Following these deeper insights leads to the flowering or blooming in trust of divine timing and fulfillment. This opportunity is always present, but we must revisit this place of awe and reverence to overcome our shadows time and time again to remind ourselves of our true nature.

Solitude can be an incredibly beautiful and clarifying time … and it may also be profoundly lonely. When we go through periods of loneliness, we can view these as an opportunity to move deeper into our aloneness, an empowered place of solitude. As this process unfolds, we often discover yearnings that arise sometimes as fears, anxiety, pain, and struggle in relation to our desires and human longing—to be close to others, feel connected, or be part of something greater. The dance between aloneness and connectedness is familiar territory for many people in the modern world; we value our autonomy at the expense of community and the sense of connection with others. How do we cultivate a sense of connection while still in our aloneness?

In the Waite-Smith deck, the Hermit is in the snow, evoking a sense of quietness, beauty, solitude, and clarity. Snow can be an obstacle, yet it is also incredibly beautiful and seems to quiet the world when it falls around us. When we see snow sparkling along the streets, hanging on trees, and falling from the sky, we are overcome with wonder and awe, a pure feeling that is the Hermit's reminder of the wild grace of the world. We see the figure holding up a lamp, symbolizing inner illumination or guidance on the path. Even when everything is dark around us, we have a light within that is waiting to be shone outwardly.

In the Crowley deck, we see a three-headed dog at the Hermit's feet. The dog may symbolize our own childhood trauma and fears as well as epigenetic or ancestral trauma that we carry with us. We become defensive or prideful, per-haps retaliating or recoiling as if in fear. Shining the light on this fearsome beast is our only hope of recognizing that the only thing we have to fear is fear itself.

When the Hermit appears in a reading, it may be indicate that it is time to embrace therapy, counseling, or healing and work on healing these old patterns. There are often moments in life when painful memories and old traumas rise up to be resolved and healed. The light of the Hermit reminds us of the resiliency of our soul and that those memories may be resurfacing because we are ready to work on them. Although the Hermit is alone—and in this way, we can only do our own work—there is still a reminder to seek help and support in more difficult healing situations.

Essential Qualities: solitude, aloneness, quiet, transformation, wisdom, beauty, wild, forest, retreat, meditation, contemplation

Suggestions: Take time to meditate. Sit and focus on the breath for a few minutes in the morning or evening. Find time to do yoga, practice contemplative prayer, or do a guided visualization. Focus quietly on a burning candle. Appreciate the natural world—notice the seasons. This week, do not hurry. Take your time in every little thing. Trust in the cycles of life and in divine timing. Remember that you are always at the center of your own being.

Hermit Layout: The Essence

The Hermit layout invites us to focus on the essence of a situation. It is simply a single card drawn from your tarot deck. You may choose to draw from the entire deck or only the major arcana in order to focus on the archetypal aspects more deeply. The one-card draw is the simplest tarot card reading yet it is quite powerful. Light a candle and spend a good ten to fifteen minutes really contemplating your question. If the question is about a person you are in relationship with, take that time to really feel into them and their essence. Slowly shuffle the cards, pull one, and spend time in contemplation with that card. Perhaps leave it on your altar for a week as you work to dive deeper into the insights that the particular card is showing you.

1

10: THE WHEEL OF FORTUNE

The next card on the major arcana journey is the Wheel of Fortune. Here the Fool encounters a date with destiny. More than any other card, this one indicates a powerful destined effect on our life journey, one that may feel fated or predetermined. If we look back over the course of our life, we may notice certain choices, moments, or meetings with others who altered our life forever. These are the moments of the Wheel of Fortune. They cannot be planned or arranged or understood; they are the times in our journey when we feel as if our lives have been "written" ahead of time. This reminds us of the possibility and potency of our soul contract, a kind of manifesto in which we determined the lessons we want to learn in life before birth.

This card is numbered ten, which symbolizes the end of one cycle and the beginning of the next. Tens are final fruitings that offer riches, beauty, delights, but also indicate that with them come endings, letting go, and dissolving. Just as fruits offer sweet, nutritious goodness they also carry the end of one cycle of a tree and the seed of the new beginning. We see that in the numerology of tens, which contain both 1 (the seed) and 0 (the beginning and end). These numbers connect the Wheel of Fortune to the Magician and the Fool cards.

On the major arcana journey, the Fool encounters the Wheel of Fortune through destined calls to action. Here we can see how we as the Fool received a fiery soul seed which later comes to fruition at this moment in the journey. To use our two examples explored in the Magician card, a next call of action appears when Luke Skywalker must face his father in the guise of Darth Vader to support the rebel cause against the Empire. Similarly, T'Challa in *Black Panther* receives another call of action when he discovers he has a long-lost cousin, decides he must reestablish a connection with him, and make subsequent choices about the fate of oppressed black people in the world. These calls to action are both seeded and destined on our path and help us to understand our own soul journey as a map or unfolding story. The Wheel of Fortune is a literal and metaphorical profound turning moment in our lives.

At the Wheel of Fortune, we return to the awareness of our magical gifts illuminated but in the context of the world: our connection to the earth, relationships, work, money, health, and communities. The seeds planted during the Magician time have sprouted into full blossom and the winds bring cross-pollination, connection, and a rich sense of growth. We cannot control change; we can only attempt to ride the energy of the wheel and embrace the movement of the winds that move through our lives.

The Wheel of Fortune may evoke images of games, gambling, and card play. There is a quality of luck and destiny sparkling within this card, the offering of a potential swift change. There may be some strategy involved in gambling or playing cards, but there is always room for error and luck. When I do ceremony, I often have a notion that in addition to creating a good and safe container, it is also wise to leave the back door slightly cracked … just enough for spirit to enter. This does not mean the container is unsafe—the opening is where opportunity can appear and magic can happen. When we stay open to the possibility of luck and chance without trying to overtly plan and force our life to go in a certain direction, limitless possibilities may unfold. The Wheel of Fortune turning endlessly is a powerful reminder of this limitless nature.

The circular nature of the Wheel of Fortune reminds us of circular sacred spaces found in medicine wheels, labyrinth-style mazes, and mandalas of east Asian traditions. Indigenous traditions often use a circular cosmological map to understand their order, place, and story in the universe's unfolding. These maps contain the entire universe in their representation and give us a symbolic way into the infinite. These various wheels or circles are usually divided into four sections symbolizing the four directions, four chambers of the heart, the four seasons, four winds, four energetic bodies, and so on. As we are embodied in mortal forms, we cannot fully conceive of the vastness of the universe; the Wheel offers us an ordered and creative way to anchor ourselves in the context of the path. This might be a good time to revisit the directional ceremony in the Magician card and perhaps perform it again to deepen your own connection to the directions, anchoring in a sense of context for your path, and creating your own cosmology of the universe.

In the Waite-Smith imagery, we see symbolic representations of the four fixed signs of the zodiac: the angel is Aquarius, the eagle is Scorpio, the lion is Leo, and the bull is Taurus. Each creature has wings, which may suggest movement as well as divinity and wisdom. This is one of the few cards that points out a possible connection between the tarot and the Kabbalah. The wheel includes the four Hebrew letters YHVH (*yod heh vau heh*), which are considered to be the unpronounceable name of God. You may want to consider delving deeper into the mysteries that connect the tarot to the Kabbalah; references appear in the resources section at the end of the book.

The Crowley image shows the Wheel in purple and blue, colors that symbolize intuition, higher wisdom, and communication. This is a time to notice the signs and omens appearing on your journey. The energy of the image is in motion, indicating change, swiftness, wind, and movement. There is an electric and dynamic quality to the stars and lightning bolts that pulse from top to bottom while the wheel swirls, its ten spokes turning in endless movement. A sphinx sits on top of the wheel, a symbol of the mystery, unknown, and destiny that affect our lives. On the right is the Typhon who holds an inverted ankh, the symbol of life, upside down. There is also a figure on the left known as the Hermanubis, a combination of Hermes (Mercury) and Anubis, who together symbolize the energy between the worlds. Both gods are psychopomps or mediators between the living and dead who help souls move from the underworld to the light, crossing over.

This powerful imagery reminds us that the Wheel is connected to our fate; when it turns up in a reading, it indicates that powerful forces beyond our control are at work. The Wheel of Fortune may be a positive or negative turn of events, or it may influence us in unlikely ways that at first appears positive but turns out badly and vice versa. It is up to us to learn how to roll with it, so to speak. While I was in the midst of writing this actual chapter, I received an email that one of my previously books published with Llewellyn would be going out of print. The timeliness and reflection on an imminent change is priceless! Tarot (and life) works like this—we are shown the way, reflect on our path, and often need a sense of humor to remind us not to take ourselves too seriously.

The Wheel of Fortune so clearly indicates a turning point—a change in the winds, a change in direction. When you were going one way, suddenly you find yourself going in an entirely new direction. Can you remember a time in your life when it felt as if the Wheel had suddenly turned? Was it when you met someone who has since had an important effect on your life? Perhaps it was a new job, a chance encounter, a loss, news from an old friend, or even a powerful insight. The Wheel of Fortune reminds us that life moves in cycles—birth to life to death and to rebirth once again. As we shift from one of these phases into another, the Wheel is at work.

In a reading, the Wheel of Fortune may indicate that something which seems like a blessing is actually not helpful; and vice versa, things that seem like an obstacle or trouble may actually be a blessing in disguise. We cannot always determine what outcomes will be from events, news, decisions, and things happening out of our own sphere of what we perceive to be in control of. The Wheel reminds us to trust in the divine timing and unfolding, that somehow there is an order to the progression of our path, our soul's development as we move from one phase of life to another.

Essential Qualities: change, suddenness, luck, destiny, movement, wheel, magic, fortune, blessing or curse in disguise

Suggestions: Find your center. Orient yourself to the cardinal directions: east, south, west, and north. Give thanks to the rising sun in the east, the warmth of the south, the setting waters of sunset in the west, and the cold ice of the north. Play cards! Invite luck and destiny into your life. Wear something sparkly just for fun. Find and walk a labyrinth near you. A labyrinth is an ancient form of walking maze that brings us more fully into the present moment. Find a labyrinth near you and visit it to make the journey into the center, bringing along an offering to leave when you reach the middle such as a flower, coin, or stone. You can set an intention before you begin walking, something to contemplate as you meander through the winding path toward the center. The movement of the labyrinth's paths has a soothing effect on the mind which allows you to relax into a more contemplative space.

Wheel of Fortune Layout: The Wheel of the Year

This reading is an in-depth look at what is coming up for you or your client in the next year. A good time to do this reading is at a turning point in life or during a solstice, equinox, birthday, or New Year's Day. Pulling a card for each month gives you a chance to look at what will be likely coming in for you for the year. However, I encourage you to recognize that these cards represent potential outcomes—futures are never written in stone.

Light a candle and shuffle the cards and simply pull one card for each month. Write in your journal about each card, allowing your mind to explore the potential possibilities of what will arise for you in the coming year. Notice any themes in the reading such as a particular suit; a prevalence of majors, minors, or court cards, or certain numbers that appear repeatedly. You may wish to pull a thirteenth card as an overall destiny card for the year to help guide and anchor in your understanding of the reading.

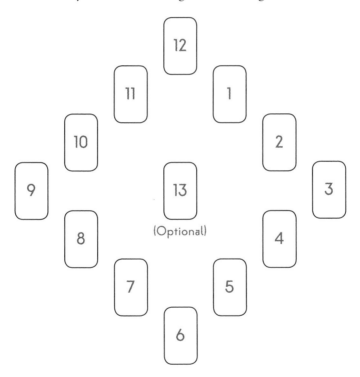

- Card 1: January
- Card 2: February

- Card 3: March
- Card 4: April
- Card 5: May
- Card 6: June
- Card 7: July
- Card 8: August
- Card 9: September
- Card 10: October
- Card 11: November
- Card 12: December
- Card 13: Overall Theme (Optional)

11: STRENGTH (JUSTICE)

As our Fool continues, they are carried by the powerful movement of the Wheel of Fortune to the next phase, the path to the Strength card (Justice in the Waite-Smith deck). Influenced by their destiny, the Fool moves on from the turning point of the Wheel of Fortune to the next leg of the major arcana journey. Here, a significant shift takes place as we delve deeper into the subconscious and the path of the heart. Personally, I prefer the Strength card here on our major arcana journey. In my perspective, Justice is a carryover of the previous seven cards at number eight, where we are still unpacking the morality, ethics, and imprints left on us from the first cycle of seven, still in preparation for the next cycle. Meanwhile, in this position, Strength follows the Wheel of Fortune and precedes the Hanged Man, which indicates a place of empowerment at moment between destiny and things turning upside down.

The Strength card indicates a time to connect to our internal strength and may indicate that we are actually strong enough to face more of the pain, trauma, or fears we have been harboring since childhood. Often we suppress difficult memories or events from our past until we are ready to face them more fully and do the work of healing and recovery. Strength is a card of empowerment and encourages us to stand up for ourselves and be the voice of truth and discovery. The figure of a woman is shown in relation to a vibrant lion who symbolizes strength, valor, ferocity, and unmistakable power.

In correlation with the Justice card, the number eleven is mirrored like the number eight and evokes a sense of passage or movement over a threshold. Imagine sliding doors and the ability to use all that has been learned in cards one (the Magician) through ten (the Wheel of Fortune) to harness your powers and offer your gifts. Eleven is two ones, like two Magicians together creating intentionality, multiplying the seeds planted at the beginning of the path. Following the Wheel of Fortune, our intentions are magnified by our soul's destiny. Eleven is a number of interdimensional power and invites us to consider the possibility of traveling through worlds to attain knowledge. The Strength card thus asks us to consider multidimensional perspectives of our life journey and healing that can happen through time and space. These invitations may appear as synchronicities and coincidences.

As I was preparing for my self-marriage ceremony, I pulled the Strength card in readings over and over again as a sign of reuniting with my own inner power. My first vow at my self-marriage ceremony was "I vow to call back all parts of myself." Surrounded by sixty-four images of the divine feminine, I committed to my life path and purpose, inviting in the many aspects of my multidimensional self to assist me in walking this journey. As indicated in the Strength card, this was a moment of empowerment and healing, and it was also the realization of a personal vision in alignment with collective impact. When visions are fully embodied, they have the capacity to work both forward and backward in our lives. Leading up to a vision, ceremony, prayer, or experience, we receive insights and guidance along the way. Afterward, we are gifted the power of the embodiment, reflections, and continued insights as the life journey continues. This is the sacred nature of the number eleven (or eight) expressing itself through the embodiment of Strength (or Justice).

In the classic Rider-Waite-Smith card, a woman strokes a lion to show how power with vulnerability is one of our greatest strengths. The willingness to be compassionate and stay open even when we have hit an edge takes immense courage. She is dressed in white, calmly stroking the lion while it licks her wrist. Although some interpretations say she is a woman taming her power, others believe she is in concert with the wild aspect of herself and is able to use it for her life's work. Above her is the infinity symbol, linking this card to the Magician, reminding us that all the power, love, and wisdom of the universe reside within us. The card has a bright yellow background symbolizing creativity and abundance; the blue mountain in the distance signifies clarity and fortitude.

Crowley renamed the card "Lust," indicating the use of sexual energy on the path. As a vital life force, sex has been traditionally viewed something to domesticate, control, lock away, and subjugate. This traditional view is ironic—we are all born out of the sexual act, our very life conception comes from the alchemical mixing of two people or essences to create new life. This card very much speaks to that power and invites us to connect more with our own sensual and sexual energies and perhaps harness it to use in art, creation, connection, and manifestation.

In the Crowley deck we see a nude woman, heart exposed, holding a vessel of fiery liquid love. She is both vulnerable and powerful, holding her essence aloft transforming the dark into light. She sits atop a creature with many heads reminding us of the many parts of our selves: our light, our dark, our shadow, our fear, our pain, our sorrows, our joys, and the myriad manners in which all these express themselves throughout life. The Strength card is also a card of compassion for ourselves, to find that inner core of care for our humble human body and its expression on earth.

When the Strength card appears in a reading, it is a call to courage and a resounding yes to personal power and life decisions. It has an overall positive impact on the reading and brings vitality, literal strength, fortitude, and energy to the next phase in one's life. In relationships, it may indicate the importance of following one's personal vision as well as tending to a partner or partners. It can also indicate the alchemical presence in a love relationship that has the power and strength to bring it to another level. In work and health, it indicates a returning vigor if it has been missing or a call to generate more strength and vitality.

Essential Qualities: strength, courage, vitality, trust, empowerment, knowing, wisdom, growth, abundance, lust, passion, beauty, firmness

Suggestions: Go for a walk or hike in the woods and reconnect with your physical body. Ask to receive guidance or wisdom as you walk, a sign to encourage inner strength. Perform a self-marriage ceremony as suggested in the Lovers card.

Strength Layout: Plant Perspective

The Strength layout uses seven cards to determine what is strong or weak in a particular area of life. Inspired by the image of a plant, this card shows the strengths found along each aspect of a plant that relates to a problem or issue that you are wanting more clarification on.

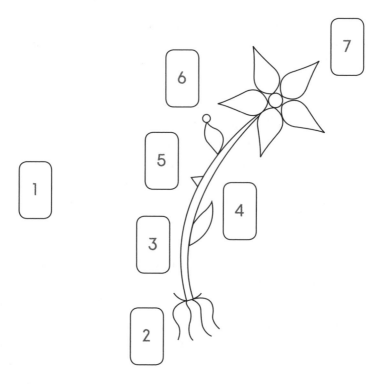

- Card 1: Querent
- Card 2: Root: shows what is grounding or supporting (or needs support in an issue)
- Card 3: Stem: what is helping the situation grow upward and develop
- Card 4: Leaf: what guidance you are receiving that gives strength and illumination to the issue at hand
- Card 5: Thorn: what is hindering or preventing you from stepping fully into your own empowered self
- Card 6: Bud: potential gifts that are unique to you and your situation, as well as the dynamic between yourself and the path's expression
- Card 7: Flower: outcome of the situation

12: THE HANGED MAN

Following either the balance of the Justice card or the grounding force of the Strength, the Fool journeys onward to encounter a literal and pivotal turning point on the path. This card is potentially one of, if not the most important card in its possible connection to the spiritual aspect of the tarot as a system of hidden, esoteric knowledge. The Hanged Man first appears as an upsetting image to most, but he is actually quite peaceful—perhaps the hanging is a choice to follow the clarity, determination, and balance of Strength (Justice) before moving into Death.

At number twelve on the path, the Hanged Man is connected to the numbers 1, 2, and 3 (1 + 2) connecting this image to the Magician, the High Priestess, and the Empress, a powerful trio! Within the Hanged Man we have the energy and potency of intention found in the Magician; the dreaming intuition and guardian of the threshold as the High Priestess; and the creative, patient, diligent approach of the Empress. Together, these qualities infuse the central card of the path, as the Hanged Man appears just over the crest of the middle part of our major arcana journey.

The Hanged Man evokes a strange quality that feels ominous or heavy, yet the wisdom of the card is more about stillness and quiet reflection. Hanging above the ground or water, he is literally doing a 180 view and turning the situation entirely upside down. This card is similar to the Hermit in its invitation to retreat and take stock of a situation in life, but to do so in a state that can be uncomfortable and completely out of our usual way of thinking. The Hanged Man reminds us that the situation we are facing cannot be resolved or understood fully in the present moment and requires not only stepping out of the box, but removing it completely in order to move forward.

In *78 Degrees of Wisdom*, author Rachel Pollack speculates that the strange shape of the Hanged Man's body signifies a deeper and more esoteric meaning than seeking out an upside-down perspective (Pollack, 1997). Most of the cards illustrate archetypes reminiscent of the times in which they became popular: kings, queens, emperors, the pope, chariots, and so on are inspired by medieval and Renaissance days, symbols and qualities of the 1500s. However, the Hanged Man imagery has older roots and is perhaps an image of initiatory practices of ancient cultures. Some historians have drawn connections between the Hanged Man and the myth of Odin in which he hung upside down for nine nights to receive enlightenment and the gift of prophecy.

Spiritually, this card indicates an initiatory experience of passing through a threshold. As in previous cards, we consider the sequence of cards that have come before the Hanged Man, and then specifically Strength (Justice) preceding, which has empowered us on the journey to handle this card's advanced initiations and undertaking. Followed by the Death card, we know that the energy of the Hanged Man is longing for a complete change and transformation in our life, one that is born out of stillness and reflection. He is literally hanging, not only upside down, but also in the middle of our major arcana journey.

Pollack goes on to discuss the possible connection between the Kabbalah, occult knowledge, and the tarot. Curiously, nothing was written about the connection between these two ancient systems until the nineteenth century, when it became a major point of interest for esoteric societies including the Order of the Golden Dawn. It is interesting to note that the Kabbalah uses the twenty-two letters of the Hebrew alphabet along the paths of the Tree of Life. Occultists such as Crowley drew connections between the Hebrew letters, the Tree of Life paths, and the twenty-two major arcana cards—the precision of the two systems mirroring each other is uncanny. Although this connection is drawn by modern occultists, it is important to note that Kabbalah is associated with ancient Jewish mysticism; traditional practitioners may disagree with this noted connection. Others may even believe it is appropriate to use the Kabbalah in a form that is outside the Jewish religion. I thus recommend readers tread lightly and do their own research.

With the Hanged Man offering an imagery that is perhaps ancient and not necessarily a depiction of medieval life, we cannot help but surmise the potential of the tarot cards to be not just a system of divination but a map of enlightenment (Pollack, 1997). On a physiological note, hanging upside down has a direct effect on the blood flow to the brain, bringing new awareness to our mind. In every moment we have the opportunity to shape our own neural circuitry. According to Harvard brain scientist Dr. Jill Bolte Taylor, ninety seconds is all it takes to notice the appearance of an emotion and allow it to dissipate (Taylor, 2006). The brain chemically produces our intense emotions of anger, fear, sorrow, excitement, and joy for only ninety seconds! That's it! The rest of the time spent fuming, weeping, anticipating, and worrying is our hardwired looping neurons that have created a story to keep a feeling afloat. What might happen if we allow that feeling to arise and then dissolve without looping the story? Can we catch ourselves in a story and do something deliberate to alter the loop? This takes focused effort to retrain the brain and uses creative thought patterning to build new neural pathways.

In the Waite-Smith imagery, a man hangs upside down from a wooden T-shaped post. His right leg is strapped to the post and the left crosses behind the right leg's knee to form a symbol of the crossroads. His arms rest behind him, evoking a sense of presence in his stillness. The blue shirt is the color of the sky and the red tights symbolize the earth and the ground, or rootedness, thus bringing the sky down and the earth up. His head is illuminated by a golden halo, a symbol of enlightenment. The answers to our questions lie in the still, reflective self when we are thinking outside the box; only then does illumination appear.

In the Crowley deck, the Hanged Man is in the same position, hanging upside down; however, his arms are extended and nailed to two pale blue disks, evoking a more intense connection to crucifixion or sacrifice. There are two snakes in the image, one at his extended foot and the other above (below) his head symbolizing powerful transformation, shedding the skin, and rebirth. The left foot is connected to the ankh, the Egyptian symbol of life and the merging of masculine and feminine energies. The colors of white and pale blue and green permeate the image, giving it a soothing or healing quality that again reminds us of stillness, quiet, and the implacable power of centering.

When the Hanged Man appears in a reading, it indicates a time for a completely new way of looking at things. This card advises against taking action in a situation but instead waiting until a new perspective that is arising becomes more clear. Sometimes solutions are found in stillness and, as indicated by the

Hanged Man, are usually completely different than anything we are thinking of now. The advice of the Hanged Man is to literally do the exact opposite of what you are doing or think you should be doing.

> *Essential Qualities:* new thought, upside down, reflection, stillness, deconditioning, hanging around, inversion, out of the box, wonder, deconstructing, initiation

> *Suggestions:* Hang upside down or do an inversion. Do a headstand or a handstand if you can! Turn your body around and be open to a whole new view on life. Practice doing a one-eighty in both body and mind. Pay attention to your thoughts. Meditate in the morning and direct your intentions for the day. Make deliberate choices to bring your awareness, thoughts, and mind back into a stream of love, acceptance, joy, and happiness. See if you can creatively create a new neural pathway or two.

Considering Reversals

This book does not include reversals or opposite meanings mainly because I do not use them in my practice. I view the cards as both positive and negative and am more interested in how the general energy of the card shows up in life and what can be done with that energy. How can we embody it more fully? What are the patterns emerging? That said, I do encourage readers to work on using reversals for some time and consider whether they might be brought into their own tarot practice.

If working with reversals interests you, use the Hermit one card layout approach to practice narrowing your focus. The traditional method of working with reversals is to read the opposite meaning of the card. For example, the Tower, which is generally destructive and chaotic, may indicate things coming back together or a restoration of harmony. Another view is that the reversals indicate a more internal process at work with the card and upright is the external or conscious view. A helpful resource for working with reversals is *The Complete Book of Tarot Reversals* by Mary K. Greer.

Hanged Man Layout: Reclaiming Initiation

This layout is designed to help uncover the deeper reasons behind a traumatic event. If we are to look at difficult situations from our past and attempt to understand them as initiations into power, love, and wisdom we can make sense of our soul journey. For this layout, you may want to separate out the major arcana cards to deepen the understanding in relation to archetypal forces. Using the full deck works as well. Decide on an event such as a loss, breakup, divorce, unexpected disaster, or another troubling event that was particularly difficult for you. However, if this is new work for you, choose something that was difficult in your life but not necessarily traumatic. Be mindful that any work which looks at difficult situations is bound to bring up complicated responses. Having a support friend, network, or counselor can help to navigate the process. As you concentrate on this issue, open your heart to receive guidance from a different aspect of yourself, a part that can view things from a completely alternative perspective. Using the upside-down stillness of the Hanged Man as our guide, we can take steps to recover, reclaim, and heal the past.

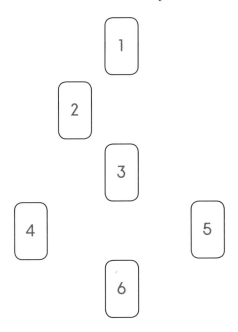

- Card 1: Querent
- Card 2: Wound: the painful past influences of the issue,
  what needed to be learned or resolved
- Card 3: Central issue or heart of the matter

- Card 4: Sacrifice: something that you gave up, that was surrendered in the initiatory process
- Card 5: Gain: what was learned or mastered from this process
- Card 6: Gift: the lesson that has become a teaching for your path; the wisdom that arose from the wound

13: DEATH

During the time of the Hanged Man, the Fool drops into the deepest recesses of a mind turned upside down. They find the very center of stillness and pass through a point of no return. Naturally this gives rise to death or dissolution, a complete shedding of an old way of being and entering the unknown of the Death card. On Campbell's map of the Hero's journey, death sits at the bottom half of the circle where the hero must cross through the threshold of death, initiation into rebirth. Similarly, this card sits halfway through the major arcana journey and thus symbolizes not an ending but a transformation. Appropriately numbered at thirteen, a number long associated with darkness, mystery, and bad luck, in truth this number corresponds to the number of moon cycles found in a year. The mysteries of Death have historically been linked to the deep, dark, feminine cycles of time, sex, birth, menarche, menses, menopause, decay, dying, illness, and death.

The Death card is the great unknown, the void, the inevitable turning of one cycle to another. The tarot is well known for this card and the fear it evokes in people who are receiving a reading. The Death card appearing and indicating an actual death is quite rare, although not impossible. Although this has happened in my readings a few times, I would consider predicting this for people unethical and fear-producing especially since the Death card usually indicates a smaller kind of death in the form of a transformation, loss, letting go, closing, an ending, or moving from one phase into another.

Death is card number thirteen, associated with the traditional thirteen-moon calendar of a year, as thirteen moon cycles is the amount of time it takes the earth to completely travel around the sun. This calendar has been used by ancient cultures all over the world until the rise of patriarchy and suppression of indigenous or folk ways. That time marked a switch into a more solar culture in which the twelve-month calendar was created, dismissing the thirteen months long associated with the Goddess, the feminine, and the mysteries. In the number 13, the one joins the Magician and intent with the number three, the energy of the Empress—creative regeneration and feminine birth, which is naturally linked to death in its opposing transitional power.

Death is a powerful mystery! It is the gateway to the unseen world of spirits, the afterlife, the grand cosmic adventure that stands, like birth, as a portal between this world and the others. Healers are known to face their own death during initiations. In some ways every loss we go through in life is a preparation for our eventual death. As explored in the High Priestess chapter, Inanna, the ancient goddess of Sumeria and queen of heaven famously descended into the underworld to meet her dark sister, Ereshkigal. When Inanna arrives in the dark chamber, stripped of all of her clothing, jewels, pride and ego, Ereshkigal hangs her from a hook where she dies for three days symbolizing the three days of the new moon. Meanwhile, Inanna's beloved servant still in the lands above calls to Father Enki, god of water and life to rescue Inanna. He does so by fashioning small genderless beings who fly down to Ereshkigal and see her moaning and writhing in pain. Instead of mocking her, they simply witness her suffering and mirror it back to her. Moved by this, she frees Inanna and restores her life (Perera, 1981). This story is one of the most ancient surviving stories speaking of initiation, death and rebirth, the sacred feminine and the power of healing through witnessing pain. All of these elements may arise in a death process and looked at closely when the card arises in a reading.

I encountered my own death journey when I lost a baby daughter soon after birth. I recall that long, lusterless terrain of grief, navigating insomnia and a heavy heart for a year and a day, leaving the ashes of my child in all the great waters of the world. Death reminds us to honor our ancestors, those who have gone before us and whom we carry imprinted in our DNA and our blood as well as our skills, our gifts, our pain and trauma. Ancestral lineages often hold intensely painful pasts and we have an opportunity to honor, heal, and release by clearing ancestral trauma through cleansing and forgiveness rituals and respecting our ancestors. When this card appears in a reading, you may refer to the Ancestral Fire ceremony in the Hierophant chapter to work with healing ancestral lines.

In the Waite-Smith imagery, we see a skeleton in black armor riding a white horse offering a black flag with a white flower. This symbolizes both the stark certainty of death as well as the peaceful nature of its arrival. Below Death lies the person who has recently died, a young child who looks up unabashedly, a youth who is turned away, and a religious figure emotionally offering their hands. These varied figures symbolize the many reactions to death. Some are at peace with the passing of a loved one, others feel intense pain or sorrow, others are in denial. Often mourning is a mixture of all of these feelings. In the background are the two gray gates found in the Moon card, indicating deep feelings receding. While the Moon brings up processes to deal with, Death is the release of those processes and the end of an era or period in our lives; it is a dissolution, a final letting go. The sun sets, or perhaps rises, symbolizing the beauty of endings and the possibility of rebirth to follow.

In the Crowley deck, a black skeleton wields a scythe across the card in an active relinquishing of the connected webs. The skeleton is cutting the cords and releasing transparent images symbolizing the spirit leaving the body and moving on to the next phase. Surrounding the skeleton are classic images of death and transformation: a snake, scorpion, and upside down datura flower. These symbols invoke a sense of power and mystery in the process of transformation that indubitably arrives with the Death card. We have the opportunity to touch into the great unknown and perhaps, while still here, bring back some wisdom to share with others.

When Death appears in a reading, there is simply no argument or anything left to process. Something is clearly ending and a powerful transformation is upon us. Often this transformation has been clear in our lives for some time and just as dead leaves simply fall to the ground, so does our own shedding of emotional issues, relationships, jobs, or places we have lived. This card will strongly affect other cards in the reading, showing that the qualities and energies moving through are at a powerful transitional time. The Death card may also indicate a fear of death, suicidal ideation, anxiety, or alternatively a time of embracing death, an initiation or a time to move willingly into the paradox of death mysteries. These are not unrelated, and the more we can sit with the truth of Death the more we can embrace life.

Essential Qualities: transformation, release, shedding, opening, mystery, unknown, letting go, magic, curiosity, endings, closure

Suggestions: Visit your local cemetery and sit on the ground, contemplating the bones beneath you. Offer a prayer of remembrance for your ancestral line and those who have put in the time of human life and all its joys and suffering. Contemplate your own death as a powerful way to remember that life is not so long after all and we can make choices of power, love, and wisdom in every moment. If we were to die tomorrow, what might we say, do, or choose differently today? If we knew we had a year to live, what would we seek out from our heart?

Visualization with the Death Card

Pull out the Death card and place it in front of you. It is often very difficult for us to imagine or accept our own death in a real way that is not conceptual. The attachment to self is strongly rooted in our way of being, and even if we have thoughts or ideas of suicide or leaving earth or don't feel at home, how many of us truly reflect on what may happen to us after death? Do we believe in an afterlife? What is the sense of being connected to our ancestors or those who have died? Do we believe our consciousness will continue? Do we believe in rebirth and reincarnation? Considering these thoughts may offer a different perspective on our everyday life. Contemplating death is a helpful way to bring more vividness and gratitude into your daily experience.

I work with hospice and often spend time sitting with people passing away. Many people die alone, and I wonder at the dissolving story of their lives, who they knew, what they experienced. Although difficult to face, these realities are happening all the time and perhaps may bring more connection to those around us whom we love.

Light a candle and sit with the Death card for fifteen or twenty minutes. Imagine you are gone from your life and everything going on after you leave. Your children, friends, and beloveds are still on earth living their lives. What might they miss about you? What are you leaving behind? Do you have gifts you still wish to offer before it is time to leave? Journal these thoughts and ideas and discover more about your own relationship and association with death and dying.

Death Card Layout: Reflections on Transition

This layout is used to reflect on what is passing away from your life, to make room for what is yet to come. This particular format is helpful to use when something is clearly ending in your life, such as a breakup, leaving a job, or moving to a new place. The cards are used to help support the necessary transitional process.

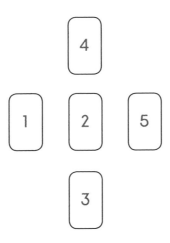

- Card 1: Past: what is influencing the current transition
- Card 2: Present transformative process
- Card 3: Ground: what is helping to support the process
- Card 4: Unseen: help or guidance that may not necessarily be apparent
- Card 5: Outcome

14: TEMPERANCE (ART)

After Death the Fool encounters Temperance, the watery, open-hearted, healing immersion that follows endings and total dissolution. Temperance is a wonderful energy that is a little wild and unexpected. After Death, who could have imagined such a beautiful rebirth? Although Death certainly feels complete and final, we learn in life that although certainly things end and finish, they also feed into the next phase of the creative the cycle that offers rebirth after death. Before a time of a big transition, before we die to the next way of being, we can cannot imagine what lay before us; it takes traversing the threshold and crossing over from one way of being to another.

Temperance is number fourteen, the one of the Magician and the four of the Emperor, signifying manifestation, a sacred container, foundational energy. Here, Temperance is at the end of the second cycle of seven, moving from the completion of subconscious energies and teachings into the realms of spiritual truths, disengaged compassion, and soulful nourishment of the superconscious.

In my own life, I experienced a powerful and literal embodiment of the transition from Death to Temperance. As mentioned in the Death card, I had a baby daughter named Rubybleu who stopped breathing shortly after birth. She was full term, yet for some unknown reason she left almost as quickly as she arrived. After a few days in intensive care, it became clear she wasn't meant to stay; we took her off the machines and she passed away in my arms. When her dad and I cremated her, the ashes turned red and blue, a total mystery! I have often been inspired by the mixing of these two colors red and blue and viewed their appearance in this magical way as a pure expression of temperance. Rubybleu's death was a catalyst for a much deeper life experience for me and my path and transformed my awareness of death and dying into a powerful recognition of spirit and beauty.

As a verb, to "temper" is to "act as a neutralizing or counterbalancing force to something." In metallurgy, tempering finds balance in metal that is neither to hot nor too cold, allowing the metal to be bent and shaped into something new. It is an ongoing process, a constant calibration. Temperance is constant reminder of this relationship with ourselves, our mind, our practice, people in our lives, our community, our world—not too tight and not too loose. The dynamic energy and creativity found in Temperance is more spiritual and refined than earlier cards such as the Empress or the Lovers. It holds the wisdom of the path walked and the wisdom of the thirteen cards before it learned, from the Magician to Death. There is more ease in the healing and can indicate an unlikely healing or mixing of unexpected forces. The work of Temperance offers loosening, mixing up, and softening.

Crowley termed this card "Art," which also invokes the passionate meeting of opposites. Whenever we bring together new qualities, we create something new. Mixing together fire and ice, hot and cold, blue and red, light and dark, this card shows a figure putting together raw elements provides the potential for infinite possibilities. This is the alchemical process of transforming raw into refined which also applies to our emotional body, spiritual work and self-inquiry process. Through Temperance we access the capability to transmute our pain into power, anger into compassion, poison into nectar.

In Waite-Smith imagery, a divine winged non-gendered being pours water back and forth between two vessels, refining, reviewing, renewing and refreshing. One foot rests on the earth and the other in the water revealing our connection to both the material world and the spiritual world. This is an essence dialogue between our form body and our spiritual self that goes beyond form. Tuning into Temperance provides us with creative, nourishing, soulful beauty and helps us to manifest this into form. The wings symbolize the connection to divine source and regenerative essence level qualities that we can tap into after Death, preparing us for the next part of the journey.

In the Crowley deck, the card's title, Art, evokes powerful creative expression. Here we see a figure who embodies the coming together of opposites—male and female, light and dark pouring the opposing elements of fire and ice into a vessel. This symbolizes the merging of opposites and alchemical creation to form something completely different, manifesting beauty following death and dissolution. The process is akin to the metamorphosis of the caterpillar who dissolves into imaginal cells before reforming into the outrageous beauty of the butterfly.

The card features the same lion and eagle from the Lovers card, but the colors have switched. Instead of a white eagle and red lion, we see a red eagle and white lion indicating the connection to the Lovers and the merging of two energies. The Temperance card is the Lovers card exalted. In the Lovers, we often express our sexual/sensual selves with a partner or an experience. With Temperance, it is still possible to have an experience with a lover but we may also discover an opportunity to use and transform sexual energy into creative expression through art, invention, writing, movement, community building, or planting our garden.

When Temperance appears in a reading, it indicates a sense of balance, harmony, and beauty. It signifies the arrival of restoration and regeneration. It can indicate an unlikely healing or newly forming creative expression at play. This card is positively indicated for relationships, work and health but may involve loosening our preconceived notions around what a partner or job or healing method may look like. When opposite forces are brought together, often solutions come in a surprising or creative manner that seem to benefit many.

Temperance or Art as the exalted lovers may indicate the arrival of new partner or someone with whom you will be potentially creating new projects. It is a call to do something that you may have done before but in a completely new way, with a new person or people or different materials. It is an invitation to mix and combine forces and be open to things you would normally be resistant or even opposed to. This card is the reminder that something new cannot be created with movement, letting go, dynamism and a willingness to explore and discover.

Essential Qualities: art, creativity, flow, beauty, tempering, mixing, melding, healing, wonder, openness, guidance, angelic, divine, source

Suggestions: Do a spiritual practice that inspires you! Visualize your energy field illuminated with rainbow colored lights and see the world around you as a mandala of enlightened glowing beings. Welcome the opportunity to transform raw emotion and negative thoughts into creative expression and compassionate actions. Mix together unlikely energies: throw a party and invite different kinds of friends, do something you don't usually do or haven't done in years, ask for spiritual guidance, paint, draw, dance, free flow!

Temperance/Art Card Layout: Elemental Perspectives

This spread is helpful for issues around relationships, creative projects, building on ideas, or anything that you feel needs deeper understanding with a fresh new perspective. Create an altar that has opposite energies symbolizing coming together: red and blue colors; a bowl of water and a candle; hard stone and soft ash. These also embody aspects of the natural and elemental world, reminding us of the dynamic mixture and interplay between elemental creation and dissolution. Make your space, light the candles and call in the helpers and guides. Take a moment to clearly visualize and center your awareness on the question at hand before shuffling and laying out the cards.

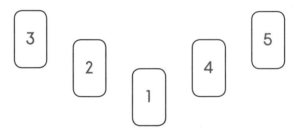

- Card 1: Querent
- Card 2: Air: guidance to support the path of bringing ideas into fruition
- Card 3: Water: guidance from the emotional realm which can help to heal and soothe
- Card 4: Fire: guidance from the spiritual realm to activate and energize
- Card 5: Earth: guidance from the material realm to help and manifest

15: THE DEVIL

The Fool continues their journey along the major arcana full of joy and tempered alchemical love only to encounter the deep, dark shadows of the Devil. Entering into the final set of seven cards begins the Fool's journey into the elevated levels of super consciousness. These cards each include a oracle vision or direct voice experience from the card's view. After creating foundation ceremonies in the first set of seven and working the cards with layouts in the second set of seven, we now move into receiving the wisdom of the higher consciousness of the last cycle. I recommend having someone read this aloud to you or recording the vision and listening while also looking at the associated card. You may also wish to explore this for yourself, writing your own oracle vision for these cards as well as others.

The Devil is an appropriate entrance point into the final cycles of human evolution as it represents all that is dark, mysterious, fearsome, and misunderstood within ourselves and in our culture. Here our inner demons rise to the surface to meet outer societal demons that may be crushing us. This card's number is fifteen, which includes the one, (the energy of the Magician) with the five (the Hierophant), the latter of whom upholds societal structures, dogmatic beliefs, and conditioned patterns. Added together, they equal six, associating the Devil with the Lovers and all that is passionate, wild, and sexually embodied but with the associated problems of trauma, oppression, and pain that yearns to be healed. In many ways the Devil is the literal opposite of the Hierophant who often was classically called "the Pope." Being a religious figure, everything the Hierophant embodies—including rules, systems, beliefs, light, outward expression, masks, conditions, religious codes, family patterns, and societal conduct—is turned completely on its head when the Devil appears.

Culturally, the Devil is the most unpopular, misunderstood, and hated figure of the recent past centuries. He is associated with Lucifer, whose name means "lightbringer," and is the one who refused to follow God's orders, later called Satan, "the accuser" or "adversary." The archetype of the Devil is the one who is against all dogma, never caring for rules, completely free and independent. In the true essence of the Devil, there are no restrictions, no limitations, and nothing is forbidden. His true origin as Satan may lie in the connection to Pan, the ancient Greek goat-footed god of the wild who had a lusty, regenerative, and joyous nature associated with growth and fertility. As it gained prominence, authority, and influence, the Christian church likely stamped him out and relegated him to what we now know as the Devil.

Since that time, anything deviating from the white, heteronormative, patriarchal Christian culture is considered devilish and even demonic. All that is dark, feminine, queer, indigenous, and of the earth has been associated deeply with the Devil, and thousands of humans have been tortured, slain, and cultures decimated in the name of a superior god that is fighting the so-called Devil. The tarot cards themselves have been and are often still viewed to be the "work of the devil," as they offer insight into the mysterious and unknowable realms. This exacerbated judgment has caused immense, unnecessary suffering for people and deeply conditioned many of us to judge what is outside the normal culture. The Devil asks us to dismantle conditioning and repression so that healing of ancestral trauma in these realms can occur. This dismantling can be an immensely painful process; however, we must recognize our internalized racism, sexism, homophobia, and judgments—they must be unpacked and processed. Equally oppressive is society's views of us and the ways in which we are boxed in based on the color of our skin, sexual orientation, gender, age, and so on.

On the personal level, we have all danced with the Devil, so to speak, when we dove into the dark holes of addiction, perhaps as excess drinking or smoking, an unhealthy relationship to sex, or eating without mindfulness. Our competitive culture itself is fueled upon the mass consumption of toxic food, excessive products, mass media, and overindulgence. We see the poisonous effects of our cultural behaviors laying waste across the earth's oceans, forests, rivers, lakes, and mountains.

And yet, the Devil is also simply our shadow, the reminder of the powerful light that shines behind the darkness. He arrives to show us our repressions, fears, secrets, and what holds us in bondage so that we may recognize how free we actually are. Without the Devil's wild, dark, disruptive dance, we would never turn to face our shadow self and thereby never bring it to the light. Staying in denial causes dis-ease; wreaks emotional havoc; and brings turmoil in the guise of obstacles, misfortune, and unhappy twists and turns.

The Devil is also a doorway into the depths of our own internal wildness and perhaps all that is truly good, not evil at all. The Devil is the wild feminine, the dark mystery, the rebel within who invites us to discover the process through change, vulnerability, and creativity. Welcoming the essence of this energy allows us to grow and expand ecstatically into parts of ourselves that we may have suppressed. The Devil can assist us in charging up mountains, doing wild creative dances, opening up to our sexual selves, and finding ourselves in a powerful place of pleasure and discovery.

In the Waite-Smith imagery, the horned figure of the Devil looks fiercely outward, gazing penetratingly at the reader. The right hand is raised upwards toward the sky and the left is holding a fire stick pointing downward, symbolizing the balance between heaven and earth. Perched on a doorway with gray bat-like wings, the figure invokes the sense of wildness, strength, and creatures of the night. The two figures below the Devil are akin to the Lovers who, exalted in Temperance, have fallen from grace. Yet, the chains that bind them can easily be slipped off as soon as they remember that their own judgments and projections are the only thing inhibiting them.

In Crowley's imagery, we see the Devil as a goat with full, twisting horns reaching high up into the sky. The goat has three eyes, symbolizing the Devil's psychic and magical associations. He stands on two possibly egg- or testicle-shaped forms with the thrust of a phallic shaped imagery behind him that represents the sexual masculine energy of potent action and change. Within the eggs are figures waiting to be freed and reborn. Behind the Devil are smears of lines symbolizing chaos and creative expression. In front of the Devilish goat is a caduceus, a staff of creative life force.

In a reading, the Devil signifies the arrival of something wild, dark, passionate, and disruptive. This may come in the form of a new lover or unexpected crush, obsession, or enchantment. Traditionally, this card may represent betrayal, lies, addictions, and negative emotions. Like the wild pigs that plow up the earth, this is not a welcome energy but it brings air and light into the soil which betters it for planting.

The Devil may show up as an unwelcome guest, coworker, or family member who is disruptive, chaotic, or unwieldy. Their arrival offers you a chance to reflect on your own judgments, stagnation, and repressions. The Devil may also indicate something painful such as discovering that someone has cheated on you, your boss has been lying, or other disappointing news. It can also indicate a recognition of long unaddressed addictions, gossip, disease, or other negative energies that are affecting your daily life and the havoc they wreak on your life that allow you to finally make needed changes.

The Devil can also indicate a time to welcome and embrace something wild such as a new adventure, lover, or form of creative expression. The energy of the Devil may actually be a breath of fresh air after the suppression of certain dynamic, creative, or sexual aspects of ourselves. It is a "coming out" energy and may signify coming out in terms of one's gender, sexual orientation, a new healing channel, following a different career, and all the ways our lives may show us it is crucial for our soul to come out rather than stay hidden. At the marking point of our evolutionary spiritual journey, the Devil invites us to reassess our own judgments and relinquish our personal demons to the fires of transformation.

> *Essential Qualities:* wild, dark, energetic, suppression, bondage, forest, secrets, disruption, chaos, explosion, sexual, addiction, freedom
>
> *Suggestions:* Notice your addictions and give some space around them. Do something a bit wild and different! Try out something new. Acquaint yourself with the energy of Pan. Create an interpretive dance that embodies a time when you "came out" in your life, when you had to be vulnerable and share something uncomfortable to someone or a group of people. Allow yourself to explore a secret fantasy.

Oracle Vision

I am the Devil. I romp into your life to awaken you from your slumbering and festering way. I disturb your false sense of security and ruffle your sedate feathers.

I create chaos and wild disturbance so that you may see where you have begun to atrophy and stagnate.

I am the Wild Pan of the forest and carry with me the wisdom of the dark, mysterious, untouchable wilderness. I am the remote reaches of land where no human has stepped foot, developing or domesticating me. I am your ancestral remembrance that you too are part of this Wilderness, waiting to awaken and play and celebrate your own delicious body and nature once again.

I am the one who brings light to the darkness, who plows the fields preparing for new seeds of life and renewal. I am the one who dances all night long, bringing down the wisdom of the stars to the welcoming arms of the earth, who makes love with the soil and the water, with the wind and roots of trees. I scream in wild pleasure and howl at the full moon crying out to be heard and lived and embodied on earth once again.

16: THE TOWER

The Fool emerges from the intense visit to the Devil's shadow self now ripe to allow even more to fall away and disintegrate. After facing the Devil's insight into the chains that bind us, breaking free and dancing with their shadows, the Fool enters the realm of the Tower. From one kind of darkness into another, the Fool journeys to the ultimate magnificent construct of ego, self, limiting beliefs, and attachments that must be broken down to reveal wisdom, insight, and spiritual clarity.

The Tower is number sixteen—the one of the Magician as well as the six of the Lovers, associated with harmony, beauty, truth, connection, and love. Although perhaps difficult to understand in relation to the Tower, this is a card that may appear troubling and disruptive but its appearance is due to a deep longing for our soul to return to a sense of harmony and love that has long been outdated. Added together, the numbers create seven, a number of friction, growth, turbulence, and resurrection. The number seven connects to the Chariot, an energy of thrust, movement, action, and obvious outward changes. While the Chariot is generally positive in nature, the Tower most often presents as obstacles, difficulties, challenges, and chaos.

In medieval times, towers were used to watch for invaders, protect and defend castles and territory, and imprison people. Warriors could shoot arrows, loft cannons, or pour boiling liquids from the high places to make it difficult for attackers to advance. In modern times, towers are tall buildings that contain large amounts of working people who usually pour their time and energy into corporate endeavors as well as communication towers that transmit information. Towers are manmade attempts to get higher, have an advantage, create a sense of power over a situation. When the Tower comes crumbling down, it is the possible actual destruction of such a structure or symbolic dissolution of power that is being misused. Early versions of the card were called "Lightning," a meaning that indicates unexpected fiery destruction.

The image of the tarot evokes a wild sense of dissolution, crumbling, and destruction of structures that are no longer able to withstand the soul's need to grow, heal, change, and discover. In many traditions, the emphasis of struggling, suffering, pain, and hardship are necessary for true, real, and rich soul growth. When we struggle the most or face our deepest fears, we discover the riches of our true selves. When we mine the depths of the dark nights of the soul the treasures of truth and love are revealed. The Tower is akin to the Nine of Swords in which the questioner has come to the dark night of the soul. From here, there is nowhere to go but up.

The brilliant lightning strike above the tower is the flash of power and mystery and suddenness that can appear in our lives, turning well-formed plans into dust. As they say, if you want to make God laugh, tell him your plans. And the Tower is the reminder of this. Belief systems, old structures, political and religious dogma must also crumble to allow the new ideas to take root. Similar to the destructive quality of lava, the Tower is the portent of chaos that leaves behind fertile new ground for something brilliant, inspirational, and completely new.

In the Waite-Smith imagery, we see a gray tower burning atop a craggy cliff against a black background and ominous clouds. Two figures are falling to their demise as lightning strikes and leaves behind smoke and ash. Above the tower is a golden crown tilted to the side appearing to also fall. This symbolizes the opening of the crown chakra or energy center at the top of our head. This can symbolize a kind of enlightenment or brief experience of illumination that follows the difficult dissolution of the tower. Flames emerge from the tower's windows signifying the burning away of old structures and conditions. There is nothing left to do but fall.

In the Crowley deck, the Tower card has vivid and sharp imagery that indicates a kind of shattering. At the top of the card is an all-seeing eye which beams outward beyond the chaos and turmoil below, indicating the part of our soul self that survives any major change or upheaval. Forceful flames emerge from a wide open toothed mouth, fierce and all-consuming, symbolizing the unstoppable change. Yet in the background is a dove flying with a peace offering, a symbol of hope and grace even in times of turmoil.

The Tower certainly brings crisis and chaos and events that will be impossible to avoid. In a reading, the Tower indicates an external major transition such as loss of a job, divorce, chaos, and turbulent changes. Internally it may signify a loss of identity, sense of well-being, or emotional upheaval. This card always indicates difficult challenges in life; the reader should look to other cards to see what the Tower will be affecting the most, such as relationships, health, work, or spiritual matters.

If the Tower is in the future or outcome placement, the reader or client can be advised to prepare for a disruptive change. Sometimes the Tower works like an initiation in which everything is taken away so something new can emerge. If this is the case, we can also prepare for a time like this and enter change willingly or with more openness.

Essential Qualities: crisis, chaos, destruction, change, rubble, deconstruction, dissolution, loss of power, lightning, initiation, turmoil, upheaval

Suggestions: Look at the belief systems and stories that are confining you and preventing you from growing. Dismantle the old and make way for the new! Have a fire ceremony and write down a list of all that you are clearing away and burn it. Burn a bunch of papers, documents, art, and/or journals you no longer need. Turn the old into ash and lay that down on the earth to fertilize your way.

Oracle Vision

I am the Tower. I destroy limiting beliefs, identities, and attachments with no mercy. When I arrive, it is a time of ultimate surrender as change and chaos reign down upon you. If you struggle against the wild will of the Tower, you will experience further pain and suffering.

I remind you that loss is necessary and surrender is the flow of life. You have built up many walls around you that you thought would keep you safe. I am here to let you know that in life, there are no guarantees. There is no security but for the song and brilliance of your soul that only wishes to emerge more clearly from the rubble I cause.

From the ashes and dust that I create comes new life. Rebirth always follows death. Let me strip and burn away the facade that keeps you from experiencing the truth of everlasting love. Allow the fires of purification to clear and cleanse what has grown old and tired. Relinquish the old stories and clear the air for new power and beauty and wisdom.

17: THE STAR

Following the painful turbulence and intensity of the Tower, the Fool finds themselves totally surrendered with nothing left but the purity of their soul's essence. When everything is stripped away, the Fool encounters the brilliant, refreshing, illuminating light of the Star card. Probably one of the most popular cards in the deck, this card brings fresh spiritual insight, revelations, and clarity in the forms of beauty, light, and cleansing. The Star is our courageous heart shining forth, connected to the infinite universe of unconditional love and brings us a sense of renewal, hope, faith, and rebirth.

The number seventeen continues to carry the essence of the Magician as well as the Chariot, number seven. The magical energy is moving forward now full of light, energy, power, and force. The combination number eight signifies creative flow, work, and manifestation of clear insight and radiance. When the Star appears in a reading, almost everyone is delighted. It carries a resounding "ta-da!" and is the kind of energy that refreshingly arrives following a sense of dread, sorrow, and the troubled aftermath of the Tower. The Star brings the confident and purposeful awareness of the soul's calling.

The Star has the ability to translate spirit directly into form without having to overly process the emotional and mental realms; instead, we are asked to rely on higher sources of wisdom. The Star is a reminder to step into our own confident selves and trust the flow of life. While the Tower completely humbles us as humans on the journey, the stars remind us we are also divine in nature. With it, the Star brings an outpouring of blessings, revelations, and clear dreams.

At night, we look above to the stars—those brilliant reminders of light that shine in the dark night—and are moved by their ancient beauty. They are so far away that when we look at them, we are actually looking into the past. We can harness this awareness and remember that although we perceive we are having a linear, mortal, progressive experience from birth to death, the truth of awakening shows us that the universe is not linear and time is a mental construct. The Star evokes the energy of compassion, forgiveness, and spontaneous healing, reminding us that these things can happen across both time and distance, through generations, and even with those who have passed away.

The Star reminds us that we are always guided, even if we don't always feel that way. The assistance of our unseen helpers, guides, dreams, and spiritual beings are always available—we only need to ask. Dreams are one of the most potent forms of guidance and are often overlooked in their usefulness for assistance. I recommend taking advantage of this rich time at night to invoke healing, guidance, and wisdom more fully into your daily life. Whatever you are struggling with simply ask out loud for assistance before you go to sleep *every single night that you remember.*

In the Waite-Smith imagery, the Star card shows a woman who is naked and vulnerable yet fully empowered and open to her pure expression of beauty in the world. One foot rests on the earth, grounded and connected, while the other foot is in the water, representing the emotional body. She pours two vessels of water, symbolizing cleansing, rebirth, renewal, and illumination. Above her shines seven smaller stars and one large star, all with eight points. The eight-pointed star is symbolic of regeneration and resurrection, the bright rebirth that follows the long, dark night.

In the Crowley deck, the Star card is imbued with vivid and bright colors of indigo, magenta, and white. A lithe and graceful figure pours a crystalline flow from one vessel downward entering the body and another down toward the earth. There are three seven pointed stars which symbolize Venus, hope, love, and healing. Behind the figure is a large celestial globe indicating the connection to the cosmic rays of the universe. Below the figure are crystal formations symbolizing the pure elemental nature of creation from soul essence to material form.

When the Star appears in a reading, it casts its brilliant and beautiful light onto the other cards, lifting their meaning into the awareness of divine purpose. The Star indicates a healing, clearing, and renewing time often following obstacles and troubles. It may indicate a surprise blessing, unexpected good news, divine inspiration, or guidance. In relationships and work, the appearance of the

Star is a positive blessing on any endeavor. The Star suggests following one's intuition and avoiding getting caught in the material or emotional world and to trust a more spiritual or essence level outlook.

Essential Qualities: light, healing, rebirth, love, brilliance, guidance, peace, restoration, ancient, ancestors, angelic, beauty, wonder, awe

Suggestions: I invite you to meditate with the starry night sky! During the time of the new moon, you have the opportunity to reflect on a more star filled sky. As you sit with the stars, imagine the brilliant silver and gold light pouring down and illuminating your energetic, emotional, and physical bodies. Set an intention at night to receive a healing dream and be open to receiving guidance in myriad ways.

Oracle Vision

I am the Star. I shine brilliantly in the vast, cosmic heavens reminding you of your own divinity. I illuminate all that has transpired, offering forgiveness, healing, cleansing, and purification. I wash away aches and pains and soothe the scars of your heart. I offer the waters of beauty and sweetness to help you remember the joy that life has to offer.

I emerge shining night after night in the sky above you to remind you where you come from. I am your ancestor that dances in fiery expression echoing a time from long ago. You are my future and I look to you and admire your willingness to fall down and rise, again and again.

I am here to illuminate your path and show you the way when you thought you were lost. I am your higher self, your innate wisdom, your unseen guidance that is always with you even when you seem the most lost, the most desolate.

18: THE MOON

Our Fool adventurer continues their major arcana journey and encounters the radiant, dark, elusive, mysterious moon. The moon is a divine and wondrous sphere orbiting the planet, its presence causing the effect of tides and currents on the oceans and a reference point for our lives, waxing and waning through the seasons reminding us of the constant, cyclical flow of one phase to another.

The Moon has the potential to aid in our healing of buried qualities, to illuminate and guide us through the murky waters of our unconscious toward transformation and the powerful reminder that all things move in cycles. The moon is a symbol of love without names or forms, its light reflecting the sun's brilliance, which is simply a star in the vast universal dance. The light of the moon dances with the Star's energy bridging us to the Sun's awareness.

The Moon is number eighteen, continuing to carry the intentions of the Magician, number one, as well as number eight, which symbolizes right effort, balance, neutrality, and empowerment. Together these numbers equal nine, connecting the Moon to the Hermit, representing solitude, inner illumination, darkness, and discovery. When used in a focused and clear way, the gifts of the Moon provide us the tools to make changes in our deep habitual patterns; when ignored, emotional problems, disillusions, and weakness may result. This card marks the turning point in the cycle of seven and is an opportunity to heal emotions with the super conscious element guiding the way.

The moon is as old as we humans know and figures in countless myths as goddesses and a few gods. It has long been associated with the dark, mysterious qualities of the feminine and the female body that also waxes and wanes in its biological expression and ability to receive the male seed and create new life within. Many myths, ancient practices, and magical workings rely on the wisdom of the moon and its dance through the constellations to guide and offer structure to magical work.

The word "moon" derives from *menses* which later evolved into our contemporary word "month." Traditional moon phase gardening is a method that follows the cycles of the moon to guide when and what to plant. As the moon influences tides and subtle bodies of water, it also affects the moisture in the earth. During full and new moons the sun and moon line up with earth exerting their influence on the earth and encouraging growth of plants. In magical work, the new or dark moon indicates clearing away an old cycle, moving into new beginnings and seeding intentions. As the moon waxes, the energy of these intentions grow and develop, reaching their maturation and full activation stage at the full moon time. As the moon wanes, the energy slowly dissipates and clears away, making room for the next cycle.

Relationally, the Moon indicates troublesome or shadowy emotions and invites us to examine our connections to others more deeply. We are required to take more and fuller responsibility for our thoughts, feelings, words, and actions in relation to one another. This responsibility can be within our personal relations as well as others in our workplace, socially, and globally. The Moon card asks us to examine limiting beliefs and victim mentality, and instead step fully into the potentiated awake sense of self walking a path.

The Moon card is the symbol of the deep unconscious rising up into awareness. This may bring to light hidden secrets, buried passions, and unrealized dreams. The Moon can act as a warning of deception, lies, dark fantasies, and tricky enchantments. The Moon card is like the pied piper—the sound of the flute is beautiful but may lead us into a dark forest. This is not the first time such an enchantment has arisen; the Moon often symbolizes the repeat of a past issue coming to the surface once again. At the start of a particularly enchanting and powerful relationship, we each drew a card from the Mana cards, a deck of Hawaiian myth and imagery. Curiously we both chose the same card, the Mo'o or lizard card which offered the advice, "beware the enchanter." I chose another card from my Waite-Smith deck for clarification and pulled the Moon card. Ignoring the sage advice of these cards, I entered into this relationship with wild abandon, only to have my entire life turned upside down by its powerful enchantments, both for better and worse.

Although the Moon may bring to rise illusory and challenging deceptions, it has with it still the watery wisdom of cycles and the power of reflection. Following the Moon is the Star, which rises illumined and brilliant, helping us to find a clear and vivid revelation on our winding journey of life. After the Moon dissolves into the radiance of the starlight, we are able to clearly see what needs clearing away with a more gentle and compassionate view.

Like the Tower card, the Moon represents another kind of initiation, however this time into the subtle realms of memory, delusion, illusion, perception, and fantasy. The Moon reminds us that things are not always what they seem and are forever changing from one form into another. Passing through the gate of this awareness allows us to more deeply navigate the waters of our own subconscious which drives so much of our behavior. Our addictions, fantasies, negative habits, and imprints are all connected.

In the Waite-Smith deck, we see a full moon shining down over a rocky landscape. Two gray pillars stand as if watching, like guardians symbolizing a gateway. A dog and a wolf howl up at the moon representing the wild and domestic parts of ourselves or the conscious and subconscious aspects. These two animals are separated by a pathway that travels from the forefront of a pond to the mountains in the distance symbolizing the path of illumination. From the pond emerges a lobster, a representation of the deepest aspects of our unconscious which often unknowingly drives us to act.

In the Crowley deck we see two huge pillars guarded by Anubis, the Egyptian god of the dead who helped spirits cross over, and Set, the god of rational thought, intelligence, and the trickster. At their feet, facing each other are the dog and the wild wolf symbolizing the battle that can happen between our rational mind and subconscious emotive self that is linked to death and mystery. They guard the river of life, the scarab beetle carrying the sun through the pillars symbolizing rebirth and illumination.

In a reading, the Moon may indicate secrets coming out into the open, hidden ideas and thoughts being revealed. Traditionally, this card may symbolize deceptive behaviors such as cheating, lying, or stealing that covers up restless and unsatisfied aspects of us. In this way, the Moon card asks us to examine what is coming up to the surface for us? What is showing up in your dreams? What obsessive thoughts haunt you creating unrest in your psyche? Although the Moon card is uncomfortable, it helps direct us into the murky aspects of self that have until now remained subtly hidden from our own healing and awareness.

The Moon indicates a time to bring something out into the light. It may be a part of us that needs to be healed, transformed, energized, or revitalized. This healing or transformation comes in the form of creative expression through art, dance, writing, or a song. The Moon invites us to dissolve our edges, doubts, fear, and insecurities through healing waters and meditation. The Moon is a time of lucidity and contemplation, watery intuition, and insight.

> *Essential Qualities:* luminous, cycles, shadows, darkness, waxing, waning, full, new, circle, birth, death, rebirth, enchantments, illusion, deception, clarity, intuition, dreams, insight
>
> *Suggestions:* Spend time with the moon. What is the feeling that fills the heart when you gaze at the waning moon during these darkening autumn days? When do you discover your true aloneness? Rest quietly in solitude either early in the morning or late at night, listening the quietness of the moon. The Moon brings the dissolution of illusion and brings about guidance and clarity beyond the darkness. Revisit the water gazing ceremony of the High Priestess card.

Oracle Vision

I am the Moon. I perfectly reflect the light of the sun, that which gives light to all of the world. I remind you that life always moves in flow and rhythms of change. My waxing and waning is reflective of the expansion and contraction that naturally occurs in all of life. I ebb and flow in concert with the tides, deeply connected to the waters of the world and the waters of your body.

As you continue to awaken to your true nature, I illuminate the residual negative patterns that persist in the deepest parts of your subconscious. I remind you that healing moves in cycles of birth, life, death, and rebirth. I am here to witness and reflect the changes that you move through.

19: THE SUN

The major arcana journey continues as the Fool meets the Sun, the bountiful beauty of the warm bright center of our universe. After traversing the lonely, enchanting, curious terrain of the Moon, the Fool arrives in the land of plenty, the place of pure desire and harmony. At this place in the evolution of the cards the spirit and form align allowing for dreams to come fully to life. Sunlight is essential to our well-being. All life on earth thrives due to the perfect alignment between our sun and the earth, a star among billions of other stars. An ordinary miracle! When the sun touches our face, we feel the imminent grace of warmth, beauty, light, perhaps even magic. It is ever enchanting to watch sunlight dance on water, reflecting and reminding us that everything is in constant, perfect motion.

The Sun is number nineteen, the last card with the number one, carrying the seed of the Magician to its final expression. The number nine symbolizes integration, flowering, beauty, and growth. Added together we have the number ten, which connects the Sun to the Wheel of Fortune a connection of fortune, illumination and destiny. Combined with the number zero, connected to the Fool, the Sun also includes the qualities of trust, innocence, love, openness and freedom.

The Sun provides an expansive and illuminated view. It is the brilliant warming energy of growth, beauty, harmony, and sharing. The sun's warmth brings unexpected opportunities, manifest dreams, and sprouts new seeds into life. When we lay in the warmth of the sun our bodies automatically relax, our nervous system rests, and our breathing slows down. These are opportune moments to receive messages and open to bright wisdom and guidance from our ancestors, the land, and the sun.

The Sun amplifies all of our blessings and gifts, reminding us of our true purpose on Earth. I think of it like a gift basket that each of our souls carries with us. We have a certain soul signature that is our unique way of sharing our gifts. When we align with these gifts, we are able to experience an abundant life rich in spirit, mind, body, and heart.

The Sun is our reminder of what is good in our lives. On those dark days when the sun peeks out from the clouds for just a moment, we may feel a rush of delight in our bones. Even if we cannot see it, the sun is always there, just as our true brilliant awake nature is always resting within only waiting to be continuously realized. This can be a helpful reminder when we are going through all of life's changes, intense transitions we may face, and in the recognition of suffering happening on earth in so many forms.

In the Waite-Smith deck, a gleeful naked child rides a white horse, arms widespread to the warmth of the vigorous sun above. Behind the child are huge, full sunflowers, symbols of the fullness and ripeness of the summer harvest. The sun radiates outward above the child and the horse with a calm and beatific look on its face. The child holds a red and yellow gold flag that unfurls in the wind to symbolize the energies of strength, vitality, joy, and radiance.

In the Crowley deck, two figures with butterfly wings dance in exultation below the brilliance of the sun. Their arms are lifted up to the sky in joy and their feet move gracefully on a green hill which symbolizes the fertile land and abundance of the sun. Along the edge of the card are illustrations of the twelve signs in the zodiac indicating the fullness of the entire astrological heavens in connection to the movement of the sun through these constellations.

When the Sun card appears in a reading, it indicates the outward expression of dreams fulfilled and may signify land, marriage, partnership, family, blessings, and abundance. This is a time of creativity, warmth, sharing and the harvest where we connect with those of like mind and open our hearts to cocreation and celebration. The Sun always warms the reading, so to speak, amplifying the gifts and messages that appear in the other cards. The Sun reminds us to count our blessings and see what is abundant and flowering in our lives, even in difficult or troubling times.

Essential Qualities: brightness, growth, abundance, beauty, love, innocence, family, blessings, gifts, joy, sharing, communication, dreams manifested, inspiration

Suggestions: There is a Buddhist practice I find helpful called Tonglen that inspires us to become our own personal sun. In this practice we inhale the dark, chaotic, painful suffering of the world and others into our hearts, transforming it into light and breathing it back out. In this way we identify with the struggles of others and generate compassion. Tonglen empowers us to step into the courage of the heart knowing we are strong enough to handle what is fearsome and painful and be of service to transmute that into love, compassion, and grace. I encourage you to practice Tonglen, drawing in the pain of others and transforming it in the courageous vessel of your own divine heartlight. Be your own sun, shining outward to others, generous without expectation. Create a gift "basket" of your soul, illuminating your own gifts to the world. Find objects or symbols to represent who you are and your personal sun power offering that brightens this world.

Oracle Vision

I am the Sun. I radiant eternal and infinite light and warmth blessing the earth and atmosphere continuously with my rays. Without me nothing could grow, thrive, flower, and fruit. My perfect distance from the earth reminds you of the perfection in all things, the harmony of ceaseless manifest forms.

I adore you and my adoration never ceases. I remind you to continuously bring your desires and dreams to life, continue to ask, and remain open to receive the wild abundance of light and love that permeates all things. I am the reminder to invite without expectation, to love without condition, to dream without worry, to dance and live without pressure. I am the offering of unlimited freedom.

I am the warmth and revitalization and bring the blessing of healing from disease, disharmony, and lower level vibrations. I offer the pure resonance of sound and sacred geometry, the illumined lines of light that move through all things. I am a Star and remind you that you too are in a body made of star dust, a brief encounter between form and light.

20: JUDGEMENT (AEON)

The Fool's next phase on the major arcana journey passes through Judgement. As the Fool nears the end of the path, they encounter the depths of wisdom and reflection of the long journey that has unfolded. When the Judgement card appears, it indicates a time of reckoning, a chance to self-reflect on events, relationships, and the life path. It is a call for clarity and perhaps a time to atone for one's actions through forgiveness, release, and compassion.

Judgement—or Aeon, as Crowley renamed it—is number twenty. At last, we leave behind the essential seed of the Magician and move into the number two of the High Priestess. The Judgement card is imbued with the essence of the wise feminine guardian who sits between the worlds and offers intuitive guidance from the unseen realms. With the connection to number zero also present, we have the Fool's sense of innocent pure and insightful truth that grounds the wisdom of judgment into our current awareness. Although Judgement is one of the last cards of the supra-conscious cycle of seven, there is a sense of embodied wisdom and human truthfulness that echoes through the elements of this card as well.

Contrary to its name, the Judgement card is more about impartiality and awareness and less about making negative judgments or assumptions about others. In the traditional idea of Judgment Day, the inspiration is a willingness to drop the egoic and attached view of our idea about how things should be and move into a more expansive and overarching view of the situation. The angelic presence in the traditional Rider-Waite-Smith card indicates a call to gather our resolve and uplift the attachments to things being a certain way, to certain stories or habits we become addicted to in our lives.

Well-grounded judgment allows us the ability to see things from a neutral perspective, above and beyond the ordinary story of our small human problems. This card asks us to take the high road from a place of disengaged compassion and a willingness to rise above the small drama so that we may grow into a new phase of life. So often, we find that this process is harder than it seems! Yet every moment is a new opportunity to step into presence.

This card invites us to move beyond our ways of reacting and being in our life path to bring in flow, magic, and creativity but without attachment or expectations for how things should look. This attitude also applies to our relationships, asking us to consider discerning and judging our true needs and desires. Judgement asks us to examine what we are giving ourselves and our friends, lovers, partners, and family members, encourages us to set boundaries, give and receive consent, to say clear yes's and no's, and stay open to those particulars changing and becoming more fluid.

In the Waite-Smith deck, the imagery shows the archangel Gabriel blowing a trumpet of grace and divine order, a profound gesture. This symbolizes a clear message from the higher self or awareness, a kind of call to destiny on the path. Below, gray-colored people lift their arms to the sky hoping to be seen and heard in this moment of divine witness. Their gray bodies indicate the mix of black and white, reminding us to move beyond dualistic and binary thinking and all its hang ups around good/evil, male/female, heaven/hell.

Crowley termed this card "the Aeon," which means a very long time, perhaps as long as a billion years. It takes a diamond at least a billion years to form, comparable in some traditions to the long and slow spiritual evolution of the human consciousness. This card then speaks of rebirth and potential of multidimensional lives and perceptions. Arching across the card is the Nuit, the Egyptian goddess of the sky. Every evening she swallows the sun and gives birth to it every morning. Also featured is Horus, the sky god child who symbolizes rebirth and potent brilliant energy. Horus's form is standing in the shape of the Tree of Life which links the journey of the tarot to the Kabbalistic path of evolution.

The Judgement card indicates a time when everything comes home to roost, so to speak. When this card appears in a reading it indicates a need to revisit past situations with the clarity of hindsight. Someone may be returning from the past either in person or in thoughts and dreams to allow for a shift in understanding around a past difficult situation. The card indicates the need to take the high road and aim for a larger perspective view on the situation at hand. In relationships and work, the Judgement card indicates a more universal connection, with a greater sphere of influence. This card may also indicate a time when suddenly things that have been clouded or unsure become clear. Insight, truth, or a strong decision are at hand guiding a newly forming destiny. This can be the arrival of a new and important relationship, change in career, or a sudden revelation about one's life purpose.

Essential Qualities: discernment, neutrality, clarity, wisdom, higher level awareness, balance, sky, above, eternity

Suggestions: Allow time to reflect and look past events. Light a candle or have a fire to honor what has challenged you the most. Write a letter to someone who you still feel a strong connection to, a letter with full heart and truth and love that you may or may not choose to send to the person. This can also be a letter to someone who has passed away with whom you feel you are still connected or have yet to resolve certain things.

Oracle Vision

I am Judgement. I offer the wisdom from high above, a hawk's-eye view. I remind you that there is always another perspective. I ask to take to the heights with me, spiraling above the tree tops into the air streams that meander the earth and wander the world.

I am divine guidance that offers you the timely hindsight to see the painful lessons of your past with new eyes. I evoke the remembrance that what is challenging is necessary growth for your soul and present new views on old memories. I invite the past into your present with a sense of meditative neutrality, dispassion, and cultivated awareness.

21: THE WORLD (UNIVERSE)

At long last, the Fool enters the final card of the journey, the World or (Universe) card. Moving from the higher perspectives and neutral discernment of Judgement, the Fool arrives at the culmination of a major life lesson or lessons learned, and then progresses to the next phase of their evolution. What has originated with the spark of the Magician has now come to completion and fulfillment.

The World card is number twenty-one, the final phase of the last cycle of seven. Here, the Fool's journey comes to a close and realization happens. This is the opportunity to look back over the path and see all the trials and tribulations that have been faced and overcome. Containing the numbers two and one, the World is infused with the energy of both the High Priestess and the Magician, when the active vital seed of intention has fully fused with and completed its journey with the guidance and wisdom of the unseen. Added together is the number three, symbolizing complete manifestation, abundance, and joy. When we reverse the number twenty-one to twelve, we discover the connection of the World to the Hanged Man, again illuminating the deeper esoteric truths that inhabit the tarot.

Entering the phase of the World we have a clear sense of what our path has been about and are perhaps suddenly open to a new kind of expression. In this way, the World holds all the potentials and possibilities. It is the myriad of pathways radiating out providing infinite options for the Fool to take. The World card is a sense of empowerment, strength, and integration. Here there is a more fulfilled sense of purpose and connection to a greater sense of self, to our higher self, as well as a deepening awareness of our interconnectedness to our relations. The World is also the earth which provides all forms of nourishment for us to sustain life, grow, thrive, and develop.

The World is also the reminder that there are as many expressions of the divine as there are human beings. We can witness the range of human expression with appreciation and respect when we dissolve our basic judgments and move into a place of love, clarity, and awareness. The World reminds us that we are all connected whether we like it or not, a global family. Each decision we make affects the world, even the tiniest of choices. We have the authority and responsibility to step fully into our empowered selves as global citizens.

Many traditions and cultures use a circle to create a container, honor the four directions, and evoke magic from a sacred space. In this way, the World card is similar to the mandala found in Eastern traditions or the Medicine wheel in Native practices. In my own Tibetan Buddhism practice, the mandala is understood to contain the entire cosmos in its circular symbolism, a representation that gives us access to infinite possibilities in an orderly form. Working with form, we can discover an infinite interplay of creativity and expression in our human journey.

The whirling stars that surround the figure on the Crowley card is usually associated with Nuit, the eternal Egyptian goddess of the skies. This imagery also evokes the qualities of Indra's net, a multifaceted and jeweled net that hangs over Indra's palace on the sacred Mount Meru. This net contains a jewel at every junction that mirrors and reflects every other jewel symbolizing the perfect patterned and multidimensional existence of the universe.

In the Waite-Smith deck, the World card shows a naked female figure in an easeful dancing posture. Her face is relaxed and content and around her is a scarf, symbolizing wisdom. She is contained within a circle of laurels indicating the infinite connection from birth, life, death, and rebirth. Anchored into the four corners of the card are symbolic representations of the four fixed signs of the zodiac which are also found in the Wheel of Fortune card. In this way, the World is a manifestation of the destiny set into motion by the Wheel, a culmination of the journey.

Crowley terms this card "the Universe," indicating an even more vast sense of the card that opens up potentiality to the cosmos' expansive and multidimensional nature. In truth, the vastness of space is a paradox—our limited form cannot necessarily fully conceive of the never-ending story of birth, creation, growth, decay, dissolution, death, and rebirth. We can only experience this during intense times of initiation, transition, or growth; put more simply, we only reach this understanding in moments of awe and wonder where our small self dissolves into the larger Self.

When the World appears in a reading, it indicates a task fulfilled on a mundane level—related to career or relationships, for example—and/or on the soul level, related to growth and change. There is a sense of completion, success, and achievement. Perhaps an award has been given. The World positively indicates fulfillment in the questions asked and presents the possibility for options not yet conceived. The World card may also indicate literal worldliness as in travel, opportunities, wealth in home and life, movement, and synchronistic connections. New ideas, options, and proposals may appear; the World encourages the questioner to stay open. This card may also indicate staying in one's power and to center the focus, trusting one's own path more fully when making a decision.

Cycle of Seven Exercise

As mentioned throughout this book, it is helpful to remember that each major arcana card contains all the lessons, challenges, wisdom, and power of the cards that have become before. As you may have done at certain points, I again recommend laying out the entire journey now from the Fool to the World to have a look at the unfolding. Following the cycles of seven, you can lay out three rows with seven cards each, starting with the Magician as the first card up to the Chariot. This way you can view the progressions of the cards, what comes before and after, and it is also interesting to note how the lines connect vertically as well as horizontally.

Essential Qualities: empowerment, totality, ending and beginning, dance, joy, expression, global, possibilities, paths, turning, understanding

Suggestions: Create a nature mandala. Spend a few hours in the woods or outside collecting things to make a simple work of art with stones, leaves, pine needles, flowers, and other small found things. Climb to a high point or look out and reflect on achievements and accomplishments. Make a list of what you are grateful for. Make a bucket list of thirty things you would like to do.

Oracle Vision

I am the World. I see and feel all things manifest on the earthly plane. I offer the wisdom of completion, of coming to the end of a journey, and recognizing when it is time to feel the confidence of a job well done. I remind you that no matter what you have done in your life, you have completed tasks and lessons, and you are walking with wisdom even if it is difficult to see this.

I invite you to discover the deep gratitude of a life in human form and to play with as many expressions as you can. I am the earth, the universe; my creative play is infinite, as is yours. I remind you that your potential is often much grander and more expansive than you can imagine. Rest in the true and open state of awareness so that you may remember your whole and eternal self.

Embodying the dance of beauty, power, freedom, expression, love, and joy is your inherent birth right as a human being. Social systems set up by man are not always congruent with the truths of the World. Seek that which gives you joy. Dissolve and let go of that which brings pain and suffering. Use every opportunity to find the center of the heart and breathe new and wild life into that moment.

THE MINOR ARCANA

The minor arcana are the fifty-six cards in the deck composed of the four suits and their association with the elements. There is a debate among the tarot community as to which came first, playing cards or the tarot? Most historical evidence points to decks of playing cards using four suits associated with the elements were around centuries before the formalized tarot emerged in the mid 1500s. Versions of cards with suits and varying numbers of court cards have been in use for hundreds of years. Contemporary playing cards clearly associate the minor arcana with the following connections, respectively: disks/pentacles—diamonds—earth; cups—hearts—water; swords—spades—air; wands—clubs—fire.

The popularization of tarot by Arthur Waite and Pamela Colman Smith portrayed figures engaged in activities, thus deepening the meaning of the minor arcana and making them more accessible for anyone to read. Each of the minor arcana cards are situational archetypes which illustrate processes moving more quickly through our lives than the major arcana. They are not as powerful as the major arcana archetypes and yet still have clear indicators to help us better understand our relationships, career, health, creative projects, home situations, and more.

The most important aspects of developing your understanding of the minor arcana besides practice is through studying the elements and the numerology of each card. Spending time connecting to each element—earth, water, air, and fire—allows you to develop an embodied and personal connection to each suit. The following explanations of the minor arcana include ceremonies, exercises, and visualizations to assist in your practice of working and using the elements in association with the minor cards helps you to embody the tarot as a living system.

Reading through and contemplating the numerology of the cards will anchor your ability to give readings for self and others more quickly and effectively.

Elemental Practices

The elements are directly connected to the minor arcana and will offer deeper insights into both the suits and court cards. To deepen your connection to the elements in relation to the minor arcana, choose one of the four elements and spend two weeks (fourteen days) practicing a fifteen-minute meditation on the element. Fourteen days allows for a practice of one day per card for the minors which include ten numbered cards plus four court cards. This also corresponds to the moon cycle and can be started on the day of the full or new moon to enhance your practice. Each day, contemplate the minor arcana and element associated with that suit. For example, if you want to work with the cups and water, start with the Ace of Cups and then follow progressively through the suit from ace to king, one card per day.

While you are working on that particular suit, also take time to delve into the qualities, insights, and essences of that particular element. It is helpful to make an offering each day before your practice. For example: earth, offer some rice or salt; air, offer incense; water, offer water in a small bowl; fire, offer flame by lighting a candle. Meditate for fifteen minutes contemplating the element and feeling into its qualities, how it shows up in your life through your body, the weather, in the food and drink you take in, as well as energetically through thoughts and emotions. Write down any insights that arise from the meditation. Link the quality of the element with the particular minor arcana with which you are working. Notice how a teaching may arise during the day that connects you to the card. Embodying the minor arcana in this way will provide powerful insights into the cards to strengthen your practice.

NUMEROLOGY

The following section explores the numbers found in the court cards and their associated meanings. Although this section is short, do not discount the effectiveness of laying groundwork for your readings with the simplicity of connecting to the numbers. Using plants as a metaphor, we explore the numbers as a journey unfolding from seed (Aces) to plant (twos through nines), to flower (tens), to seed again. Tuning into the relationality of numbers on a path opens the door for deeper understanding and insights. When you are giving a reading, it is helpful to note which numbers and in what quanitiy appear in a reading as related to their corresponding suits or elements. You may also observe the connection between the numbers and major arcana cards as a way to set groundwork for the reading. For example, if several sevens appear in a reading, we know that aspects of the querent's question is shifting, changing, or may be difficult due to the nature of sevens in the tarot system. Comparing this to the Chariot, the number seven of the major arcana, we add the understanding of an energy that is movement, change, forward direction, and a shift from one cycle of seven into the next. If you find several same suit cards but different numbers in a reading, it shows the person is working on one area primarily in their life and are at different developmental levels. Start by practicing your study with one card at a time. Use the numerology ideas presented here and then spend time meditating on your own connection to the numbers to discover more insights.

Aces: The Seed

Aces are the first card of each suit in the tarot and act as a doorway or gateway into the next level of growth and understanding. They are powerful cards and, unlike the rest of the minor arcana, are considered and equal in strength and potency to the major arcana. Within an ace contains all the wisdom and knowledge, gain and loss, power and lessons of an entire suit. Like a seed which contains all the information to grow an entire tree, the ace contains all the information of an entire suit. For example, within the Ace of Disks or Pentacles is contained every disk card from two to ten as well as how it relates to financial issues of gain and loss, material wealth, and its relation to other aspects of our lives in addition to the building up and taking down of structure and form. When all of these are combined together in an ace card, it symbolizes a profound opportunity that is arriving for growth and understanding on the next level.

Aces are a new beginning. It is as if we stepped up and into the next round, or the next act of a play. One act has finished, we have learned and completed those lessons and are ready for the next. Aces come with the awareness that a doorway is opening, but it is ultimately up to us to say yes to that opportunity and move forward.

The ace is huge seed of potent potential. When we receive an ace in our readings, we know that a new opportunity awaits us. This could be a new job offer, a new friendship, a new avenue for learning. In the Waite-Smith deck, the aces are shown as offerings—outstretched hands bear the associated suit symbols. When an Ace appears, it is up to us to take a hold of the opportunity and choose to move forward. When more than one ace appears in a reading, it is a particularly strong indication that a big change is coming that will involve opportunities for growth and learning.

Twos: The Dance

Twos follow the ace, the one. Like the plant that often sprouts into two single leaves, the twos sprout from one. Two enter into duality; here we begin the dance of reflection between self and other. This relationship may appear in the form of ideas sprouting, connections with others, or a need to resolve something with someone else. Because twos are still close to the beginning of the journey, they carry with them the energy of the one, which is embedded in dreamtime. We see this dance in the High Priestess card, in which she has one foot firmly placed in this world and the other in dreamtime, or the world of spirit. In the minor arcana, the twos signify the energy of movement, juggling, dancing, reflecting, seeking an answer, and receiving a message. This card can be negative or positive; it depends more on the surrounding cards.

Threes: Growth

Threes move into the energy of dynamic growth. The sprout of the plant begins to pour more energy into moving upward, toward the sun, toward light. This kind of growth may be physical, as in the Disks, or spiritual growth, as in the Wands or Swords. In most desks, all the threes appear positive and harmonious in general, except for the three of Swords which is one of the most negative and difficult cards of the deck. This reminds us that growth may happen through pain and struggle at times, not simply the wealth of growing money or relationships. Threes are the energy of the third party and the duality is opened up to bring a perspective that allows room for movement, creativity, plans, and deepening connections. The Empress is a three and is shown growing a field of plants, the hint of a child within her, illuminating the serene wisdom and growing beauty of the mother archetype.

Fours: Foundation

From the dynamic growth of the threes we settle into the firm foundation of four. Fours are square and like the foundation of a house, or the sides of a container, they offer structure and a firm base. The four of the Emperor is connected to the father or masculine energy of building, setting structure and rules into place to contain the growth so that it has form and direction. Fours solidify and are also the number of elements/suits found in the deck. When fours are positive, they indicate stability and grounding; when they are negative, they indicate stifled growth and inflexibility. Four also connects to the four directions—east, south west, and north—and thus orient us to our place in life and anchors us firmly in the center of the directional compass.

Fives: Adjustment

After the stability of the fours, we move into the dynamic shifting and changing of the fives. Foundations only last so long before they begin to wear and crumble, inviting change and growth to a situation. Adjustments are needed as unresolved shadow issues are forced to the surface to be integrated and healed in a situation. All the fives are difficult cards in the minors, indicating the tension, loss, and disappointment faced through various struggles and obstacles. Associated with the Hierophant, we are asked to confront what is holding us back from connecting to our spiritual selves. These are complicated cards, but they also offer us a tender and vulnerable look at a situation and what needs to be purified, let go of, changed, and cleared away.

Sixes: Balance

Following the difficult and challenging aspects of the fives, we come into a sense of balance, harmony, and vitality with the sixes. Here, healing and equilibrium are restored after the storm; there is a sense of calm and beauty. Often sixes indicate restoration and sometimes the need to travel or move, as in the case with the wands and swords, that the energy of travel will help to clear, restore, and provide needed nourishment in the situation. Six is connected to the energy of the Lovers and can indicate a blossoming of the heart, connection, joy, and renewal in our lives. Sixes include the four directions as well as above and below, bringing us into a connected awareness of our human selves between earth and sky.

Sevens: Reflection

Sevens are a turning point in the progression; here the energies of the suit begin to reach a maturation level as seen in our relationships, projects, careers, and so on. Sevens indicate a time to rest and reflect, to see what is no longer serving and make clear decisions about how to move forward guided more strongly by our intuition and heart and less from our rational logistical mind. If we haven't done our work in the fives, the sevens will encourage us to let go or release that which is no longer serving us after we take time and space to reflect. The number seven is connected to the Chariot, which moves forward with energy and vitality but is also guided by the divine forces of will. We must be in alignment to move quickly and surely, and the sevens invite us to find that guidance within.

Eights: Effort

After a pause and some reflection, the eights follow to provide us with the nurturing energy to work, create, stabilize, and heal old wounds and patterns. The energy of the wands and disks is fruitful and restorative, bringing in energy and support for our projects, health, and career. The swords and cups show old wounds rising to the surface but offer the opportunity for healing and transforming the pain for healing these fully, allowing the pain and suffering of our own trauma to be turned into power and love. Connected to both Strength and Justice, eights offer a course-corrective view to bring us relief from the past by transmuting our personal pain and poison into beauty and medicine. Very often our gifts are closely associated with what has hurt us, and the eights provide the stable ground to anchor these into in our lives.

Nines: Integration

Three threes coming together creates the power of nine, the energy of integration. Here the different aspects of ourselves unite holistically offering a deeper view and understanding on the path. In the disks and cups, this is a number of fruition, right effort, flowering, connection, and abundance. In the wands and swords, nines are an intense challenge to grow, change, and move through our pain with even more surrender than the eights. Connected to the Hermit, the nines are an opportunity for incredible soul growth whether that comes in the form of bliss and beauty or pain and burden. Although these seem disparate, the highs and lows of our life are often deeply connected and provide the intricate lessons of soul growth and wisdom.

Tens: Completion

Here, the cycle of the suit comes to completion and one phase ends before the next cycle begins. This is akin to the flowering of a tree in which the beautiful offerings of the flowers are also the precursor to fruits and seeds. Only in the short life and death of the flower can we make way for new buds and growth on the tree. The offering of fruit to the earth and its decay brings the seed into the darkness of beginning the cycle anew. Ten is the Wheel of Fortune, which indicates the turning of the path and the influence of destiny on our journey. Here we have the opportunity to fully surrender, release what no longer serves while also celebrating what has been accomplished, learned, and shared.

EARTH: DISKS OR PENTACLES

Earth is the manifestation of physical matter. As an element, earth is the mountains, stones, hills, and land; the still matter of time that has been here for millions of years before humans. The earth element is often connected to the ancestral realm and reminds us that these bodies we inhabit come from thousands of people in a long lineage before us. Our bones and our blood carry their stories. We use stones and coins to create simple ceremonies and exercises in the tarot. You may also develop your own ways to work with the earth element using seeds, grains, or other physical, earthy manifestations.

This section begins with the earth element as a way to set the ground for our ceremonial and magical work. You may choose to work through this book in any order you wish, however, touching into our earthly self is a good way to create a strong container to help with divination and strengthening your intuition. Working with the earth, we learn to ground, manifest, and work with the solid forms. Using stones and our bodies, we anchor the energies of the tarot. Depicted in the tarot as disks or pentacles, the manifestation of our emotions, thoughts, dreams, issues, obstacles, and creations come into form through the earth element.

The disks pictured in the Crowley deck signify the currency we use to exchange for goods and services. Disks are responsible for laying a foundation and creating a container or structure for feelings, thoughts, and spiritual energies to inhabit. In the Waite-Smith deck, the coins are Pentacles that contain the five pointed star of magical manifestation. The five pointed star symbolizes the four elements plus oneself and reminds us that all material objects are interconnected with our earth as a living form and the elements of earth, water, air, and fire that combine in a multitude of ways to create the various forms on earth.

In the tarot, disks or pentacles are directly connected to the physical realm of money, matter, and earth. The Latin word *mater* is akin to the words "matter" and "mother." We can think of our own mother, parents, or caretakers and how they provided resources for us, just as disks and the material realm are our resources. Financial issues are a common concern for people seeking tarot readings, and the disk cards help illuminate issues with money and physical resources in combination with the other suits of wands, cups, and swords and their respective realms of spirit, emotional issues, and thoughts.

The material realm is a physical manifestation of spirit. Spirit is not necessarily concerned with the how or when but instead is simply energy that reveals itself through physical manifestations. When spirit moves through emotional and mental states, the outcome is affected according to the positive or negative aspects. For example, guidance may indicate for us to move somewhere new, but if this intuitive message from spirit is then overlaid with mental doubts and emotional anxiety it can make the physical manifestation difficult to realize. Alternatively, if the feelings are one of joy, excitement, and trust, doors can open that seem to almost magically manifest this new reality. These concepts and ways to work them are explored further in each of the disk cards and how we can better relate to the earth element that manifests as money, finances, health, and home in our daily lives.

Exercise: Connecting to the Earth

This is a basic grounding exercise to reconnect to the earth. Many people are disconnected from the experience of living on the earth in a real way. To do this, simply go outside and lay down on the earth. Use a blanket or whatever you need to make you comfortable. If you can, lay your entire body on the earth so that you can feel the contours of the land.

Feel into the earth's aliveness. Lay by a tree and look up into the branches. Reach back the roots of your essential being. After a while, close your eyes and feel your breath moving through your body. Listen to your heartbeat. Feel the supportive nature of the earth below you. Imagine the soil and dirt that lies under your body, the rock below the soil, and the water below the rock. Visualize the roots of all the different plants and trees growing in the soil, supporting the plant life all around you. All the insects and creatures that bury themselves through this earth. Allow your awareness to extend all the way to the center of the earth, to the inner core of the earth, the pulse and heartbeat of the mother. Rest in this pulse, opening your heart in gratitude and thankfulness. Ask the earth to remind you to be reverent on its surface as we *are* the earth—our bodies, tears, and bones will one day return to soil and waters.

Exercise: Make an Offering

This act is a symbolic gesture that opens your heart to your life, to the day, to receive teachings and wisdom. Traditionally, cultures all over the world make offerings of rice, flowers, a leaf or fern, salt, or light a candle or incense to begin the day and connect in with the divine aspect of ourselves. We may choose to practice yoga or qigong as a way to bring health and life force into our morning and also offering our body, as a physical temple to the unfolding of the day. Taking a moment to light a candle or place a small amount of rice in a designated altar space touches our physical self into our spiritual. As you work through this section on earth, disks, and pentacles, use the simple act of making an offering to connect you to your earthly self and rest in openness before receiving guidance. Before you begin a tarot reading, I recommend lighting a candle or offering a flower as a way to open yourself to the wisdom of the cards.

Ace of Disks or Pentacles: The Seed

The Ace of Disks or Pentacles is like a seed which, when planted, opens us up to infinite potential in the material realm. Like an acorn which contains the entire oak tree within its tiny interior, the Ace of Disks carries all the wisdom of the disks. This includes material loss and gain within the realm of financial, career, home, health, and the physical aspects of our lives. This card symbolizes new beginnings and a fresh perspective. This is a concrete, physical card and can help jumpstart us into the next level of working with money, finances, physical health, building a business or career, acquiring a new home, or starting a project.

In the Waite-Smith deck, the pentacle is being offered from a cloud like a revelation or an opportunity for gratitude and awareness. The disembodied hand that appears in the card symbolizes that doors may open unexpectedly and reminds us to stay open to opportunities and even miracles. This also shows that generosity is an act of openness and is not necessarily connected to a specific person or place. Often we pour energy into a person, project, or idea with the expectation that we will be rewarded directly back; however, our return may come from many other sources and keeping our minds open in gratitude allows for abundant flow to happen naturally.

In the Crowley deck, the green and gold colors symbolize growth and the vital life energy of the earth. This card acts as a doorway to the next level of understanding and activation in our daily physical wealth. When a shift happens in our mindset to move from scarcity toward abundance, the Ace of Disks will appear to show that we are about to receive an opportunity that mirrors our view.

The Ace of Disks is a gift from the universe and may come in the form of a specific opportunity. We may be offered a new job, receive a check in the mail, or find a new place to live. We may receive good news about health, a financial windfall, or a promotion. This may indicate a time to plant a new seed, such as a garden or project, and that assistance is on its way from the universe to help with that. However, if the Ace of Disks appears with Five of Cups and Ten of Swords, which are negative cards, the indication could be that an opportunity, idea, or investment could fail or is not necessarily a good idea.

Ceremony: Finding a Stone

To work with the Ace of Disk or Pentacles, we open ourselves up to the wisdom of earthy manifestation. Go outside and find a stone. Pick a place where you can look for one uninterrupted such as at the coast, near a river bed, or in a forest. Spend time wandering around this place, asking to find a stone or rock that will be a touch stone in your life. When you come across a stone or rock that feels right, take some time to sit with it and reflect on its journey on earth. Around every rock and stone is a family of other rocks and stones surrounding it. It is part of the dynamic web of the natural world you are visiting.

Ask the stone if it wishes to come with you, and respect its response. In some traditional cultures, rocks are viewed as our relations or ancestors. Set an intention that you will work with the energy of the disks or pentacles in harmony with your relations. If the stone agrees to come with you, leave an offering such as a hair or dried herb you feel a connection to. When you return to your home, place the stone on your altar created in the Magician chapter. When you feel down or troubled by health, finances, or other physical issues, use this rock as a literal touchstone to feel back into that place where you found it and center yourself. This stone can also be a way to ground yourself and a simple reminder to connect with the earth.

Two of Disks: The Dance

Following the gift of the Ace of Disks, the energy shifts, and things in life begin the process of creation. After the seed of the Ace is planted, it sprouts into a slender green shoot with two tiny leaves forming on the stem. Similarly, the two of disks or pentacles holds the vital life energy yet is vulnerable to other elements. The two of disks is a card of change and movement on the material realm. This is a worldly card, affecting and affected by the world around you in a physical sense.

In the Waite deck, a figure dances while juggling two disks along a cord of infinity. These disks are intricately woven together—one relies on the other, and they each depend on each other. This playful approach reminds us of constant movement and the dance of energy, even with fixed things in our life. Behind the figure is a clear blue sky with a turbulent ocean and ships cresting the waves, symbolizing the importance of clear communication, listening, and being open even if emotions and situations are in a state of unrest. The green cord that holds the disks reminds us that things are always in a perfect balance even if it does not appear that way in the current situation.

In the Crowley deck we see the word "change" and the energy of the yin and yang. The eye of the yin rests within the yang and eye of the yang within the circle of yin. This is a dance of dark and light, masculine and feminine, winter and summer. We cannot have one without the other. In winter time, on the longest night, we honor the light returning at solstice which contains the seed of summer to come. And in summer, on the longest day, we honor the dark returning in the seed of winter to come.

Because of its suit, the Two of Disks is practical and suggests a positive time to make plans, confirm appointments, and reach out to people. This could be a literal move in location, opening a new office, or the need to shift things in your personal space. The card can indicate an external change that is coming, such as a new roommate or pet, or new garden plot. It can also signify a message that causes some change, or even disruption in your life. This card is highly influenced by the surrounding cards so look to the other cards in your reading as well.

Ceremony: Two Stones

In the yin and yang we see the continuous interplay of light and dark, masculine and feminine, up and down, right and left. The dance of opposites encourages us to see that within all things. We cannot have one without the other. In our own selves, we are the unique mix of a father and mother, a male and female ancestry. When you receive this card, you can use this simple ceremony to help you honor the dance of duality in life as well as what may arise between the binary opposite forces as well.

Find one dark stone and one light stone. Find a place outside and take your shoes off. If you wish, do the grounding cord exercise from the Emperor Card. Hold the light stone in your right hand to symbolize the inner masculine and your male line. Hold the dark stone in your left hand to symbolize the inner feminine your female line. Feel the stones resting in your hand and visualize your parents next to you on either side of you and your four grandparents behind them and their parents behind them. Even if you did not know one of your parents, simply invoke the presence of them.

Hold your right hand up with the light stone and state the intention: "I honor and thank my male line, my right side. I now release any and all blocks from my male lineage." Then throw the stone as far as you can. Next, hold up your left hand with the dark stone and state the intention: "I honor and thank my female line, my left side. I now release any and all blocks from my female lineage." Then throw the stone as far as you can. This is a very simple act and of course will not clear ancestral trauma in one throw. However, setting this intention and embodying it is one way to begin the process, like a seed to help open the channel for healing to occur.

Continue to feel the presence of your ancestors, and allow them to admire you as the sum total of thousands of human beings who have come before you. See them stretching out like a triangle in support of you and your path, loving you and honoring you without hesitation, without any blockages. When you are done, feel gratitude in your heart and center yourself by touching the earth.

Three of Disks: Manifesting the Vision

As the two progresses into three, the energy opens up to both receive and express more energy and substance. In the plant symbolism, the sprout develops more leaves and growth becomes evident. The roots below the surface reach further down for nutrients as the leaves extend upward for more light. This is a card of outward manifestation, work, and putting one's mind to creating with effort.

In the Waite-Smith deck we see two architects with a diagram of the cathedral. A young apprentice under mentorship discusses a plan with the other two, sharing ideas. This is the image of artisan work, creation, and physically crafting a labor of love. The work here is shared so that feedback may be received—an important aspect of developing one's path in career, working with money, or creating a project.

In the Crowley deck the keyword is "work," and this card indicates that it is time to work hard on something but do so with joy, dedication, and in delight of the creation process. The image shows three disks in the shape of a triangle with clouds clearing behind the triangle. Each of the disks are equidistant, indicating a balance of threes such as a three-legged table where each leg is necessary to balance the table top. The clouds indicate that effort is needed to complete the task at hand; development of a plan or setting realistic goals can aid in this unfolding.

The Three of Disks indicates your willingness to take an idea and make it grow further. Use the ceremony below to add energetic juice to something you wish to create further in your life, as the card is a positive indication of growth and a strong sign of encouragement. This card may also indicate coming together in a group, forming a team or collaboration to bring an idea toward manifestation. As shown in the Waite deck, receiving feedback is an important element in the creative process and gives energy to push the project along, as well as constructive criticism to see where the project is not working or is flawed. When this card appears with major arcana, it strengthens the energy of that particular card.

Ceremony: Energizing a Project

This ceremony is to energize a project or something you are working on. Gather one or two images that symbolize something you are wishing to grow further in your life such as: a hobby you want to learn more about; a skill you are developing; a business plan that is happening; a creative project that you are developing. For example, if you are learning how to juggle, then find or draw an image of a juggler. Choose a project that is *already in motion*—this is important in the

Three of Disks. Unlike the Ace, threes are already happening and the seed has already sprouted. You are adding illumined energy and light to your project to fertilize and develop it.

You will need three stones or coins, preferably gold, and one small yellow candle. Choose a candle that burns down in twenty minutes. The optimal time to practice this ceremony is at night, before you go to sleep, so that you will also seed your subconscious to assist in the growth of your project.

Place your image on your altar with the gold coins or stones in a triangle shape around your image, with one coin at the top of the image and two coins at the bottom. Set the candle just above and beyond the top coin. Call on your directions and guidance.

Light the candle and sit quietly watching the flame burn, illuminating the gold in the coins and brightening the image of your work that you are developing and strengthening in the world. If possible, sit and concentrate on your image, sending it love and light as the candle burns down. If you find this focused concentration difficult, allow your mind to rest every few minutes and focus on your breath.

As the candle burns, state aloud your gratitude for the manifestation, *as if it has already manifested or happened.* This is an important key to manifestation, as it draws your vision and desire into your current state of awareness. As you state this aloud, then continue to visualize the manifestation with the feeling of love, completion, accomplishment, joy, gratitude, and so on for having manifested your dream. This amplifies the manifesting process and brings it quickly into your current life.

When you are finished, release and thank the directions and guidance. You may do this three nights in a row, burning the candle each night. Another option is to practice this over a twenty-one-day period to add energy to your work. With this kind of focused effort, the project, skill, or practice will be energized triple-fold.

Four of Disks: Setting a Boundary

With the Four of Disks, we move from the dynamic and creative qualities of the three into the foundational and structure of four. This card indicates a solidifying of outward manifestations. Fours symbolize stability and strength, allowing for the creative energy of the three to ground and take root. Four corners of a space or building are connected to the four cardinal directions, four elements, four suits of the tarot, et cetera. With the earth element, fours are successful and empowered in the process of manifestation, money, and resources.

In the Waite-Smith deck, the image of the four of disks is very similar to the Emperor. Both figures are wearing crowns and the color red, and have both feet firmly planted on the ground. This indicates a connection to the earth, strength, grounding, and authority. Unlike the Emperor, the figure in the Four of Disks is holding a disk or pentacle squarely in front of his chest, like a shield. There is a sense of distrust, wariness, and a feeling or need to protect one's interests.

In the Crowley deck, four disks are placed in the four corners of a square symbolizing the foundation of a house or four cornered structure. The background is peach and orange colored indicating creative energy and growth. Bridges connect each of the four squares that rest atop of pillars that rise up out of a human-made water stream, such as a moat or channel. This may indicate the need for boundaries and protection between outer and inner expressions. The word here is "power," inspiring you to call in your resources and give them a sense of shape and container in focus and direction.

This card may indicate the need to examine a conflict and perhaps confront the issue by standing squarely and looking at it directly in the face. There are two main ways to look at this card, depending on the other cards in the reading. It indicates that the issue is either withholding resources or love or a need to protect these resources from others ... or maybe a bit of both. Likely, there is a need to set clear boundaries and firm up one's resolve in material matters and how they affect relationships and development of a project. This card encourages the seeker to examine what should be withheld and what should be more freely given in terms of material wealth as well as emotional energy. The card encourages less dreaming and more action needing to be taken; or to notice the actions one is creating in the world in relation to business, money, contracts, and physical needs.

The Four of Disks may also be encouraging you to form a specific physical container for your work such as getting a studio space, putting more energy into how you dress or present yourself, or solidifying an investment plan. Creating a specified container for a project, relationship, or health issue can actually allow and encourage more healing and growth as the intention is focused and vision is crystallized.

Exercise: Setting Clear Boundaries

This exercise is to create boundaries to prevent taking on issues from others and also cultivate a strong container to build your personal energy. This can be used if you are struggling with financial issues, an unresolved relationship conflict, or a nagging feeling about something that you haven't really taken the time to face.

Gather four stones. Go outside and arrange them in a square, each stone in the four cardinal directions: east, south, west, and north. Sit down in the middle of your square facing the north. Call in your helpers and ancestors. Notice yourself sitting on the earth; feel the breeze. Practice the grounding cord exercise from the Emperor card to firmly root yourself energetically with the earth. See and feel the energy of your grounding cord extending down from your root chakra, or the base of the spine to the center of the earth.

Call into your mind the issue you are working on. Visualize the stones forming a protective field of light around you, creating a container to help you see and clarify the issue. Ask yourself: Do I need better boundaries with this person/issue/conflict? Be open to receiving guidance as to how that might look. Do you need to lessen contact with the person? Is there another way to communicate? Do you need to set boundaries with yourself?

As you inhale, imagine the protective stone qualities immersing your aura and body. Feel your connection to your bones, teeth, and structural body. Acknowledge your connection to stones through the minerals in your body.

When you are finished, you have the opportunity to set a vow for yourself if you wish. Make a decision to face the issue and take a step towards resolution, even if it is a tiny step. For example, if you have unresolved debt, determine how much debt you have and begin the necessary conversations to work on resolving it. If you have a project that needs to be finished, map out a series of small, realistic goals.

Five of Disks: Carrying the Burden

After the four of disks in which one is trying to protect or withhold resources, we move into the five which indicates a loss. This is one of the heavier cards in the deck, a card of physical loss that affects us emotionally. We are confronted with the loss of our security, something we hold dear and which threatens us on a deeper level as well. This may indicate a time of loss that affects us and others around us including friends or family members. The energy of this card along with the number five indicates a kind of burden and the need for change or adjustment in order for the way to clear again.

The Waite-Smith card shows two figures out in the cold snowy winter, struggling to survive. They are hungry, cold, and desperate. They pass a church, a sanctuary, but are unable to see the refuge that could help them. This card reminds us that loss is often felt with another, as the two figures huddle together, looking to each other for support. There may be love and connection even amid depression and sorrow.

In the Crowley deck, we see five hardened disks arranged in a downward pointing pentacle symbolizing loss and negativity. The word for this card is worry which indicates the conflict that appears when we are faced with loss and challenges to our material security. The heaviness of the card is a reminder to rest and settle for a moment before taking action, to take a moment to feel the weight of gravity and the pressure of our body and physical reality.

Often the five of disks indicates a difficult and challenging loss such as a contract falling through, something stolen, losing money, a forgotten bill, or a debt suddenly resurfacing. Although this is a troubling card, this minor arcana offers us the opportunity to clear the way before moving forward. We do not progress on the path without obstacles and this card reminds us to stop, take stock, and remove the burdens that are weighing down on us. Often our burdens can be relieved through asking for help, shifting our perspective, and remembering gratitude.

Exercise: Making an Offering

When a loss threatens to appear on the horizon or there a loss has recently happened, it is helpful to make an offering to assist in the situation. Offerings soften our hearts and help dissolve our smaller selves into the larger, expansive oneness of the universe. We often take loss personally and forget to find the opportunities or lessons that are inherent in any kind of loss or struggle in our life. When we make an offering we allow the feelings of sorrow, grief, sadness, or fear to move through us instead of taking hold and growing larger. Also, if the card is set in the future, making an offering can actually help prevent the loss from happening as it sets out to right the balance. You can use the offering ceremony in the Ace of Disks card to make an offering and open your heart.

In some traditional beliefs, when something is stolen, lost, or disappears, it may indicate an imbalance with our relations and our ancestors in particular. We may need to cultivate a stronger connection with our ancestors and feed them with our tears, or blessings, or honoring. Also, this card brings to mind the concept of tithing. In prosperity books, one of the ways that we can open ourselves to experience more flow and abundance in our life is to tithe 10 percent of our earnings as well as offering reparation funds to organizations that support vulnerable communities. The idea is that if we don't do that, then it will come off another way from our earnings, such as loss, theft, unexpected bills, and so on. It's like a spiritual cleansing of our income to assist in keeping our energies flowing and hearts open.

Take a moment to offer something generously to someone in need, create a flower, herb, or candle offering for your altar or set an intention to pay off a bill or debt. Remember that in times of burden you can ask for help and also be open to receive as well.

Six of Disks: Collective Wealth

The Six of Disks is a card of balance and restoration after the loss in the Five of Disks. This is a card that reflects from outward things happening in our life to help guide us to understand where we may still be out of balance regarding wealth and generosity and how we can work to stabilize this in self and our work with others. Sixes bring the qualities of harmony, balance, beauty, and joy.

In the Waite-Smith deck, we see an image of a wealthier man giving to those who appear desperate and poor. It appears that the wealth is out of balance, a reflection of the wealth distribution in our economy. Traditionally, this card indicates that someone is getting something materially, however it may be at the expense of others. Perhaps there is a power imbalance in the relationship between friends, co-workers, and family that will manifest through material wealth and goods. This card may indicate that someone is trying to take advantage of you or you are taking advantage of someone else, perhaps being used or using someone for their skills and gifts, or making money off a situation that is not on equal footing.

Digging deeper into this image we also note that the man distributing the wealth holds a set of scales which indicates the need for measure and balance. In Rachel Pollack's *Seventy-Eight Degrees of Wisdom,* she explores the idea of giving, but not the right amount. In this way, we cannot give love or wealth generously if the other cannot receive; and we ourselves can only receive what we are open to. What comes into our lives may be a kind of mirroring of how much we are open to receiving.

Crowley's view on this card indicates a more harmonious meaning with the word "success." The image shows an even number of pastel colored disks coming together in a circle. This card encourages us to change our views and perspective about wealth distribution to make it more inclusive, community oriented, and collective based. These views are often considered idealized, as our culture is so deeply embedded in our current social system of wealth inequality.

Either way, this card encourages you to look at a group situation in your life and how you view collective wealth and sharing. Perhaps you need to undo old patterning around sharing in a community mindset, and release the mental constructs that encourage a hierarchical view. This card indicates the need to soften and open to others, listen, exchange, and share. In work matters, it may indicate the need to have a meeting with staff members to break down boundaries and resolve issues regarding financial or energetic resources. In personal relationships, it encourages the help of others to be present and find solutions that work for both parties in a family dynamic. This card can also indicate that success is on the horizon in a project, and resources or funding may become available for use with the help of others.

Meditation: Bowl of Light

In the Hawaiian tradition, the soul and life journey are viewed as a bowl of light. We come into the world with a clear bowl filled only with light. When things happen to us in life, such as trauma, pain, disease, loss, divorce, and heartache, they are like stones that find themselves into the bowl. If we don't take time to empty out our stones, we carry them around and inhibit our ability to receive and express love and light. Here we use a bowl, a vessel that holds water, a link to the emotional symbolism of water and cups. This connection is important—as we begin to deepen our connection to the earth element, we find that our material and physical resources are intimately linked with our emotions and relationships with self and others.

Find a bowl and several stones. Find time and space for a quiet meditation. Sit in a comfortable meditative posture and focus on the breath for a few moments. Feel back into your life as child and slowly walk yourself through your life journey. Focus on times of pain and sorrow in your life: when you lost a friend, got hurt, betrayed by a loved one, or when someone important to you passed away. For each traumatic moment, place a stone in the bowl. Keep going until you have tracked your life to the present. Hold the bowl full of stones on your lap. Perhaps you can feel into the sorrow, heaviness, and trauma of those times. Send healing love and light into the bowl and back through time to yourself in those difficult moments.

When you feel ready, deepen your breath and practice the Ha breath: inhale fully through the nose and exhale while making a *haaa* sound through the mouth. Repeat the breathing cycle several times, then dump the bowl over and free the space to receive light in your soul once again. Allow the bowl to rest in your lap again, empty and symbolically free of your past traumas and difficulties. Feel gratitude in your heart and remind yourself that at any moment in your life, you can choose to dump the bowl of light.

Seven of Disks: Contemplate and Compost

The Seven of Disks brings with it a time to contemplate and reflect. After the work of understanding giving and receiving in the Six of Disks it is time to reflect on what is going well and what is not. We often find that it is time to compost what is not working, to return parts of our project or ideas to the earth to become soil. Sevens are the number of reflection, taking a pause to turn and look back on the path of our projects, relationships, health, and so on. Everything moves in cycles and the seven indicates a transition into the last stages of development, fruition, and completion.

In the Waite-Smith deck, we see a figure resting from his hard-earned work. The garden is established and growing on its own, and he can take a rest and step back to view this progress. This card may indicate the need for patience in a situation and to take stock before making a firm decision upon the next course of action. The wisdom of the Seven of Disks asks you to notice when things are in the flow or not. When something is not coming easily, we may consider it is not the right course of action for us and can make a choice about stepping into the flow or out of the flow. This is not a card to push or try, but instead discern and observe.

In the Crowley deck, the disks are gray and heavy and seem immovable. The word is "failure"—some aspects of the project, work, or relationship are no longer working. The leaves are dead and heavy, needing to be discarded and reworked into the soil. This card also encourages you to use the resources you already have in a new way. I have always called the Seven of Disks the "compost card," in which we take the scraps of stuff we have used and, with time and turning, transform it into the opportunity for rich, fertile soil that feeds the plants we are currently growing. Applying this to your life is a useful way to gather, reduce, and reuse what is not working well in your life and recreate something new with the same energy.

Emotionally, this card may signify relationships; work or projects that have come to a standstill. Taking time to reexamine what no longer works and let it go can fuel other projects or relationships that you are more committed to keeping. This may be an opportunity to also clear out a closet, clean up clutter in your home or throw away old papers, photos, and things that are just no longer useful. Making a fire and burning old papers, creating ash that can be used to fertilize plants is a nice symbolic way to clear away the old and literally compost something you are growing.

Exercise: Stone Stacking

Stacking stones are an ancient way to mark the trail, make offerings, and leave prayers at sacred spots in nature such as on mountain passes. In this practice, taking the time to gather and stack the stones opens the mind to quiet contemplation and reflection.

Gather many stones that are somewhat flat. The best place to gather stacking stones is around a river bed or at the ocean where the water has worn down the stone, smoothing it out. Choose a place to stack your stones, a place in your yard. The direction west is a good place, as it signifies the time of death, rebirth, and reflection.

You can dedicate your stack of stones to something specific, like a prayer for something that you are reflecting on and trying to work out in your life. Take time to sit and carefully stack your stones. If they fall, stack them again. Perhaps you need to choose a different stone. When you feel you are finished leave the stone as an offering to this place and a reminder of the situation you are working through.

Eight of Disks: Perseverance

After the fallow energy of the Seven of Disks and time spent contemplating and composting, our work and effort begins to flower. In the plant symbolism, the Eight of Disks reminds us of the diligent perseverance it takes for a tree to grow, flower, and finally produce fruit. Eights are fours doubled and symbolize the energy of strength, foundation, and grounding with more structure and deliberate manifestation. This card indicates the value of patience and long, hard work, but a kind of work that is incredibly joyous and to be treasured in its undertaking.

In the Waite-Smith deck we see a figure carefully crafting with tools and then artfully hanging his work. Traditionally, this card is linked to the artisan of old, the real time it took to master a craft, beginning with apprenticeship at a young age. The gray sky behind the figure symbolizes the energy of focus, quiet, diligence, and practice which can be dull at times but is eventually rewarding. Six of the disks hang completed, showing the pride in perseverance; one disk is being finished, and another lays on the ground showing work is still at hand. The disks figuring as artistic pieces in this card (rather than coins) remind us that our work is also our offering, our gift, and our wealth.

The image of the card on the Crowley deck shows a beautiful, balanced, flowering tree. The huge pink flowers are at their peak and yet still in the shade, symbolizing the quality of divine timing and trust in the right moment for the flowers to be revealed and turned to fruit. Work is still needed on projects and right effort is important here to continue to bring a vision into fully blossoming form.

My grandfather was a traditional cabinet maker from Hungary, which he learned as an apprentice in the Old World way. He never used nails, only wooden pins crafted perfectly to bring the pieces of wood together. Today's world is the antithesis of this kind of craft; things are made cheaply and without diligence. We want instant success, instant results, and instant gratification, and our technology supports it. We often focus on the fruits that a tree produces, and so many fruits! Yet it took countless right conditions to produce the fruits: the right soil, water, sunlight, and pollination. Similarly, in our work we must be sure that it is being properly nourished by not just money and finances, but also healthy relationships and connections.

This card indicates success in a project or venture, but only through hard work and careful deliberation. We must pay attention to the process and be willing to learn if we are not doing it right. This card may also indicate becoming either a mentor or an apprentice, learning a craft. If your work has hit a plateau, seek out more advanced and successful people who can help guide you on your path. The appearance of this card indicates the need to continue our hard work, make a plan, that efforts will be rewarded particularly through our own pride at our hard work and focus.

Meditation: Nature Walk

Find several hours where you can take a long walk in nature alone. Don't bring along your phone, music, or other distractions; instead make a commitment to be fully present in the woods, park, field, mountain, beach, or any natural place. Bring offerings with you such as a small amount of grains, flowers, or herbs to leave at different points along your walk.

As you begin your walk, first notice the season. Take time to observe the different creatures you see along the way. Try to see them with fresh eyes even if you have already seen a thousand squirrels or sparrows or geese. Perhaps they have something new to show you. Observe the diligence of plants, trees, flowers, and their innate knowing of when to blossom, when to fruit, when to seed.

As you walk, find eight points of interest to stop and connect deliberately with the land. Leave some of your offerings and reflect on the interconnectedness of land, sky, water, and sun. Here the earth element expands to include all aspects of earth and material form. Without breath and air, water to drink, and metabolic fires, we would not be alive. Feel gratitude for the earth and all its creative manifestations; in its perseverance to create and continue even in the face of great adversity, namely humans. Feel into the humility of your presence in a natural world that doesn't need us.

Nine of Disks: Fruitful Efforts

The Nine of Disks indicates a time of incredible richness, growth, abundance, and fertility. The progress, effort, focus, and concentration of the Eight of Disks begins to fully show on the outer level. Nines comprise the number three and six and contain the harmonious qualities found in each of these cards with even more manifestation, complexity, and depth. Plants receive their life force from the air they breathe, the soil, and the sunlight. Similarly, we take in nourishment in a variety of foods and drinks, as well as air, water, and sunlight.

In the Waite-Smith deck, we see a radiant woman delighting in the bounty of her garden. She is dressed in fine clothing and surrounded by lush beauty. She appears full of vital life force in an effortless manner without struggle or sacrifice. The energy of easefulness and enjoyment fills this card as she enjoys the fruits of her labors as well as the labors of others. The sky behind her is yellow symbolizing creative manifestation, illumination, and success. At ease, she holds a trained, hooded falcon on her wrist indicating the deliberate training of something wild into a flourishing intentional space.

In the Crowley deck, the image shows three disks at the center of the card crossing over and connected to one another like a triple circle Venn diagram. This symbolizes the growth of three and that once two energies unite, a third is born. Surrounding the central three are six disks accompanied by vivid rays of light indicating vital life force, growth, abundance, and clarity. The concentric colored rings in the background symbolize the connection different elements and energies in the manifest world.

The key to this card is diversity and remembering that resources and whatever sustains us comes from many sources. Oftentimes these resources may come from different places that are unique or unexpected. Perhaps a check shows up in the mail or we receive an inheritance or a bonus from work. We can receive support for projects, ideas, and relationships from many different places. This support may come in the form of money or physical funds but also emotional and spiritual support, as well as skills and practical help.

This card may also indicate a flow of life in which people are coming and going, bringing us gifts and joy. Friends, family members, and coworkers are part of our everyday world, and we are in a positive grace of sharing and receiving, the interconnectedness of our relations. This is a card of abundance and growth where we are truly able to see our efforts flowering in the manifest world.

Visualization: Interconnectedness

This exercise is to recognize the interconnectedness of all things. When we do this we recognize we are a single strand in the great web of life. This practice is both humbling and awe inspiring to do as a reminder of our relations to others. Take something as simple as an apple. Hold the apple in your hand and notice its smell, texture, and taste of its skin. Then close your eyes and imagine the tree from where the apple came. Imagine how the trunk looked, the branches and leaves. Notice how the soil looks and the other trees in the orchard next to it.

Envision the laborers coming along to pick the apple and how it got put into a basket, then a bag, then a box, then a truck. Imagine in your mind's eye following one of the laborers to his home. See his wife, perhaps, and children. See the extra apples he brought home to his children. Notice what they are eating for dinner.

Bring your attention back to the apple and envision the seeds that you know are inside the apple. View them being planted into the soil knowing that at some time in the future, they will yield fruit year after year. This time connect even more deeply in with the feeling of the tree and imagine yourself as this tree. Feel your body as a trunk of tree bending slightly in the wind. Extend your roots deep down to receive the nourishment of the soil and minerals in the earth. Push upward and outward as if you have branches toward the light and the sky. Fell the individual leaves growing effortlessly on your branches, forming into flowers and then fruits or apples. Take a moment to notice the feeling of creating apples that are each filled with seeds, each holding the potential to create another tree full of apples. Breathe into the natural abundance of creative effort and beauty. Affirm your own life giving abilities of creation, beauty, abundance, and radiance.

Ten of Disks: Nourishing the Inner Wealth

Following the coming together of the Nine of Disks, the Ten of Disks is the final card in the suit and the highest expression of elemental earth energy. This is a card of flowering and abundance, a coming together like the six and nine of disks, but on an even greater spiritual level. This card suggests connection to many relations and celebration of a time to dance and make merry, to dress in finery, to give and receive gifts.

The Ten of Disks is a card of radiant joy and expresses itself in the Waite-Smith deck showing a family with the sun shining down with many blessings. The card shows the power and wealth found in personal relations and the importance of community and interconnectedness with others. Building on the Nine of Disks, the energy reaches a full expression and indicates that many gifts and resources are flowering. Connections with others open and are filled with love. It seems as if everything you touch has the potential to turn to gold. We see a wise elder wearing a robe of fruitful wisdom, a couple in love and connection, and a small child playing with two dogs. The family dynamic is healthy and strong and the structures and arches indicate a developed and full expression of one's dreams, creative endeavors, work in the world, and fulfilling relationships.

The Crowley deck shows ten golden coins in the shape of the Tree of Life, the sacred system of Kabbalah backed by several violet coins behind. This indicates the spiritual manifestation of inner wealth into outer wealth. The inward, alchemical process of transmuting pain, fear, and shadow into light, beauty, and power is the true wealth, the true gift of the human spirit. This card illuminates this process of welcoming inner abundance first, only to experience it outwardly. When this becomes a state of being, true joy, then the outward experiences matter less and we find gratitude and radiance in every moment, even in challenging situations.

Tens indicate the end of one phase, the beginning a new phase, and is the time of flowering and blooming. Often this happens just as the energy shifts; this is the peak card, the card that indicates something has reached its height or has the potential to reach it. Of course, following a peak is usually a descent, a shift, a change, so it is wise to acknowledge the flowering beauty and abundance of this card as well as the natural ebb that will likely follow.

Creating prosperity and abundance in one's life, true prosperity in the form of joy, love, and radiance, always begins within. I had a dream where I was walking along a path in Hawaii and suddenly an enormous *ulu* (breadfruit) fell directly at my feet. The *ulu* symbolizes wealth in Hawaiian and also has the potential to feed many people, particularly a large one! It is a very nutritious fruit that is full of starch similar to a potato. In the dream, this *ulu* was huge and in perfectly ripe condition with no marks or bruises, a symbolic image of wealth, nourishment, and gratitude all together.

When this card appears in a reading, it signifies fulfillment of a dream, wealth, and abundance. It also indicates the connection with family, friends, and/or beloveds for this dream to be fully realized. Wealth is truly nourishing when shared with others. This card also indicates that the path is in alignment with the divine energy of the higher self that naturally moves to benefit others.

Ceremony: Stone & Seed Gratitude

In this exercise, we affirm our own inner wealth by feeling grateful for all that enriches our life. Becoming wealthy in life is often as simple as tuning into the wealth that already exists in our daily reality. Gather ten stones, paint to use on them, and ten seeds and small pots with soil. Make a list of ten things you are grateful for and ten things you wish to activate or manifest in your life. Before you start, create an altar with pictures and symbols of things you are grateful for and what you wish to manifest. Choose one or more candles to use during your ceremony.

Next, set aside time to create your stone and seed ceremony. Create a sacred space, calling to the four directions, your guides, and your ancestors. Light the candle and then spend time painting each stone with a color, symbol, or word to represent your gratitudes. Then take each of the ten seeds, blow into them what you wish to manifest and plant them in a pot with soil, water, and love. Place a gratitude stone next to the pot, directly linking your manifestation wishes with your gratitude. This is also a symbol of endings and beginnings, as the cycle of disks has reached a new phase in your life.

WATER: CUPS

Water is life. We are composed of 57 to 60 percent water and can barely live more than a few days without its nourishing presence. The forms of water are as varied and dynamic as human expression. Water can be slow and placid, stormy and wild, rushing and cleansing. The movement of water from ocean to mountaintop through the water cycle is an incredible process of cyclical movement across land, creating rivers, streams, and springs. Water is a natural carrier of both physical elements such as minerals and salt, as well as pollution and toxins. As discovered by Dr. Masaru Emoto, water also carries emotions, mind states, and moods. Dr. Emoto observed a variety of different water crystals and how the molecules rearrange themselves in response to different qualities that surround or affect them including emotions, songs, and prayers.

We have cycled through the earth element discovering a range of expressions in the material and physical realm. As the understanding of money, finances, job, career, wealth, and resources deepen, we see how these aspects are intimately linked to our emotional well-being and relationships. There is a dance between these two realms in both the natural world of earth and water as well as the tarot through disks and cups. These two elements have a strong and relatable dynamic, perhaps more than any other suit relationships in the cards. This is because our emotional selves are so intricately linked to our physical bodies and worldly manifestations and is something we can identify easily and clearly in our day-to-day lives.

When doing readings, you will want to consider the emotional aspects of disks cards when they appear as well as the physical expressions of cups when they appear. For example, when the Ace of Disks appears in a reading, it likely indicates a new job offer, contract, or monetary gift. Also consider the emotional qualities that accompany such a new offer; we are usually excited, joyous, delighted, and feel affirmed and encouraged by life and the universe when this happens. This emotion helps to fuel our next steps and energy put into the offer presented to us.

In the tarot, cups are water and represent our emotional states in our lives. This includes personal emotions and our emotional well-being, relationships with others, and emotional intelligence. When we were babies, many of us were allowed to express our physical pain and emotion through crying and were usually held and comforted. However, as we got older, our strong emotions of pain, discomfort, anger, sorrow, hatred, and rage were often seen as something unacceptable and we had to repress these stronger emotions.

Our emotions are ever changing, like water. They work best when in continual motion, otherwise stagnation sets in. When we are overcome with fear, anger, sorrow, or other difficult emotions, we have a choice: lean into it or repress it. It is important to revisit our emotional bodies and find safe spaces to express our emotions. Only then will we be able to reach levels of emotional maturity and experience the divine connection to emotional intelligence.

In this section, we use the varied expression of water to connect to our emotional body and work on this rich source of information. Water in tarot is connected to our intuition, dreams, creative subconscious, and how that information moves through our emotional body. Emotions are the signposts to our deeper connection to source. Several cards in the suit of cups appear heavy, stagnant, and difficult to work with; yet it is these harder emotions that are often are most precious resources to show us where we are stuck in growing on our life path. Just as rushing wild water has the power to destroy in the case of a flash flood or tsunami, it also contains the power to cleanse, refresh, and wash away the old to make room for the new.

Meditation: Water Source

This is a simple practice to help you touch into the water element that guides you along your life path journey. One of my Hawaiian teachers often begins a circle by having the participants connect to the mountain and waters that were closest to us when we were born. If we do not know this water source it is worth our while to look it up and in particular to find out which watershed we lived in and where our water came from. This helps connect us to place at our birth, which in some indigenous perspectives is deeply imprinted on our soul the moment we emerge from our mother's womb. I had no personal connection to the water near my birth, as I was born in North Carolina and we moved when I was eight years old. I had to look up on the map and research to find the watershed that sourced the first eight years of my life.

Once you know your water source, take a moment to connect into this source. Fill a bowl or cup with water as a symbolic way to connect to water. Sit in a meditative posture and create a simple sacred space. Focus on the breath for a few moments and then tune into the body and contemplate it as primarily water. Try to sense yourself as a container for the fluid nature of water. Send your awareness back to the watershed of your birth as well as the other waters that were near you, such as rivers, streams, lakes, or an ocean. Spend a few moments cultivating awareness between yourself and your birth waters and feel gratitude for this connection.

After working with the watershed of your birthplace, then begin to work with the watershed you currently live in and with, if it is a different place. Following the same guidance, research the ways that you get your water, where it is sourced from, and how it is affected by the geography and land you live on. As you work through the cups section you may want to consider collecting waters for your own ceremonial and sacred work. This suit will culminate in a water ceremony in the Ten of Cups and incorporating waters from different rivers, streams, lakes, and oceans helps us to remember our connection to water and that water is sacred, water is life.

Ace of Cups: Seed of Love

The Ace of Cups marks the beginning of the suit of cups and its progressions through the myriad emotional expressions, relationships, and fluidity of life. The ace holds the potential for the entire suit, containing all the expressions of how water and emotions move through us. Although the Ace of Cups traditionally signifies the experience of love with another, it also holds a deeper meaning in the importance of self-love. We can only love another as much as we love ourselves. Similarly, we can only give as much love as we can receive. The appearance of the Ace of Cups indicates a willingness to open ourselves to a loving experience, one which deepens and also reflects our capacity for self-love.

In the Waite-Smith deck, an outstretched hand offers an overflowing golden cup as a gift of delight and beauty. This hand symbolizes an offer or generous gift of love, compassion, and openness, and it is up to us to reach out and grasp the cup and drink from its contents. Sometimes we are stuck in our old patterns and we may have a challenging time opening up to a pure gift of love. Love does not always come in the form we expect it and can herald a time of cleansing old patterns or habits as the joy and bliss help us to move toward the next stage in soul development.

In the Crowley deck, the image of the Ace of Cups is radiant and glowing, showing the potential to outwardly affect a network of intricate lines. These represent our relations in our life and symbolize that love promotes healing on all levels: physical, mental, emotional, and spiritual, as well as through time and space. For the Ace to work its magic on all these levels, we have to be open to receiving this gift of eros, beauty, love, and bliss. Sometimes we are afraid and may feel uneasy or believe that the timing may be off.

The Ace of Cups indicates an offer of love, perhaps a declaration from someone you are already with, such as an engagement or taking a relationship to the next level. If not in a relationship, the card may signify someone arriving in your life, someone who has the potential to open you up to new feelings of love, beauty, and joy. The card may indicate a birth of a new baby, creative project, or a new garden; something that brings with a sense of joy and delight. This may be a situation as well, an opportunity to experience love in a deeper and more heartfelt way with the land, with a group of people, or with something material, such as a new home or job even.

The Ace of Cups may also symbolize a seed of beauty that is planted within but not necessarily expressed outwardly. When we receive blessings from spiritual teachers, praise from a colleague or friend, or a gift of beauty, this may rest in the soil of our soul before emerging later to bloom. The feeling of the Ace of Cups is pure heart and reminds us that the heart has its own language and timing often very different from the way our mind and thoughts work. The quality of the heart language is pure, clear, and based in the essence level experience of life.

Ceremony: Heart Waters

To draw the beauty and love of the Ace of Cups into your life, create a simple heart ceremony using water, flowers, and a clear glass bowl. Sit with your bowl and slowly pour water into it. Then visualize clear light moving through your heart center and into the water. Imagine breathing in this clear light and breathing out the clear light so that you become a vessel of clear light with no boundaries or end.

As you form this connection to pure, clear light, begin to think of all the people in your life. Start with the people you are closest to that you feel love for; then those you feel neutral toward; lastly those who you do not like, even enemies perhaps. As you do this, offer the flowers into the bowl of water symbolizing an offering of beauty. When finished, you can take the bowl of water and flowers and pour it into a jar to offer at a river, lake, pond, stream, or ocean. Feel your connections to the people in your life like fluid streams that move across the earth.

Two of Cups: Cherishing the Beloved

Following the ace and its beautiful seed of light and love, watery emotions split into two vessels, two cups. Here the reflective quality of the two becomes apparent. From the fullness of one we move into the dance of two and can see the love reflected outwardly with another. This develops and deepens our capacity to love and is the core to spiritual growth, discovering love with others as we move through the earthly plane.

In the Waite-Smith deck, two figures face one another; blessings pour forth between their open hearts. Above the two figures, we see the symbol of the caduceus which represents the combination of different synergies or essences of the two persons. This can be in romantic partnership, friendship, or even business indicating positive support leading to a desired common goal. They are creating a sacred union. In this moment, they feel the profound grace of love that comes from the divine but only meets with others at certain, compelling moments in our lives. The Two of Cups reminds us to take sweet pleasure in this moment, as it is to be cherished. The card encourages creating a ceremony, stating vows, or making a declaration of love to someone.

In the Crowley deck we see a lotus pouring our divine, clear waters through two intertwined fishes and into two overflowing cups. The lotus is an ancient symbol of enlightenment, a flower of beauty and grace that grows through the muck and mud before blooming. The journey of the lotus flower growing through the heaviness of the mucky soil symbolizes the path that humans take through suffering, pain, and obstacles to reach the beauty and bliss of enlightenment. This is not an easy, quick high but instead the lasting clarity of true love and peace. When we make a deep connection with another human being through love, we glimpse this radiant divine grace; it is up to us to see that that connection is a spiritual signpost on the journey toward enlightenment and not a temporary fling with another person.

In the Two of Cups, the love reflects itself in the eyes of a beloved. This card indicates a deepening love with a lover or friend or that a friendship may be turning into a romantic relationship. Often this signifies the wish to take vows with another and may be in the form of a love ceremony, marriage, or intimate partnering. This card indicates the meeting of two hearts and the formation of a lasting bond. The reflection of another pouring love toward us, through their gaze, their heartfelt honoring is a profound and sacred gift. This card is intimately connected to the Lovers card of the major arcana, signifying a deepening commitment between two people.

Meditation: Eye Gazing

Eyes are windows into the soul and reflect beauty and love back to us when we take time to look into one another's eyes. The simplicity of this mediation is marked by the profound sense of love we feel for others even if they are not our partners or beloveds.

Choose a partner to practice this with—it could be a lover, beloved, partner, or friend. Set aside some time and, if you wish, create an altar with flowers, incense, and two cups filled with clean spring water. Then, create sacred space using the five directions from your work with the Magician or simply visualize a clear ring of light around you as learned in the High Priestess card.

When you are ready, sit with your legs crossed on the floor or as close as you can in two chairs. Then, simply gaze into one another's eyes for five minutes. Notice feelings and your breath as you look into the other's eyes. If you feel uncomfortable or awkward, that's okay! By being intensely present with another you are being present with yourself and we often hide from this. This is an opportunity to be fully present with self and marry your inner and outer expressions. If you wish to deepen the practice, you can also place your left hand, the receptive hand, on each other's hearts. This allows you to not only connect through the eyes but also the pulse and embodiment of your being and breath.

Notice the love you feel that naturally arises for the other person—the sense of gentleness, kindness, and compassion. During one of my women's circles, we practiced this with one another, switching partners. I found it to be an incredible experience, feeling the natural expression of love for each of the women in the circle. Each set of eyes was so unique and beautiful in a different way and also incredibly capable of passing love and light.

When you are finished with the eye gazing give each other a hug and thank the other person for being present with you. Each drink the fresh spring water from the two cups or offer it to one another as a way to seal in the loving experience. Take a moment to feel gratitude before closing the circle.

Three of Cups: Abundant Flow

The Two of Cups expands into the Three of Cups as the flow of love increases. As we move from two into three there is growth and beauty that is shared not only among two beloveds with but a growing group of friends, family, and other relations. This is card of continual giving and receiving, that to open and receive we must also give away freely without expectation. For the waters to flow the way must be clear and the movement constant like a waterfall flowing freely from mountaintop to ocean.

The Waite-Smith deck shows three women merrily dancing together in the sunlight, delighting in one another's company. They hold three cups aloft and celebrate the joy, love, friendship, and connection they find when they are together. This is a card of sisterhood in which the women are able to relate through creativity and sharing in a heartfelt manner. The fruitful harvest at their feet symbolizes the outpouring of abundance that appears when relating this way as a close circle of friends.

In the Crowley deck we see three lotus cups filled with pomegranate seeds and golden lotuses that beam rays of golden light onto the seeds. The pomegranate seeds symbolize fertility, fecundity, and growth as well as a much deeper meaning with ancient roots. When Demeter, the Greek goddess of the earth, lost her daughter Persephone to Hades, god of the underworld, she lay the earth barren in her grief. This time became winter, a time of loss, sorrow, and death. Upon her daughter's return, Demeter's joy results in the beautiful blossoming of spring as the earth comes to life once again. However, while Persephone was in the underworld, she ate six pomegranate seeds, the fruit of the dead, which bound her to that place forever. The pomegranate seeds are symbolic of the cycle of seasons on earth and in life. Winter follows summer which follows winter, just as grief follows joy which follows grief. This can be celebrated in each passing as different colors or shades of the human experience

When this card appears in a reading, it usually signifies a creative time in life, abundance, flow of resources, and positive connections with others. You may be entering a burst in creative expression through writing, painting, singing, or another form of passionate expression. This card may also indicate a time of celebration following the completion of a project or after a crisis when the need to come together and honor one another is necessary.

The Three of Cups may indicate an unexpected blessing in seeing old new friends or forming a sudden kinship with new friends. There is a flow of love and joy and spontaneity in this card that may give rise to celebration, dance, grace, and beauty. This card is about sharing with others; sharing our joy and laughter, as well as our sorrows, but in a way that is with beauty and honoring. We lift one another up, look into one another's eyes, and feel the joy moving through us.

This card also indicates play and sensuality and may indicate a time of sexual exploration. This exploration may be openness to expressing intimate fantasies or sharing crushes we feel on others with our primary partner as a way to be tender and vulnerable. It may also be embodied through an experience of having more than one lover as a short-lived experience or longer, as in polyamorous relationships. The key is the willingness to remain open in the heart and allow the love to express itself through all people with respect, clear communication, and boundaries.

Ceremony: Have a Party

One lovely way to honor the message of the Three of Cups is to create a festive ceremony—in other words, have a party! Celebrate yourself and your friends by creating a time to gather, connect, and share. Include beautiful cups or vessels and fill them with wine, kombucha, sparkling juice, or other fun elixirs. Share drinks, laughter, and fun with your friends. Do a party exercise where everyone writes down what they are grateful for on a big paper. Showing and sharing gratitude has been shown to open the heart, create connection, and gives a reason to gather with others in community. This is an essential part of experiencing happiness and joy in our lives.

Four of Cups: Reflective Dreams

Progressing from the festive Three of Cups, the energy slows into a dreamy state, one that is both reflective as well as listless in the Four of Cups. Fours are often stable, however with cups, this stability is momentary and is threatened by the movement that is water and emotion. The Four of Cups indicates a luxury and temporary delight but also the possibility of delusion or illusion. Sometimes our emotions distract or even deceive us. They may be projections of what we wish, and not necessarily what is happening in our lives.

The Waite-Smith deck shows a figure sitting under a tree with his arms crossed in front of him symbolizing protection from the emotions of the cups and a disengagement with the world. He is looking downward, perhaps toward the three cups in a row before him. Meanwhile, a hand floats in a cloud, offering a cup which he is either ignoring or cannot see. The energy of the card is passive, dull, and lackluster. There is not much movement and the water seems to have stopped flowing. This card indicates uncertainty and doubts. We may be unable to make decisions about what direction to take in our life path and our relationships with others.

In the Crowley deck, the card at first appears to be more illustrious and positive than the Waite-Smith deck. The picture shows four gold cups receiving radiant flows from a lotus. However, this lotus is turned downward, indicating a move away from the path toward enlightenment and a focus on relationships that can be obsessive or unhelpful. The curling vines between the cups are dark and heavy, reminding us of the energetic cords connecting us with other people.

The Four of Cups indicates a time of indecision and lack of forward movement. There may be an experience of beauty, luxury, and outward monetary gain, but it is likely to be illusory and temporary. The deeper fulfillment of the spiritual path is hard to access here, clouded by unclear emotional states. Continued mental and emotional processing does not help the issue but instead drags us even further into the rut we have found ourselves in. We often need a shift of perspective to break out of the heaviness of this card or, on a deeper level, a clearing of emotional ties from people who are no longer positive presences in our lives.

Ceremony: Clearing Emotional Cords

Emotional cords are energetic or psychic cords that are formed between people who have relationships with each other. The stronger and more intimate the bond, the stronger and more numerous the cords. When we have toxic and intense connections still left over from previous relationships, it is helpful to clear and heal the cords. Some practices encourage cutting these cords; however my teachers have shown me how this can cause even further harm, so I offer the practice of clearing and healing instead.

First, create a meditative space. Then focus on your breath for a few moments, settling your mind and going into a peaceful place free of worries or concerns about the past or future. Then, visualize yourself surrounded in a golden or clear brilliant light, one that protects and energizes. If you cannot visualize it, simply intend protection and love and call upon guardians, helpers, and ancestors.

Now, visualize the person you are clearing cords with coming toward you, also surrounded in the golden, clear light. Once the person is in front of you, have a dialogue with the person from the compassionate part of yourself. First listen to what the other person needs to express. Then respond all within your own mind. Give yourself time to complete this dialogue, as both parties may need to express their feelings and listen more than once. In this moment, we often begin to resolve a lot of the issue, truly communicating with someone from our soul essence. When you are in safe space illuminated in this way, often the true nature of the connection is revealed and can be deeply healing for both parties.

After the conversation is finished, then notice where the cords are between you and the other person. Notice where they are in the body and how this may have been affecting you and the other. Then imagine clearing the cord between you and the other person. After this is done, visualize golden light between you and the other, healing the cord. You are still connected but not in a way that is harmful. Finally, visualize the other person floating off and away into the space, healing and recharging.

Five of Cups: Disappointing Loss

After the illusion and possible delusions of the Four of Cups, there is a letdown or letting go in the Five of Cups. Throughout the cups we experience periods of ecstatic highs and disappointing lows, a true reflection of the ups and downs of our emotional bodies. Life is rich in both of these experiences and the challenge remains to navigate these ups and downs without becoming subsumed by negativity.

When we feel low, it is important to honor this time and perhaps reflect, to be kind to ourselves and remember that we are only at where we are at. Grief is the winter of the heart. Without being able to honor letting go, our sorrow turns to unspent emotion resulting in resentment, anger, even rage. It is important that we allow the letting go to move through us.

The Waite-Smith deck shows a figure hunched in a black cloak looking out over the river passing by. The sky is gray and leaden, and two cups have been knocked over while two remain in an upright position. This image shows that although there is a loss such as a breakup or disappointment in something that isn't going to work out, there is still steady emotional grounding in this process and there is a kind of purpose to this shift in energy.

In the Crowley imagery we see five cups at the point of a downward facing pentacle. This symbolizes power turned inward and upside down. The flowers droop and dark vines curl around each other showing a tightness in growth and immobility. Two dark leaves arch over the cups threatening loss and disappointment. These images are not easy to swallow, and yet behind the translucent cups (indicating a stark reality or awakening), the background is orange and red, symbolizing creativity. It is often amid disappointment that we experience the latent creative force come to life and an outpouring of emotion.

Traditionally, this card indicates that someone or something has been taken from us and we feel the loss. Perhaps something has been stolen, or we have lost the competition or didn't get the job we had wanted. Feelings of disappointment or even shame or guilt may accompany this feeling of loss. We might even feel bitter about our loss or depressed if it carries on for a long time.

Ceremony: Letting Go

This ceremony is a beautiful way to honor loss, to grieve, to let go. Additionally, as this card can forecast imminent loss, if we face it before it happens and make offerings in preparation, it can both soften the blow and even affect the out-come of a situation, moving it in a more positive direction.

This ceremony can be done alone or with others. You may wish to do the first part at home and then go to the waters, or you can do the entire ceremony at a water's edge. Choose any place that is somewhat private such as a quiet beach, a river's edge, waterfall, or stream. Gather flowers, a bowl, a jar to put the water in, candles, crystals, and salt. Create a beautiful altar with the items you have gathered and call in sacred space and connect with your guides and ancestors as provided in the major arcana ceremonies.

Pour the water and cleansing salt into the bowl and let it rest in your lap. Call to mind something that is particularly troubling you, such as what showed up in your reading or any traumatic or challenging incidents that have hap-pened. You may also wish to track back in your mind the hardships you have faced in your life along the way. Try to bring up the sadness, pain, and sorrow you felt in these situations and, if possible, bring yourself to tears. Feel into not only your own pain but the pain and suffering around the world and all the intensity of poverty, humanitarian issues, genocide, rape, conflict, loss of species, and land and climate change… the list goes on. As you do this, release your tears, knowing they are helping you cleanse, soothe, and heal your pain. Tears are an offering to our ancestors.

When you feel the sorrow subsiding and you move into a calmer state, offer the flowers to the bowl with the expression of gratitude. When our grief sub-sides, we usually feel lighter, calmer, and sometimes even brighter and refreshed. We can tune into this heart opening by feeling thankful for all the experiences in our life. So often what we are sorrowful about we are also grateful for, as these challenges are our greatest teachers. As we offer the flowers, we see the beauty of the world filling up the bowl.

As this completes, either pour the bowl of water, salt, tears, and flowers into the waters you are next to, or put it in the glass jar to take to a river, ocean, or stream when the timing is right. Be sure to do this in the next few weeks after your ceremony as a way to honor the letting go and gratitude of your heart. When you are finished, close the sacred space and release the directions.

Six of Cups: Forgiveness

Following the loss and sorrow of the Five of Cups, we move into a very tender place in our heart. Grief and loss invoke a sense of vulnerability that can feel painful but is actually the process of our heart softening and opening up in the Six of Cups. Here we experience the power of forgiveness and the soft touch of compassion may well up within—to feel more is ultimately the ability to love more.

In Waite-Smith we see children playing among flowers, a reminder of innocence. We have all experienced the joy that children bring and the openness they can show toward their relations as well as complete strangers. They haven't yet built up hardened and bitter walls around their hearts. As we grow older, we often shut down after traumatic experiences, heartache, and painful things in life that happen to us and those around us. This card is a reminder of what is still pure within us and helps us to see the essence level of who we are and those around us.

The Crowley deck shows a delightful array of six golden cups appearing to dance and move on waves. The word is "pleasure"—a reminder to practice self-care and delight in the pleasures and beauty of the world. The gray background and vines remind us that pleasure is often temporary and fleeting and to not invest all of ourselves into the outcome of a situation but rather be present in the passing delight.

Martin Prechtel, visionary author and healer, speaks of the inextricable relationship between grief and praise. It is powerful to give praise in great gratitude for something in our life because we recognize that it is passing and impermanent. Conversely, when we are in sorrow for what is passing, we recognize the sweetness and beauty, and we feel deep gratitude to experience this. This is the essence of the Six of Cups, to recognize the blooming flowers and the simultaneous beauty of the moment and passing through.

When this card appears in a reading, it indicates the need to soften the heart, to have "honey in the heart," as Prechtel writes. We may need to let go of certain cruelty or judgment about ourselves or others. A time of forgiveness and healing is happening, and perhaps our perspective is shifting so that we may feel more compassion to those who are hurtful. Often people in our lives who express anger, hatred, or act negatively toward us are full of their own suffering and clouded mindset.

This card also encourages us to practice self-care and be kind to ourselves. Take baths, rest, spend time in nature, reflect on the beauty in your life. Give thanks for your relations, soften your approach to others, and cultivate a soft heart. This may also indicate a time to spend with children and/or older people who are closer to the beginning and end of life.

Meditation: Tonglen

This is a simple meditation that comes from the Tibetan Buddhist tradition. The intention of the practice is to transform heaviness, suffering, and pain into light and clarity. You do not need to be a Buddhist to practice this. The meditation is shared by Pema Chödrön a Buddhist teacher, nun, and author. In the Buddhist view, "buddha" simply means "awake," and practices are meant to remind us of that already existing brilliant, compassionate, and awakened state.

For this meditation, set up your altar with the Star and Six of Cups cards, a small glass bowl of water, and a candle. These items symbolically connect you to light and cleansing. The beauty of the Star figure pouring her vases of water into the earth reminds us of our own constant inner divinity and grace. Light the candle and reflect for a moment on the simple beauty of fire reflecting in clear water. Acknowledge the three aspects that form the core of Buddhism: the Buddha, the dharma, and the sangha. Again, you don't have to be Buddhist to practice this. When you acknowledge the inner Buddha, you are acknowledging your own inner awakened state; with the dharma you touch on the teachings of enlightened beings who have gone before you; and with the sangha you recognize that there is a community of people around the world who devote their lives to benefit the beings and alleviate suffering.

Sit in a meditative posture and focus on your breath for several moments. After some time has passed, feel into a particularly troubling emotion or problem for yourself. Extend your awareness out to recognize that if you are feeling shame, anger, sadness, or pain, it is likely that thousands if not millions of others are as well. Reach out through your heart center and envision this pain as a cloud of dirty smoke.

Pull this smoke into your heart center, trusting that you have the power and strength to transmute this into love and light and clarity. Envision your heart as a transforming and powerful center that takes in the dirty smoke of pain and suffering and transforms it into the brilliant light of love and compassion. Practice doing this for several minutes. If you wish, you can continue with different emotions and painful situations, transforming them into compassionate light.

When you are finished, dedicate this practice to benefit all beings throughout the world, for self and others. Feel the lightness and open spacious quality in your heart and acknowledge your connection to all the beings in the world and beyond.

Seven of Cups: Illusions

Following the cleansing and compassion of the Six of Cups, we encounter another tide of fantastical wishes, illusions, and dreams in the Seven of Cups. It is often after we practice a heart opening ceremony that we find old patterns rear their ugly head yet again! It seems the journey of human evolution is wrought with endless layers, and nothing more clearly illuminates this then the progression of the tarot cards. Sevens symbolize a time of reflection and reorienting oneself along the path. With cups, we reflect and take stock of our relationships, intimate connections, and inner emotional landscape.

In the Waite-Smith imagery, seven cups filled with jewels and enchantments hover alluringly above the figure. Each cup holds its own illusory possibility, each symbolizing a distraction and unfulfilled fantasy and wish. This is a card of laziness and the inability to progress because we have too many options or perhaps too much time on our hands. We are indecisive, lost in our dreams, and unable to manifest what we desire. This card is similar to the fantasy of the Four of Cups but may be even more illusory and delusional.

The Crowley imagery shows seven cups rising up out of a mucky swamp. They are overflowing with heavy, thick liquid that oozes in a toxic manner, symbolizing a need to detoxify and cleanse the systems—emotional as well as physical and mental. This card indicates the need to fast or practice self-discipline in cleaning up your life. There are too many distractions. Perhaps you are watching too many shows, smoking or drinking a lot of alcohol, eating foods that aren't nutritious, or engaging in toxic behavior with friends, family, or coworkers.

This card may also indicate taking on another's energy such that it affects you. Perhaps your intimate relationship is codependent and needs to be reexamined, or a friend, family member, or coworker is pulling on you and asking you to be or do things that don't feel right or balanced for you. This card indicates a need to check in with your boundaries around emotional relationships and reexamine the choices you are making in life.

Visualization: Aura Cleanse

This meditation is used to cleanse the aura through visualization as a way to clear any negative or excess energy from the field surrounding the body. You can also use other methods to cleanse and clear, such as smudge smoke from herb bundles, taking a salt water bath, or spraying the aura around you with essential oils or rose water. This particular practice is useful to do at the end of the day or after you have been in an uncomfortable situation or with people who feel negative or toxic.

Sit comfortably in a meditative position. Visualize your grounding cord from the Emperor exercise, extending it down to the center of the earth. Imagine that your aura is a bright color, forming a full sphere, like an eggshell around your body. The aura boundary should extend about two feet above, below, behind, and in front of your body. If needed, push out any of the edges that are too close to your body, or pull in edges that are too far away. Allow your energy field to show you any parts that need to be smoothed out. Let your mind and/or your hands do the work.

After your field has been straightened, recheck the color. Then make your grounding cord the same color. Enlarge the grounding cord so it is a foot in diameter. This way, whatever comes up in the cleanse can easily be thrown or pushed into the grounding cord and taken back to the center of the earth where it will neutralize.

Bring the aura boundary in so it is only an inch away from your body. Visualize the aura boundary pulling in toward you so it is squeezing out anything dark or muddled. See your aura like a tube of toothpaste, pushing out the unwanted or excessive energies, allowing them to flow down and out through the grounding cord. After a few moments, pop the aura in its original place and visualize your energy field filling up with a bright, vivid healing color such as violet, electric blue, or clear yellow. Notice the difference in your energy field, how you feel lighter and brighter.

Finally, recheck the grounding cord and bring it back to six inches in diameter. Choose any color for the day. Then come back into the awareness of the body. Touch the earth to reground and slowly open your eyes. Write down any experiences you had. What color did you see for your aura boundary? How did you feel after you pulled the boundary in then popped it back out? Continue this exercise at the end of the day to feel cleansed and renewed.

Eight of Cups: Leaving Behind

After the illusory dreams of the Seven of Cups, we awaken to the reality that we have been overindulging or living in a fantasy world. With the Eight of Cups, we are inspired to shed what is not working and go within again, to clarify our emotional landscape and touch into our inner divinity. Often, negative emotions are viewed as wrong and judged by the outside world. Yet when we make friends with our inner darker emotions, we discover that by working with and transforming them we can release immense creative power.

In the Waite-Smith deck, we see a figure walking along a stream under the moonlight. The person's back is turned toward us, indicating a time of turning away and slowing down. The moon symbolizes the unconscious, the dark hidden parts of our soul. This card encourages us to slow down to access our interior depths and discover what is not working, to find a new way, one that may be very different from what we "think" we should do. This can be exciting for some, daunting for others. The figure is leaving behind the cups that are still full in order to move on to something new. Although the way is dark and unknown, there is a sense of trust in the movement from one shore to the next.

In the Crowley imagery, the water has become stagnant, lazy, heavy, and thick. It is full of the toxic residue from the Seven of Cups and sinks into an earthly state calling desperately for clarity and release. Lotuses hang heavy and downward and the clouds behind the cups are thick and need to be let go of their heavy rains. Old patterns are dredged to the surface, and although the way forward is completely unknown, what is known is that the old ways won't work anymore.

When this card appears in a reading, it encourages you to quiet and center yourself or go within. Similar to the Hermit, it often indicates a time of self-reflection, a needed retreat or time away from a busy life full of distractions. This card can also indicate the realization that certain relationships are no longer working the way they were. Perhaps you realize there is a level of codependency or a toxic way of communicating that is not serving you. Finding ways to make changes in the relationship become essential for your health and well-being.

Ceremony: Offering a Relational Gift

When relationships, jobs, homes, and chapters in life come to a close, we often feel a sense of sadness and letting go as we transition from one phase to the next. It can be helpful to offer an object or item, a letter, or some hair from that time as we make time for moving from one phase to the next. When one of my most powerful love relationships ended, I created a ceremonial offering, drifting a piece of wood, ring, and crystals that had been part of our connection out on to the river. Letting go of those items were a symbolic way to both honor the connection and let go.

For this ceremony, choose something that was a significant or symbolic object of what you are letting go. This may be something specific you shared or worked on with someone, or it can be a symbol of your connection. Choose something that is not trash—no plastic or other synthetic materials—it should be biodegradable or found as a surprise gift for someone in the future. Once you have your object, find a piece of wood that will float. During the waning moon at sunset or sunrise, go out to the river or ocean to create your ceremony. Make offerings to the water and call in the directions, helpers, guardians, and set the space. Take time to sit with the memories of the person, work space, or time you spent. Feel the connection and sing or speak in a good way back to the past to honor what has happened. Float the piece of wood with the object(s) out onto the river, continuing to offer flowers as the sun shifts in transition into the day or the night. Continue to sing or offer words of honor and letting go as your wood floats out into the world. Remember the fluidity of life, the interconnectedness of all relations, and welcome the openness of new discovery as the sun moves over the horizon. Close the space when you feel complete, thanking the helpers and guardians.

Nine of Cups: Fulfillment

At long last we reach a stable and beautiful place in our journey through the cups! The Nine of Cups is an emotional deepening and connection with our relations in a way that benefits us and brings us more in touch with our inner joy and beauty. We are able to share with others and discover lasting connections with people who are able to accept us fully for who we are and we can share our gifts with one another.

The Waite-Smith imagery shows a wealthy adorned man who is full and jolly. Above him arch nine vibrant cups indicating success, pleasure, happiness, and contentment. This is a time to celebrate our dreams as well as add our own inner wealth of gratitude and creative vision to the unfolding of our lives. The background is yellow symbolizing abundance and creative manifestation, accompanied by a high table with a lush blue tablecloth indicating grandeur and nobility. This is a very full and nourishing card but may also indicate a sense of false pride or ego.

In the Crowley deck, nine cups are arranged in three rows, three cups per row. The cups are violet colored indicating a connection to our higher self, refined wisdom, and intuition. Radiant light pours from nine lotus flowers, one over each cup. Arched vines against a blue background symbolize clear communication, understanding, and higher learning. This card reminds us that we are interconnected with all of our relations; although we seem alone on the journey, we are connected to so many.

This card indicates a time of coming together with others in groups with family and friends. In particular, the Nine of Cups points toward the importance of community and sharing our gifts with many others. Perhaps it is time to bring a vision, project, or creative endeavor to the next level and include others. This card indicates a positive time to invest both financially and emotionally in a project and to consider the offers that others have to assist you in building your dreams. This card is a reminder that we do have the potential to cocreate our lives the way that we wish through harmonious connections with others. The appearance of this card in a reading may also symbolize wealth appearing, an inheritance, a pleasurable vacation, or a well-deserved weekend of joy and fun!

Ceremony: Full Moon

This simple ceremony is a way honor our relations. Think of all the people in your life whom you consider close, who have the greatest effect on your life, who you love, and who bring you challenges. Especially honor and recognize the ones who challenge you for they are often the greatest teachers! You may also include people who you may not believe directly affect your life but pop into your mind anyway.

Once, after a friend of a friend passed away in our community in Hawai'i, we did a journey so I could attempt to access her spirit and receive messages. As I reached out to connect with her, I was struck by two things: I saw hundreds of flowers (I later learned that she grew many flowers in her garden) and she impressed upon me the importance of each and every person in an individual's life. She conveyed to me that no encounter is random; every connection down to the tiniest glimpse of a person in an elevator has meaning, and we are all interrelated whether we are aware of it or not. I was left with the understanding of how important it is to treasure all our relations and attempt kindness and care as much as we can.

For this ceremony, gather nine cups and label each cup with a person's name on it. Fill each one with water and place near the window on the full moon light. Add a drop of honey to sweeten each of the cups and soften your heart especially to relations that are difficult to deal with. Recognize the gifts that each relation brings to your life and feel love and forgiveness (if appropriate) for each person. In the morning, offer the water at sunrise and ask for peace and harmony to show themselves in all your relations.

Ten of Cups: Joyful Connection

As the joyful connection continues from the Nine of Cups, we experience even more radiance, beauty, and love with the Ten of Cups. Here the emotions reach a level of bliss and purity and we feel a powerful divine connection to all of life. This is also a ten which signifies the end of a journey and a kind of completion or resolution before the next phase begins.

The Waite-Smith imagery shows a family standing together under an arching rainbow with ten glowing, golden cups. The parents or adults embrace one another, hands to the sky in a seemingly joyful and exuberant expression while two children dance in delight next to them. This card symbolizes the joy of a fulfilled life, again similar to the Sun in its outward expression of fulfillment. It indicates the harvest, the joy of celebrating a job well done, good work celebrated. The rainbow is a universal symbol for love, beauty, magic, and illusion. Its appearance is beautiful while also temporary, reminding us of the reality that the end of a cycle is nearing.

In the Crowley deck, ten golden cups are arranged in a pattern called the Tree of Life, one of the most ancient symbols in human history. The Tree of Life is a map that chronicles the journey of the Fool through the phases of the major arcana. I encourage seekers to study more of this connection (see the resource section at the end of the book) as it offers rich study that will help deepen your understanding of the tarot, should you wish to incorporate the Tree of Life into your tarot practice. This card holds a spiritual component that signifies not just bliss and harmony, but true awakening and even self-realization. The background is a rosy orange glow indicating harmonious creations and growth.

This card indicates a time of beauty, peace, and domestic harmony. Related to the Sun card as well as the Ten of Disks, this may herald a new beginning such as a birth, acquisition of land, a marriage, flourishing business, and success in projects and creative developments. It may also indicate the deepening connections of these aspects of life such as a growing love in partnership, a developing business, or the extension of a trip.

Ceremony: Sacred Waters

During the writing of this book, several crises related to water became more apparent in our daily reality. We are coming to a crossroads as humans on earth and water is fast becoming a scarce commodity. In order to recognize this important fact, I recommend sourcing the closest natural springs to you not just for spiritual connection but also as a practical resource for clean water.

To create this ceremony, gather your water, as well as a large bowl, candles, flowers, incense, and any other offerings. It is important to do this with a few people; the more the merrier to amplify the experience. Bring the waters and your offerings to a place where you feel the water needs your prayers and attentions. Perhaps you wish to pray that the rainfall would be steady for the winter to ensure a solid snowpack and enough water for everyone to drink the following year.

Set up an altar with the waters and the offerings. Create sacred space, call to the directions, guides, and ancestors. Have each person step forward and pour some of the water they brought into the large bowl mingling them all together. Have people offer their prayers, songs, and chants to the water. Be creative! People will want to share different songs from traditions they know or say certain prayers connected to the waters they brought. Perhaps you could also offer tears as in the Five of Cups ceremony.

After everyone has taken their turn, bring the circle together with a closing song for everyone to sing together. Offer the bowl of mixed waters to the river, waterfall, stream, or ocean where you are connecting to your place on the earth and with all the waters on the planet. Release the directions, thank the ancestors and the guides. Feel the gratitude for one another and the precious beauty of this earth.

AIR: SWORDS

As we move into swords, we move into the air and winds around us. This is the realm of the mind and the intellect. The winds have the power to both clear and illuminate as well as cloud and confuse which we see unfolding in the path of the Swords. Swords connect us to our mental thoughts, patterns, habits, and attitudes about the world around us. The realm of the mental energy in the Swords is connected to ideas and how they manifest or are blocked in our path. Swords are also quite heavy and should be taken with some measure of care. They show up in a reading to get our attention. Imagine lifting a sword and the physical strength required to wield this heavy, sharp, metal object that is primarily a weapon. Knowing that this quality is symbolic of the mind helps us to understand how we can learn to wield our own mind with clarity and control rather than weakness and self-sabotage.

When we imagine swords, we may naturally think of them swinging through the air, indicative of their power and relation to the wind and air. They have the power to cut through, free, and open the way, and they also have the power to wound, cause pain, and create suffering. When we look at the cards in this suit, we see several negative cards, more than any other suit in the deck. The indication is that our own mind is often the crux of many issues within our life. Many of the cards in this suit are associated with symbols of darkness and blood. Figures may be shown confused, blindfolded, in despair, and under attack. The cards illustrate the power of the sword as well as the importance of addressing the mental issues that often underlie questions around career, money, love, and health.

Swords have a powerful connection to the acts of speaking and listening and will indicate when these are positive and useful in our lives, when they are absent, or at worst, when they are negative or demanding. At their best, swords encourage us that a new kind of approach to life is possible, or that it is time to move more into the realms of learning and sharing and seek out new teachers. They may indicate the arrival of an "a-ha" moment to help turn our path in a new kind of thought. On the negative side, swords indicate a time to cut through harmful or limiting habitual thought patterns that no longer serve us, the need to rise above negative speech or gossip, and a call for action to help us shift our perspective.

The element of air is connected to the winds and the winged ones, the ability to soar over and through problems. Birds have the capacity to fly high—think of the "bird's eye perspective"—which the suit of swords encourages. The air can be cleansing or it can be turbulent, as in a wind storm. Finding our connection to the wind and the air helps to anchor our understanding with swords. We can connect to the air through the use of feathers.

Exercise: Finding Feathers

Feathers as a part of bird wisdom are symbols of air, wind, flight, and communication. Feathers and wings have been used for healing in countless cultures to evoke the energy of wind, breath, light, and clarity. Often associated with the air element and energy of the east, feathers bring a sense of fresh awareness and aliveness. Feathers are also everywhere! They are a gift from the winged creatures that fly throughout our day, offering song, sound, feathers, and the reminder to look up and connect with what is above us. We can set an intention to find feathers and may start to discover them in our path more. Take time to learn about which feathers you find, which birds they belong to, and their unique sounds and ways of communicating. Learning about the birds in the area, their habitat, and relation to the trees, we are able to connect more to our surrounding environment. This process naturally soothes and relaxes our nervous system, allowing our mind to quiet and awareness to center on the breath in the present moment. In quiet moments we can open up to deeper inspiration and guidance that brings us into alignment with our path. This is a helpful reminder when we are feeling overwhelmed, stressed, or anxious—states of being that are so prevalent in the swords of the minor arcana.

Ace of Swords: Clear Insight

Aces contain all of the teachings within them, and this one carries with it the full spectrum of the swords suit. Swords are connected to the element of air and our thoughts and mental patterns. They have the potential to clear the mind, to help us move forward with ideas and thoughts, and the possibility of wounding and obscuring. Within the Ace of Swords, the mastery of thought, ideas, creative discipline, and mental realms is possible.

In the Waite-Smith deck, a hand offers a shining silver sword pointing toward to the heavens. The sword bears a crown with green herbs symbolizing growth, vitality, strength, and vigor. The crown indicates a powerful insight, a crowning thought, so to speak, and certainty of direction. Here, the gray background symbolizes a steadfast awareness, solid like the landscape below the sword.

In the Crowley deck there is a vibrant green sword with crescent moon handles and a radiant crown. Behind the sword is the sun rising and illuminating sacred geometrical forms symbolizing the inspiring quality of guidance, a new idea that has the power to change and affect our path in a clear and dramatic way. Clouds clear, allowing for this new path to unfold.

When the Ace of Swords appears in a reading, it signifies that a new opportunity of learning and discovery is on the horizon. It may be going back to school, receiving spiritual teachings from a new teacher, or simply taking classes in something that you have been interested in for a while. The Ace of Swords may also indicate the time to teach, to pass on what you know, and an opportunity to share knowledge and wisdom will be presented to you.

The Ace of Swords often indicates a form of mastery of the intellect, of higher learning and discipline, a crucial aspect of working with the mind. Often, we are overwhelmed by our emotional states, the pain body, or life issues because our mind turns toward worry, concern, even despair and sadness. We may need to implement a positive mental practice to help move through the challenges in our lives. In Buddhist practice, the focus is on the mind; it is by changing the mind that we change everything around us. When we develop and cultivate lovingkindness, one-pointed focus, and concentration, we are able to balance our mind and approach life with right attitude. Committed, disciplined action can help heal an issue. In bringing our minds into alignment with our body and emotional selves, we can naturally create a mental shift that fosters an environment for deep healing.

Exercise: Cultivating Discipline

This works to help shift, let go of, or manifest something in your life—or a combination of all three. Choose something you wish to change, such as a negative relationship pattern, wanting to manifest more abundance in your life, or letting go of something that no longer serves you. Create an affirmation to use during this process. Affirmations keep our mind focused and engaged in positive thought instead of swirling off into negative thinking or wallowing. For example, if you wish to bring more abundance, love, or health into your life, you can use: "I am abundant," "I am healthy and strong," "I am love," or "I am loving awareness." If you are wishing to let go of something, be sure to turn the idea of letting go into a positive affirmation. For example, instead of saying, "I let go of my ex-boyfriend," change this to "I am free and whole in myself," or "I cleanse and heal my emotional body."

Once you have decided on your affirmation, create a simple action that you will do every night to put it into a ceremonial context. If you are creating more abundance or love or light, you may wish to light a candle every evening while stating the affirmation. If you are letting go of something, do an artful practice such as folding paper cranes to encourage healing. Through the repeated action of this work, you will find yourself on a journey to unlock certain aspects of the mind and make changes. We have the power to change, release negative thoughts, and turn our minds back toward love and clarity. The Ace of Swords is the reminder that this change is always possible, even if the swords or the mind become heavy and troublesome.

Two of Swords: Temporary Peace

Moving from the Ace of Swords, an opportunity for learning and expanding our mental horizons, we shift from the all-encompassing power of the ace to the two. Twos are the moment of separation, when a dualistic view emerges. This card in particular offers the opportunity for mental reflection and deep listening, the clear recognition that a situation is no longer working and there is acceptance. Although one may not know the way forward, what is clear is that the current method no longer works. This card indicates it is time to approach things through a practical and logical method; emotional currents have run their course. Obstacles may still be evident, however, resting in the knowing of peace and understanding will have a long-term influence. The Two of Swords encourages a stable mind and a willingness to look at both sides of a situation.

In the Waite-Smith deck, a female figure is blindfolded and holds two swords crossed over her chest. She is protecting her heart and is unable to see; her perceptions are limited. Behind her stretches the waters of emotion, feeling, and intuition. The sky is clear and unobstructed, symbolizing the potential for inner insight and perhaps even an initiation into deeper wisdom from within. The figure's ability to stay relaxed, yet also upright, while holding two heavy swords crossed indicates a unique quality of tension that rests in the balance of heaviness. Inner peace may arise amid conflict and tension, but only at the counterbalance between two opposing views.

In the Crowley deck, the word is "peace," and this card indicates a momentary time of peaceful resolution. Two swords pierce a blue lotus, symbolizing the cutting awareness of conflict and the opportunity to see things from another point of view. Behind the swords, four pinwheels dance across a pale green and yellow background indicating the need to pause and feel into a fresh perspective—lightness and opening are possible.

In a reading, this card signifies that two parties have decided to temporarily halt a conflict or issue that has arisen. Listening and quiet reflection are more useful than fighting out a disagreement. However, this card does usually indicate that this peaceful resolve is temporary in the kind of way that two people agree to disagree. There is not usually a clear resolution in sight, only the opportunity to listen, reflect, and acknowledge one another.

Like the Hanged Man, this card may also indicate being at a crossroads and needing to make a decision about a relationship, job issue, health concern, or spiritual matter. Resting for a moment and allowing yourself to be in the crossroads can give time for an insight to occur that you may not have thought of.

Exercise: Partner Listening

This exercise is helpful to practice both processing and listening with others. The need to be heard and seen, and witnessed on our path is one of our most basic ones. When I read cards and offer sessions to clients, this card signifies the importance of creating and holding space for someone to allow their process to emerge. By acting as a witness while offering quiet guidance, it allows for someone's own insights to occur. This practice requires trust that others involved are capable of carrying intuitive intelligence regarding their own life paths.

In this exercise, find time to create space to listen and process with a trusted friend, partner, or family member. If you are having a particular issue with someone, do this not with them but instead a neutral person who is not involved in the conflict or issue. Create a sacred space and altar with candles, flowers, and anything that symbolizes receptivity, such as a shell or bowl of water.

Then, simply take time to allow the other party to speak their heart freely. In this exercise, practice fully listening without comment or asking questions—just give them space to process whatever is on their mind. You may wish to use a prompt to start such as, "What is bothering you today?" or "What are your concerns and worries about [a situation]?" or "How do you feel about _____?" After asking the question, establish eye contact and allow them space to explore verbally any response that emerges. Though you are simply listening, this is a kind of active listening in which you are not giving advice or opinion or waiting for the person to finish so you can add your own thoughts. With this type of listening, you are instead allowing the person to open and process their thoughts and feelings, giving them the chance to be full in who they are. When they are finished, you can provide reflections by repeating back what you heard and allowing for them to express anything left unfinished. Then, simply change places.

When finished, notice any reflections that have come up, emotions that surfaced during the process, and the underlying awareness often hidden under conscious thoughts and problems. Perhaps take a moment to write down any reflections. Thank each other for holding the container for listening and processing and close the space.

Three of Swords: The Terrain of Grief

The peacefulness of the Two of Swords is not lasting. Moving into the Three of Swords we find a disruption in the quiet, one that is painful and heartbreaking. One of the most difficult cards of the tarot, the Three of Swords is a time of intense sorrow, pain, loss, or fear. Because it is a swords card, the situation at hand often creates a sense of mental anguish and worry—even if the situation itself is not terrible, the mind certainly processes it as terrible, which in turn dramatically affects the emotional body.

In the Waite-Smith deck, we see a large heart pierced by three swords. The background shows gray clouds and streaks of rain. The tone is somber, and there is little light in the picture. The heaviness of the clouds indicates that there is no light at the moment; the only way to get past the pain is to go through it.

In the Crowley deck we see three swords piercing the heart of a white lotus, the petals falling away like tears. Two of the swords are curved, symbolizing a distortion in the mind that can cause anguish and pain. The swords are surrounded by rippling layers of gray and blue clouds, indications of turbulence, obstacles, and a very difficult process.

When this card appears in a reading, it often indicates sorrow, trouble, or a predicament between three people. Someone may be cheating on someone else, falling in love with someone else, or there is pain between three family members. It could also signify a conflict at work with other employees or an experience of loss in a relationship. This card indicates the importance of paying attention to the conflict and trouble in your life so that you can begin to walk through the pain toward healing.

Reframing a Personal Story

As explored in other sections in this book, I was profoundly affected by the loss of my baby daughter many years ago. When I was pregnant with my first baby girl, Rubybleu, her father and I decided to pull one tarot card on her imminent birth. He pulled the Three of Swords. Disturbed, I reshuffled and pulled a card myself. Again, it was the Three of Swords! A few months later I gave birth to a seemingly healthy girl who then died few days later for unknown reasons. As I found myself recovering from the shock of losing a baby, I was numb and hollow as the image of three swords filled my mind. This was one of the worst possible case scenarios one could encounter, and it reaffirmed my understanding of the depths of sorrow carried by the Three of Swords.

The year that followed was a long heavy walk of pain and suffering. Three souls, forever interconnected—my baby daughter, her father, and myself—taught me the pain of loss. As I grieved, I also received many gifts in the form of teachings around birth, death, karma, loss, and beauty. My daughter taught me all of these things and continues to do so year after year. One of the most powerful lessons of learning about what I call the "Terrain of Grief" is to reflect on a painful time in your life and reframe it as a powerful initiation or teaching. This activity helps us make sense of things that seem hopeless, painful, or confusing, and it empowers us to see our life as a mythic journey.

Similar to viewing the Fool on an unfolding path through the archetypes of the major arcana, we can also choose to see a difficult time as a teaching on our journey. You may also wish to use the Hanged Man layout, which helps us to reframe a traumatic event as an initiation. Choose a particular painful time in your life and set the intention to understand the process from the perspective of the soul or higher self. Create a sacred space on your altar with candles, a bowl of water, and flowers. Light incense to honor the air element and call on your guides to help you track back to a painful memory in your past. Set the intention to view this from a healed and whole place. Visualize a clear blue and gold light moving back toward the painful memory and sending healing. Then track back to the time and view the issue or memory as if you were simply an observer. Allow any feelings or observations to arise. Be open to receiving insights from this time in your life.

When you are finished, send healing light again to your past self and acknowledge you are learning on your path. Bring your awareness back into the present moment, and write down anything that feels important about this process. Close the space and honor the helpers.

Four of Swords: Momentary Rest

The challenges and conflict presented by the Three of Swords is followed by the temporary rest and peacefulness of the Four of Swords. Four indicates the ground, rest, and stability; however, similar to the Two of Swords, this card indicates a passing or temporary rest. This card may be also an impasse, knowing that further force or push will only aggravate the situation and it is best to pause and take a moment to reflect, rest, and even retreat.

In the Waite-Smith imagery, we see a figure lying in repose on a long flat board or concrete panel. Below him lays one sword parallel, suggesting the quality of being at rest. Three swords hang above him against a gray backdrop of solemnity and quiet. Pictured in the stained glass window we see a figure on his knees. Perhaps he is asking for forgiveness from a priest or teacher as well as receiving a blessing from Christ. This is a gesture of humility, the quality needed to listen to our inner divine wisdom, our own higher self who is consistently guiding us.

The Crowley deck shows four swords pointed inward resting in the center of a thousand-petal lotus. Behind the lotus is a soothing peaceful green color; the word is Truce. This indicates a quality of rest and peacefulness.

This card can indicate not just rest and retreat but also the need to create a contract or the appearance of a peace contract, negotiation, or pact to give a sense of balance and harmony in a situation. When we don't know how to solve a problem, coming up with guidelines to follow that feel right and correct can help to lay a foundation for moving forward, step by step. For example, if we wish to make a change in our workplace and are having conflicts with our boss, we can choose to take a pause from reacting, gossiping, and complaining and instead take a step back. We can find our center and make a time to meet with our boss and speak our truth about what is bothering us. We can seek alternative solutions and approaches to a situation. Resting in the unknown and allowing the reactive energy to pass often gives the space and time needed to come up with creative solutions that are born out of insight and awareness instead of urgency and anger.

Meditation: Resting in the Breath

So often, we strive to resolve things from a place of urgency, fear, and concern that is not necessarily patient or wise. The Four of Swords encourages us to slow down and take a breath before acting on something or reacting to something. Swords are connected to air which is the breath that moves through our body. By tuning into our breath, we are able to slow down our awareness and rest in our natural state.

During this meditation it is helpful to burn incense, spray an essential oil blend, or inhale a soothing oil from the bottle. This way of connecting to our sense of smell helps relax our mind state and tune in even more distinctly with our breath and the air element of the swords.

Sit in a meditative posture either in a quiet space in your home or outside in a natural environment. You may sit in a chair with feet resting flat on the floor, or sitting cross-legged in the lotus or half-lotus positions. Focus on the breath for a few moments. Bring your attention to the outflow and inflow of the breath through the nostrils. Notice the gap between the air flowing out and the air coming in. Acknowledge that peaceful, restful quality, that stopgap between. Throughout your day, see if you can find that stopgap between activities, thoughts, and exchanges with people in your life. There is always an opportunity to stop, drop, and rest, so to speak, and remind yourself of the inner peace that dwells within. You can do this even if you don't feel peaceful all the time!

Five of Swords: Internal Strife

The Five of Swords evokes a sense of tension, strife, and disappointment. With this card, we may feel a tearing at our heart. Although it is similar to other fives such as the cups and disks, this loss is primarily in our mind and we feel plagued with doubts, discomfort, fears of the future, and dread. The source of this pain is usually a past trauma or sorrow that is unresolved and likely has no bearing on our current situation beyond the mental drain that thoughts can cause.

The energy of the Five of Swords often appears in relationships that cause us suffering and haven't yet been resolved. We may find ourselves in continued conflict with family members, exes, or coworkers. In these situations, we have to contend with being triggered into doubt, anger, fear, and sadness. Although it is difficult, this is actually an opportunity to work with those more troublesome emotions and gives us a chance to practice forgiveness. In traditional Buddhist practice, we welcome our enemies or the ones who make our lives difficult because without them, we would not be able to work toward becoming more compassionate. It takes effort to move back toward a place of gratitude and kindness, and work on taking the high road rather than sink into the defeating mental storms. This card may also indicate a need to set clearer boundaries particularly with toxic people or people who carry toxic emotions that influence us in negative ways. Forgiveness may not always be possible or feasible in certain situations, and the anger that one feels may be a good way to clear the path and move forward without getting dragged down. In this way, peace may not be an option. In any kind of conflict where there seems to be no resolution or peaceful end in sight, we find ourselves confronted with the lessons of the Five of Swords.

In the Waite-Smith deck we see several figures who are in displacement from one another, symbolizing a lack of harmony. Sharp gray clouds indicate confusion and hint at the possibility of a storm. One figure holds the power of the swords upright, but two have fallen to the ground. The figure looks back over his shoulder in concern about the other figures who appear to be lost and unhappy. This figure is either overly concerned with how these others think and feel, or he is fearful and distrustful of their intent... or both.

In the Crowley deck, five swords bleed with pain and misery. The quality of the card is dark and indicates defeat and an inability to move forward. The energy tears at the heart which causes bleeding yet also invites us to open further toward the possibility of healing. As we know, it is often darkest before the dawn. Pulling other cards to assist in ways to move through the heavy clouded energy of the Five of Swords can help to navigate this troublesome time.

This card may indicate disappointing news, particularly about something we were hopeful for. We may experience a loss in communication with friends or loved ones. We may have found out we lost a job, a chance to share our gifts, or we have realized that an idea or plan is not going to work out after all. Although this can be painful, this is usually a passing occurrence unless accompanied by a stronger card of loss such as the Three of Swords or the Tower. If accompanied by the Star or Sun, this loss may turn out to be something in our favor after all.

Ceremony: Purification

Swords represent the mental realm, and the heaviness of this card is connected to doubts and insecurities that we burden ourselves with in our mind. Negative thoughts have a powerful influence on us and can become stories that bring our emotions down, eventually resulting in disease in the body.

To help clear some of these doubts, use smoke to clear and heal your energetic space. Gather or purchase a bundle of sacred herbs or wood that are gathered in an appropriate and eco-sensitive way.

Use the smoke to cleanse around your body and also your space, in your room, and the house. Start in the eastern corner of the house and make your way around each room, filling up the space with smoke. Smoke of sacred plants clears away negative energy in the home, including unwanted entities and negative thoughts that become energetic patterns in space and around objects. If you are sensitive to smoke, use a spray bottle with purified water and essential oil such as lavender, lemon, or rosemary.

After clearing and cleansing your space, sweeten it by either burning sweet-grass or setting out fresh flowers in a bowl of water. This attracts the sweet energy in life and helps to affirm a more positive outlook in mind and body. We need continual resets in our lives to realign ourselves with the beauty, magic, gratitude, and love that flows through the life experience.

Six of Swords: Crossing Over

After the heaviness of the Five of Swords clears away, the restoration of harmony appears in the Six of Swords. This may come from an outer change that appears, such as in travel, or in a new inner way of the turning of perspective and outlook. This card also encourages taking a retreat, getting away, or setting aside some personal time.

In the Waite-Smith deck we see a literal crossing over water on a small boat. Two figures are hunched behind the steadiness of planted swords. They carry their ideas with them, yet the movement across water suggests a change is coming. This may indicate travel across water or encourage the questioner to take a trip over or near water, be it across the ocean or a visit to a river, lake, or stream. The interdependent relationship between water and air is relevant here. In the Five of Swords, we touched on the connection between mind and emotions in clearing our mental patterns and shifting our negative emotions. In this card, the emotional aspect of water is soothing to the mind.

In the Crowley deck, this card shows six swords coming together at a point centered on a rose in the middle of a cross. This evokes a dialogue between the parts of us based in faith and reason. On the one hand, our logical mind needs evidence, certainty, and assurance; on the other hand, our heart seeks mystery, divine connection, and the touch of the beloved. The Six of Swords invites us to dance with these two aspects of ourselves and recognize how we need both to feel fulfilled. These are the qualities of wisdom and compassion, the knowledge that it's useful to be of service and feel compassion for those we choose to serve.

This card may also indicate travel or the need to take a journey either by air or over water (or both). The movement of passage is present here; even if the journey is not a physical one, it can indicate a journey into a different aspect of ourselves, in our minds and hearts. When this card appears, it indicates a time of looking and reflecting on those parts of us within that are having the connection between faith and reason. We may be moving away from one or the other and toward its opposite to find more balance in our lives. For example, if we have been doing a lot of faith-based practices of devotion to a spiritual teaching or teacher, we may find we need to follow more intellectual pursuits for a while and learn more practical things, or vice versa.

Ceremony: Crossing a Bridge

In this simple ceremony we bring the idea of crossing over into actual form. First, find a bridge to cross over! This can be anything from a road bridge that is also walkable, a rope bridge over a river, a small bridge in a park, or even a homemade bridge in your backyard. Once you find a good bridge to cross over, set an intention of what it is you are leaving behind. Gather flowers to drop into the water or land as you cross over, dropping the petals to symbolize clearing the way and being willing to move from one phase of your life and into another.

When you arrive on the other side of the bridge, close your eyes and feel gratitude for having made it across this bridge, for the courage to leave behind something and enter something new. Ask your guides or intuitive self to show you a physical move you can do that embodies this new self, such as a dance move, spinning around, jumping up and down—anything to symbolize you have left behind the old and moved into the new.

Seven of Swords: Futile Efforts

After crossing over our bridges in the Six of Swords, we enter the Seven of Swords, a time of surrender and release. In the sword progression, we are not charging forward, but instead continuing to reflect and let go of that which no longer serves us. We may be so deeply in the process of letting go here that things may seem futile and like they are not working. In some ways, this card is a necessary dead end, where the trail disappears into a field of unruly grass. We must decide if we want to carry forward or choose a new way.

In the Waite-Smith deck, we see a figure sneaking away with two swords, leaving five behind. This card often indicates a kind of betrayal or not facing something directly and avoiding responsibility. The thief thinks they are getting away with something, but perhaps the soldiers in the background see what's going on and are ready to call out the thief.

In the Crowley deck, seven swords hang without purpose and are listless against a pale blue background. The card's word, "futile," indicates that any action will not serve the situation and it is instead best to wait until the situation is more favorable. This color is also associated with communication and an effort to listen more closely to your true self, rather than any doubts or inhibitions that can cloud the mind.

When this card appears, it reminds us to take a step back and reappraise our situation. Are we being betrayed or betraying someone else in some way, either obviously or on a more subtle level? Are we betraying ourselves? This card is difficult yet giving us the opportunity to reexamine a situation such as an investment, relationship, job, or health decision. The Seven of Swords may also indicate trickery, deception, or untrustworthiness. Your coworker, partner, family member, or teacher may not be completely honest with you about something. This card would advise waiting before making or committing to any large decisions, particularly involving money or relationships.

Exercise: Free Write

Free writes are a way to express ourselves without limitations. Set a time such as five to ten minutes and write without interruption, allowing words to flow out of you. We begin a free write with a prompt to bring our mind and awareness into one direction. For this one, we use the prompt: *I have betrayed myself when...* Allow yourself to respond to the prompt without thinking about what you are writing. Let the words flow forth to give a voice to anything that might be stuck or undeveloped. When you are finished, look back over your writing and see if anything surprises you. Are there some insights about what you have experienced? Perhaps it will be helpful to do a purification ceremony or grounding exercise to honor your energy when you are finished.

Eight of Swords: Psychic Obstacles

As we move from the doubts and standstill that is the Seven of Swords, we enter a series characterized by heavy, mental darkness—the Eight, Nine, and Ten of Swords. This next series of cards are some of the toughest aspects of our human condition and also indicate the incredible vulnerability that arises on our journey in these small bodies with the capacity for infinite expression.

The Eight of Swords indicates a time of confusion, doubts, worries, and fear. The swords remind us that these are all in our mind and we are producing our own mental state. On some level, we have a choice, whether to stay in our stormy and troublesome thoughts or do the work to shift out of this thinking into a more neutral and loving awareness. This takes practice and discipline! Over and over again we are given the opportunity to work through these storms and, as the great Vipassana teacher Goenka remarks, over and over we must "start again." And yet, at times this shift or a sense of choice around thought doesn't always work. When we have been deeply affected by trauma, suffer mental distress, or have mental anxieties that can't be worked out simply, we may need to ask for help. Seeking the advice of a well-trained therapist, counselor, healer, or support network is a way to help assuage some of the issues that may be plaguing our minds.

In the Waite-Smith deck, we see a female figure blindfolded. Her arms are bound up around her chest, abdomen, and hips. She is standing in stagnant water, the swords thrust into the earth around her like a wall. The gray background behind the figure indicates a heaviness and lackluster ability to receive fresh insight. This card indicates the loss of our usual ways to move forward; we must rely instead on intuition. This is very difficult when we are plagued by our own doubts and insecurities, to know when and how to trust our inner voice. With this card, it can be helpful to pull another to clarify what will assist us in moving forward.

In the Crowley deck, we see a variety of sword styles, shapes, and sizes in a heavy display behind two solid, long, straight swords. These indicate the multilayered qualities of our anxious mindset that can cause disruption and interference. The two long swords are a heavy overlay preventing us from fully accessing our path forward and showing us that we may need to resolve issues of anxiety, doubt, fear, and identity before moving forward.

Behind the swords we see a shattering of red lines against a purple background. This symbolizes the mental anxiety that can be shifted and moved, particularly if we find a way to tune into our intuitive self. It is important to remember that so often our fears and anxieties are *not* real but mental distractions we churn up inside of ourselves. Taking time to meditate daily can help to alleviate this greatly. Spend at least five minutes a day concentrating on your breath every morning and evening. Even if you are filled with thoughts, meditation will help to settle yourself and bring more peace and mindfulness into your life over time.

Ceremony: Identity Release

The identity ceremony is a way to become aware of the ways our own identities obstruct or block us from moving forward in our lives. Often, we hold onto old identities, outmoded views of ourselves and others which can prevent us from growing in new directions in our lives. A good time to do this ceremony is during the new moon when the dark night reminds of us shedding away the old to make room for the new.

For this ceremony, you will need paper, a pen, a pair of scissors, several small sticks or toothpicks, a fire either outside or a candle inside, and incense or smudge stick/spray. Create an altar to honor the wind, air, and breath including, for example, yellow candles, feathers, images of birds, knives, and smoke makers. These help to remind us of the mutable and changing nature of the air which governs the mental states in the tarot. Light your yellow candle and the incense, bundle, or stick and invoke the element of air. Honor the spiraling and drifting quality of the smoke. Take a few moments to watch and follow your breath and feel gratitude for the breath that moves through you.

Write down all your identities onto your piece of paper. This might include: mother, daughter, boyfriend, uncle, teacher, caregiver, writer, artist, chef, and so on. Think of all the roles you play for others as well as yourself, roles you wish to let go of and roles you wish to keep. The idea is to clear away identity as a construct and give yourself permission to reset who you are. You may wish to burn your gender, sexual orientation, race, and religion—even if you still identify with these roles, this ritual gives you an opportunity to recognize yourself as pure spirit.

After writing these all down, cut them out, one by one. Scissors, like swords, have the ability to cut and define, to create new shapes out of something old. Cut out each identity and wrap each one around a stick or toothpick. After you have cut and wrapped them, place them all together in front of you. Place your hands over them, acknowledging how these identities have served you and that you will now be letting them go. When you feel ready, burn them in your fire or candle, one at a time, honoring the embodiment of release. After you have finished and the fire ends, collect the ash and spread it onto the earth as a witness to your release.

Nine of Swords: Dark Night of the Soul

This card is one of the hardest cards in the deck, indicating a shadowy heaviness of the mind and heart. Following the Eight of Swords, we descend into the depths of rejection, pain, abandonment, and cruelty. This card may be directly linked to an actual breakup, divorce, loss, or accident in one's life either currently or in the past. Oftentimes, traumatic patterns are buried within us, and something may trigger them to come to light for further healing. At these times we may be flooded with suppressed memories which force us to look at and face the shadowy depths of our being. It is a time of crisis and change.

Although we may have a negative reaction when this card appears, it may actually be a blessing in disguise. The Nine of Swords is the dark night of the soul and a powerful reminder that crisis can also be the catalyst for deep healing. This is connected to states of grieving, loss, and sorrow that are often neglected in our culture. When we don't allow these emotions to move through us fully, we stagnate in anger, frustration, and inner turmoil. Burying our painful emotions results in addiction, depression, anxiety, and even psychosis. When this card appears, we have no choice but to do that inward shadow work that we may have been avoiding.

In the Waite-Smith deck, we see an figure sitting in bed, his face buried in his hands, sobbing. Behind him hangs nine swords in straight lines against a black background. This indicates heaviness, immobility, and the push of darkness down on our mind, heart, and soul. The dark night of the soul weighs down and we must look inward for guidance. Often in these moments we call out to the divine, as well as trusted friends, support network or counselor to assist us.

In the Crowley deck, nine swords hang suspended in air, dripping with blood. The word "cruelty" is used to describe this card, indicating the intense pain of the situation. Pain contracts and pulls in and requires us to pay attention to it. If we ignore pain, we only make the issue worse. The imagery of the blood as well as shattered shapes behind the swords reminds us of the necessary breaking through illusion and denial.

Exercise: Healing Through Time

In my healing work I practice sending Reiki or energy healing across time and space. Although our human experience is usually perceived as linear, we know through quantum physics that often time moves in more than one direction. In energy healing work, we have the capacity to send our own current power, love, and wisdom back to a time that still needs to be healed. This can be a personal moment, a fight with a loved one, or to a time when we wish we had acted or said something differently. By sending out this energy to the past, we are asking for forgiveness of self and others. We release the burden of anger, sorrow, pain, and regret in this way and are able to move on with more grace and love.

In animist practices, we use soul retrieval to bring back pieces of our soul essence that have fragmented during trauma. In the animist view, a part of us may disassociate during intense pain, accident, violence, or abuse in order to protect our psyche and allow the soul to continue until it is ready to integrate that piece back into its journey once again. This practice could be thought of as a way to set the ground for eventual soul retrieval, which can occasionally happen through spontaneous healing but often needs the help of an experienced healer, shamanic practitioner, or therapist to coax this piece back into us.

For this practice, choose a time when you felt the weight of your own pain, fear, or sorrow and wish to heal. Sit in a comfortable, meditative posture and light a candle and/or incense to set the space for healing. Close your eyes and visualize the time you are wanting to heal. First, send golden light as a compassionate energetic bond between yourself now and then. Take a few moments to view yourself with disengaged compassion from that time. Ask if there are any messages from your old self that you need to hear. Listen and then give your past self love and guidance along with more golden light. Do this for a few more minutes, as long as it feels comfortable. When you feel finished, thank your past self and honor the wisdom and love that has moved through you. Close the session with a prayer of gratitude and recognition for the healing work you have done.

Ten of Swords: Hitting Rock Bottom

After facing the pain and troubles of the Nine of Swords, we finally reach rock bottom on our journey of hardship, mental anguish, anxiety, and suffering. In yet another difficult card, we find ourselves continuing into the darker aspects of human troubles; however, this card does offer a glimmer of hope. At this point, with the number ten ending the cycle of swords, we have nowhere to go but up. This is a card of utter loss and heartbreak so shattering that we are complete in our ego dissolution. Although incredibly challenging to navigate, the treasures that are offered up from going through this process only make the human experience richer.

In the Waite-Smith deck, we see a figure lying face down, at the lowest possible point of despair and anguish. Ten swords pierce the back down the spine, literally pinning the person to the ground. This indicates immobility and inability to move forward. When this card appears, we know that change is inevitable and can either be embraced or resisted. The manner in which we react to our life situation will affect how we walk through this intense and powerful change in our life. This card indicates a time of crisis, chaos, heartbreak, as well as opportunity. We are being forced or encouraged to let go of old ways, relationships, patterns, ways of making money, where we live.

In the Crowley deck, we see ten swords pointed inward toward one another piercing a central heart. Behind the swords is an orange and yellow background, the color of healing, vitality, passion, and energy. Along with the fractal movement of shapes, this reminds us that with the intense process of despair and pain comes the shattering of illusion and the power of spiritual breakthrough. This card may indicate a time of incredible breakthroughs, creative inspiration, and the return of vital life energy amidst intense changes and disruptions. Although seemingly problematic, it may signify clearing the old so dramatically to make room for a new and vivid aspect of love, work, money, or health.

The Ten of Swords is a powerful and unrelenting initiation, a transformation from one way of being into a completely new way. This card indicates a definitive ending and dissolution, a kind of painful death in which there is a certain letting go, sorrow, and ending. In a reading, this card will often indicate a breakup, end of community or a friend group, being fired from a job or project, or potentially even disastrous news about health or a loved one. Although this card indicates breaking up or apart, it also brings the potential of a breakthrough and may signify a profound new insight, a sudden and unexpected solution to a problem, or the appearance of help from an unlikely source. Often this card indicates a time that we recognize that darkness is part of our life, whether we like it or not, and trouble, obstacles, and difficulties are a part of the path, things we cannot fully escape in the human journey.

Exercise: Shadow Journey

When we think of shadows, it is helpful to remember that they are produced by light. The form and shape of the shadow is reflective of whatever form or shape we happen to embody, physically as well as emotionally and mentally. With this ceremony we delve into our shadow to recover and reclaim the darkness as a teacher for us. We honor our shadows and that which has been difficult in our life; not to suppress or get rid of the trauma, pain, or shadow, but instead learn to walk with the darkness. Often that which is the darkest in our life is our most potent gift.

For this practice, we journey into our dreamtime garden sanctuary that we established in the Empress card. This time we visit the dreamtime to set the intention to visit with our shadow in a safe place and then rest in a healing waters place within our sanctuary. We can also ask to receive guidance from a compassionate spirit helper. Many ancient myths tell the story of a journey to the underworld to pass through an initiatory experience and receive wisdom and guidance. Similarly, this is a practice to enter another part of our psyche and be open to facing our shadow and then honoring the truth and wisdom that our shadow carries. By setting the intention to meet the shadow in a safe place, you have the opportunity to understand and potentially transform deeper unhealthy patterns or painful issues.

It is helpful to either record the visualization and/or use a rhythmic drum beat or binaural beats to establish a relaxed brain pattern. You may want to lay down or sit in a relaxed upright position to do this practice, using headphones for the sound or voice. Set your intention to visit your personal garden sanctuary and meet your spirit helper, who will take you to your shadow and then to a healing waters place. Imagine you are walking down a set of ten steps, counting down from ten to one. At the bottom of the steps is a doorway. Pass through the door into your healing garden sanctuary.

Enter your healing sanctuary and find a healing water such as a river, stream, lake, or ocean. Visualize collecting some of the water and carrying it with you to meet your shadow. When you are done in the waters, move to an open space. In the middle of the field or space there is a tree. Take a moment to connect with the tree and feel its presence in your sanctuary. Ask to meet a guide and notice who shows up. Is it an animal? Human? Light or color? Perhaps you don't see anything and just sense a presence.

Once you feel supported by your guide, ask it to take you to your shadow self. Be open to what shows up. You may meet something that is obvious, frightening, funny, or unlikely. Ask the shadow if it has any guidance for you. Use the wisdom of your guide to help you dialogue with your shadow. Ask your shadow what it needs. Usually it responds in a way that needs or wants love or attention. Visualize giving the shadow love and attention by pouring the healing water over the shadow. Notice if the shadow transforms into an ally, protector, or guide. Remember that shadows are cast from light hitting a form.

When you are finished, thank the shadow for its presence and your guide for supporting you. Return to the healing waters and rest in it again. Make an intention to remember what has happened. When you are finished, leave the sanctuary and climb the steps back into present awareness, counting from one to ten. Take time to write down anything you have experienced.

FIRE: WANDS

F ire is the element of spirit, that which is the least definable in our lives. We know that we have a vital life force energy, an essence, a unique quality that is sometimes called our soul or spirit. Our spiritual aspects are the part of us that connects us directly to the divine. When we create ceremony or read tarot cards, we are opening up a method of communication between our mundane daily life and our spiritual essence.

Fire has the incredible ability to not only transform but literally transmute one thing into something else entirely. Wood and paper turn to ash, water turns to steam, solids turn to liquid. This is symbolic of the divine creative spark that illuminates us from within, enabling darkness to turn to light, blockages to soften and melt away. The symbol of the fiery, flaming heart is a beautiful image that reminds us that through our heart and the voice of the heart comes the whispering of the divine and our illuminated self.

In the tarot, the fire element is related to wands, the stick of wood that figures carry and use in a variety of ways in the images of the cards. When wands turn up in readings, it indicates a spiritual aspect is at hand. If the person has asked about money, relationships, career, or health, there is a deeper aspect to the issue that may require a deeper look into the person's heart and soul voice. Wands or fire indicate qualities of passion, creativity, dynamic energy, transmuting, and transformation. The appearance of several wands in a reading may indicate a time of creativity and power and possible spiritual initiation that may be connected to a particular spiritual teaching or teacher.

Fire also carries the ability to burn and singe, to harm us if we get too close. In the reading it may show that there is too much passion or creativity, that it can burn out the situation. There is a delicate balance when playing with fire and opening up to spirit is not always an easy process. In the teachings of alchemy, in order to turn lead into gold one must move through the fiery resources of spiritual change.

Ace of Wands: Fiery Seed of Intention

The Ace of Wands is a brilliant, fiery, and dynamic card. As mentioned, aces are equivalent in strength and power to the other major arcana. The Ace of Wands contains all the energy, potential ,and opportunities of the entire suit of wands. The element of fire is in full blaze. When the Ace of Wands appears in the reading, it has a significant symbol of energy, intention, dynamism, and force.

This card is the seed of spirit, the brilliant idea, the "a-ha" moment, the passion of a creative idea coming into our awareness. Fire symbolizes our spiritual nature, creativity, dynamic force, beauty, and play. The Ace of Wands is like a magic wand being offered out to you as an opportunity to align yourself more fully with your spiritual, artistic, and creative walk. This is like a fiery ember that has the potential to create a huge and blazing fire. This card is naturally linked to the energy of the Magician and Knight of Wands, both of whom hold magical wands that extend our intentions out into the world through a blazing, dynamic, and energetic fiery form.

In the Waite-Smith deck, a hand holding a wooden wand emerges from a mysterious cloud. Notice that the wand has green leaves on it, symbolizing growth and vitality encouraging the power of spirit and life into manifestation. In the background is a gray, calm sky which illuminates a stark contrast between the moment of arrival of the Ace of Wands and the context surrounding it. Behind the wand is a castle on a hill, indicating the potential of reaching one's dreams through creative manifestation.

The Ace of Wands in the Crowley deck is full of brilliant, fiery, and dynamic energy and power. A huge wand rises up from the base of the blaze, ready to ignite the path and way forward. Lightning bolts crackle in a red background around the golden glowing wand, symbolizing the dynamic play and transformative power of fire and spirit. This card indicates a new way of thinking, creative power, and possibly a connection with someone who ignites the heart and mind.

Ceremony: Fire

As old as humankind, fire ceremonies are an important way for us to reclaim a connection to the natural world through the fire's light, warmth, and beauty. Since the first fires, we have been entranced by their flickering forms to tell story, cook food, and warm our bodies. When we are seated by the firelight, everything around us softens and our heart naturally opens. Bringing the element of fire back into our lives is a powerful way to reignite our inner passions, open our heart center, and burn the old to create anew. Fire ceremonies can be used to activate more of your gifts in your life, release negative energies, and help open you up for divine inspiration and guidance.

Fire ceremonies are a wonderful way to honor and celebrate as well as purify, cleanse, and activate our gifts. Lighting a fire in the morning or evening, such as a candle, oil lamp, or even a small fire in a safe bowl helps us immediately reconnect to divine beauty and inspiration. By giving offerings to a fire or feeding it, we are honoring the act of feeding our own inner light. If we are in need of cleansing negative energy or releasing stagnation or blocks, it is powerful to create a fire ceremony.

On the new moon, call in guidance and then write down what you wish to clear or purify in your life. Burn what you have written and release it into the flame. As you watch the paper transform into ash, contemplate the power of transmutation. Put the ash back into the soil or your garden to complete the cycle.

Two of Wands: Igniting the Passion

Following the ace, there is a burst of power and creative energy. This is the moment when the quiet, glowing ember that rests at the bottom of the fire pit bursts into flame. Both the number two and the element of fire indicate a dynamic quality. This card opens us up further, taking the sacred dreaming in the Ace of Wands to the next level, the level of creative manifestation.

In the symbolism of the Waite-Smith deck, the figure contemplates a crystal ball, looking off into the future. He is visioning or dreaming all the possibilities. He moves through two wands firmly planted in the earth, as if they are a gateway. This card indicates a time to make a commitment to a dream or vision and take creative, passionate action! The landscape behind him is rich with possibility, showing mountains, a lake, forests, a path, and houses symbolizing the potentials of dreaming one's life into reality.

In the Crowley deck, two Tibetan dorjes cross over one another to create a passionate, energetic connection. Dorjes symbolize lightning energy, indicating endless creativity, potency, and skillful activity. This card symbolizes a passionate union between ideas, creations, and people. Fiery embers glow around the dorjes against a cooling blue background. Together, they indicate the connection between fire and water with an element of love and beauty in focused creative form.

This card indicates that passion and creativity are present in a project or relationship. There is a coming together of ideas that provides a spark for growth both spiritually and creatively. When this card appears in a reading it often indicates a fiery and creative connection between two people artistically or romantically and may also signify conception of a child, creative project, or new wave of thought.

Ceremony: Candle Commitment

This ceremony is to honor taking a strong, directed, and committed step toward something in your life. Many of us do not wish to make commitments to ourselves such as self-care, working on a project we care about, or taking a class that we're passionate about; we may even sabotage ourselves. By doing a simple candle ceremony, we can take a committed step that aligns us with our divine self. This can be a tiny commitment or something bigger and more spiritual. The power of commitment is the power of showing up. When we show up in our lives, we honor ourselves and allow for divine alignment to unfold.

Perhaps you want to commit to taking a class, doing a daily meditation, or having a needed conversation with a friend or relation. Decide on something you feel you want to commit to and write it down. Then gather two candles and a mirror. Find a place outside where you can be comfortable and create a ceremony in the evening or night time. If you wish, create sacred space and call in the directions. Then, face the east, the place of the rising sun where the holy fire rises every morning. When you are ready, hold up the mirror and state your commitment while looking at your own reflection. You may want to do this with a friend or two and take turns standing between the two candles while stating commitments. The two candles work as a threshold, signifying willingness to walk onto the path of commitment, to take the next step.

Three of Wands: Creative Alignment

After the fiery conception in the Two of Wands the energy becomes more balanced in creation and alignment in the Three of Wands. Here the ideas that have been ignited begin to take form and manifest in a clearer sense of purpose and inner truth. The Three of Wands is about putting our creative visions into speech and action. It is akin to the Buddhist dharma practice of aligning right thought, right speech, right action, and putting it into practice. This is a card of integrity, to align and harmonize our way of being, moving, speaking, and acting in the world.

In the Waite-Smith deck, we see a figure moving deliberately through two wands, firmly grasping a third. The ground below him is dissolving and breaking away as he gazes out onto the fiery landscape, the commitment from the Two of Wands carrying him further along his path. The background is yellow and vibrant, symbolizing creative energy, potency, and the power of will. Here passion becomes a steady fuel for creative manifestation.

In the Crowley deck, three golden wands cross at the center, bringing together the alignment of thought, speech, and action. Flower heads sit atop the wands symbolizing the blossoming nature of creative manifestation and opening up to our will in divine alignment. The background color of warm light orange indicates the creative fruition infused with light, beauty, and truth.

This card is a reminder that everything we speak has an energetic imprint carried into the manifest world. Becoming aware of our ability to manifest through speech is an empowering process that enables us to create more clarity in our life and also clean up toxic speech such as gossip or false promises. When this card appears in a reading, it encourages us to walk our talk, so to speak. This is a way to bring our spirit's beauty and intrinsic self-worth into our work and our relationships.

Exercise: Creative Manifestation

As human beings, we have the infinite creative potential to manifest all kinds of dreams, thoughts, ideas, and visions, yet we often struggle because of our awareness of alignment. We may come up with ideas that are not our own soul's inspirations but are instead others' ideas about us and our path. This is an example of being out of alignment, and it takes practice to discover what creative ideas are in alignment with our soul's journey. A clear sign of this is when things begin to flow in our lives effortlessly from one phase to the next. There are times when we set a clear intention guided by our soul and clearly in alignment with our speech and actions as things bear fruit. Noticing these times of flow and calling on them during other more confusing times can help to clarify the flow of our lives.

In this exercise, you will practice manifesting intentions through the alignment of will in thought, speech, and action. In large blue letters, simply write down something you are wishing to call forth into your life. Start with something small, like a certain amount of money, an item you need, or an experience you would like to have. Then, walk or drive around your town and yell it out to the world. This may sound odd, but putting the energy of your voice out into the universal consciousness has a powerful and often immediate effect. It also requires you to be firm in what you want, as calling out is a kind of commitment to self and creation. When we do this, we also are accountable for our creations, dreams, wishes, and intentions.

Four of Wands: Celebration

After the alignment of the Three of Wands, we enter the grounding phase of creation and manifestation bringing form into reality or completion in the Four of Wands. Here we anchor in dreams and visions and have the opportunity to stabilize these currents of passion into a more earthly and embodied state. This card symbolizes passing through a gateway of our own personal sense of creative visioning outward to include others on our journey. This is a card of balance and unity, two wands in connection with two other wands creating a synthesized union.

In the Waite-Smith deck, we see two figures joined in joy, celebration, and love. The four wands hold a wedding bower symbolizing union, beauty, love, and connection. This card indicates a time to step into a place of gratitude and joy. When we focus on what is good and beautiful, abundant and joyous, we naturally feel connected with others and help cultivate even more joy and abundance. The yellow background and castle behind the figures indicate a time of expansion and growth, when dreams and visions come into fruition with the help and connection of others.

In the Crowley deck we see a wheel (similar to the Wheel of Fortune) made with four wands. This indicates a turning, a celebration of one cycle ending and another beginning. Although not as strong as the Wheel of Fortune (as it is a major arcana card), there is still a potent sense of something ending and making space for a new kind of energy to come in. The golden ring around the four crossing wands symbolizes movement through cycles sealed with the blessing of beauty and fulfillment.

With the power and dynamic thrust of the Ace, Two, and Three of Wands, the four indicates a time to open up to fulfillment on the path, a new level of success and joy, a clear connection with others that is radiant. In a reading, this card may indicate a wedding, love ceremony, joyous occasion, new home or wonderful travel opportunity. It is an outward feeling of connection and delight, one that may involve others as well as land—or, more specifically, a beautiful place. It may also symbolize a finished project, a job well done, or success after hard work. In the Crowley deck, the image is similar to the Wheel of Fortune and can also indicate luck, good fortune, and destiny, especially when both cards appear in a reading.

Exercise: Count Your Blessings

Make a fire, or light several candles. If you are at the fire, speak aloud what you are grateful for. Spend several minutes reflecting on the infinite blessings you have experienced: your life, your family—even if there are difficulties or obstacles—your health, the many gifts in your life. Giving thanks to elements of your life literally rewires the neural network in your brain, thus allowing you to experience more joy, peace, and satisfaction.

Once you have acknowledged your life, continue to give thanks and blessings for the expressions of nature, the miraculous beauty of water, firelight, the warmth of the sun, the rivers and mountains, and so forth. As you speak these aloud, notice how you begin to attune more clearly into what surrounds and nourishes you. Plants and trees exhale air which we inhale. Creatures and living beings move through our lives offering actions of play, focus, and connection to the infinite variety of nature's wealth. Fruit trees and flower bushes offer not just a few fruits and flowers but an overwhelming abundance of beauty and nourishment. Spending time in this state of gratitude allows for an opening of the heart and deeper connection to the world.

Five of Wands: Scratching the Itch

As we move from four wands into five, we discover the breaking apart and disruption so classic to the number five in the minor arcana. Following the time of harmony and blessings comes the needed friction and tension that arises as we continue to grow and develop on our spiritual and creative paths. In the Five of Wands there is anger, discomfort, and fiery energy arising. When we look carefully at this feeling, though, we can see anger—not necessarily a bad feeling or wrong. In spiritual practice, we look toward the essence of the emotion without getting caught up in the judgment of it. What is the essence of anger? Vivid, clear, bright, strong, fierce. Although we may think of anger as a negative emotion, it can also be very useful in clearing outmoded thoughts, helping us fuel a necessary stand we are taking, and in setting clear boundaries or outgrowing an old truth.

In the Waite-Smith imagery, five figures holding large wands are at odds with each other. There is clearly tension or conflict in the image, as each tries to gain ground while clashing and forcing the wands into a direction that has obstacles. Although the situation between the figures is rough, they all have firm footing and the sky behind them is clear, symbolizing the fiery energy of clarity and transformation into awareness and communication.

The Crowley card shows four wands crossing parallel over a fifth larger wand topped by outstretched wings. Known as the Wand of the Adept, it uses the energies of strife and burning away what the ego no longer needs to clearly anchor inner power. The other four wands are topped by phoenix heads, symbols of transformative rebirth, and lotuses, representing receptivity and healing. Although this card can indicate difficulty and pain, it is ultimately the gateway to creative healing and spiritual transformation. It may also indicate healthy challenges with others in creative manifestation; a kind of disturbance or pruning that allows for more growth, vitality, and fruition.

This card indicates a shift in perception that is often uncomfortable, like a snake shedding its skin that needs to itch itself out. This is not a comfortable or relaxed feeling but one of irritation, angst, and even aggression. We may be experiencing spiritual growth that involves facing turmoil or conflict with others' perceptions and their discontent. When this card appears in a reading it is inviting us to take clear and strong action in voicing our needs and concerns.

This card may also indicate the need to set strong and clear boundaries against situations or people that are causing us or others harm. This can be a problematic discussion or microaggressions that need to addressed at home, in the workplace or in a relationship. Sometimes it may be asking us to defend or protect others who are on the receiving end of negativity or toxicity, particularly in relation to abuse that may be linked to racism, sexism, homophobia, or other community or societal issues.

Ceremony: Fire Clearing

For this fire ceremony, the intention is to burn something that is holding you back. Take some time to write down what is bothering you, maybe something that feels unresolved or an area that still carries tension in your life. Perhaps it is a relationship from the past that still needs clearing or healing, a conflict or tension with a coworker, or anxiety about an upcoming event in your life. After writing your thoughts on a couple pages, create a fire or light candles and burn the pages. You may want to burn other specific things associated with this clearing such as old photographs, letters, diaries, or documents. As you do in a new moon ceremony, spread the ash into the soil or your garden to finish the cycle of transformation.

Six of Wands: Victorious Rebirth

After the fiery cleanse of the Five of Wands, we arrive in a time of rebirth, renewal, and revitalization that is embodied by the Six of Wands. This is a card of beauty, love, and replenishment. Here, the fires find a place of deliberate expression through care and integration, allowing for the light to expand and illuminate more gently. As a card of rebirth, it may signify a kind of initiation or blessing on the soul journey.

In the Waite-Smith imagery is a figure gallantly riding a gray horse, confident in purpose and clarity of vision. The figure holds a wand that is topped by a circular wreath symbolizing beauty, love, protection, vitality, and generosity. Around the figure's head is a similar wreath indicating the importance of honoring one's path and celebrating the success and connections that are unfolding. Often this card can indicate a party, gathering, a wedding, a time of celebration, and the prosperity of spiritual wealth. The clear blue skies indicate the clarity of vision and communication and the outward expression of one's intention that began in the Two of Wands, was generated by the Three of Wands, and is now delivered here in the Six of Wands.

In the Crowley deck, six wands lay across one another forming a kind of balanced lattice. In each cross is a small and beautiful flame, illuminating the formation evenly. The raging fires of earlier cards have settled down into a contained fiery brilliance that offers the light of intuition, clear sight, and keen knowing. Each of the wands are topped with lotuses, phoenixes, and eagle wings, symbols of the union of spiritual energy, expansion, beauty, creativity and fulfillment. This card may indicate a successful birth of a child, business venture, partnership, or creative endeavor.

Six is the number of harmony and balance and finding the way of ease and grace. Here, support that is needed flows in effortlessly and there is likely to be success in one's actions. This is a time of clear purpose; intuition is heightened and may indicate a positive time to follow signs, dreams, and omens. There may be more luck than usual and help from unlikely sources.

Exercise: An Act of Beauty

Beyond a pretty face or pleasing landscape, true beauty is a pure expression of the heart, something powerful and healing. In many cultures an act of beauty is a way to mark a moment in one's life through gratitude or celebration. We can be inspired by the sand mandalas created by Tibetan monks, a flower arrangement at a wedding, or a piece of artwork to embody a phase of life. Performing an act of beauty is a statement of gratitude that resonates outward to all our relations. To create an act of beauty is not necessarily to make something beautiful, but to do something pure and of the heart such as sharing a prayer, song, or piece of art.

To create an act of beauty, take a moment to reflect on what you are wanting to embody and honor at this time in your life. What are you grateful for? What challenges have you overcome? Who do you want to honor and respect who has helped you or taught you something important? Decide how you wish to embody these qualities in a beautiful, ceremonial way. Take the time to create your work in a way that resonates and holds the preciousness of a part of your life experience.

Seven of Wands: Courage

Following the initiatory journey of the Six of Wands, we move into the Seven of Wands, the shifting, movement of spirit, energy, and action. This card is a call to power, a call to step up even more into our integral truth as a soul or spirit in form. This card, fueled by the practices before it, is a card of courage. The Seven of Wands is a dare, a bid for power. It is as if the metaphorical gauntlet of power has been thrown down before us, asking us to take action in a focused, direct, and conscious way.

In the Waite-Smith deck, the figure moves to balance and wield the wand as a staff, a staff of power. In front of the figure are six wands presented as obstacles or a barrier between self and the other. This warrior figure is defending themselves against others but doing so in an act or place of power and truth. The staff is wielded in such a way that embodies the truth: real power ultimately comes from within, not from others.

In the Crowley deck, we see the blazing staff of courage standing out as an offering to the reader, supported by six wands in equilibrium behind it. Now is the time to reach and take the staff without hesitation, even if plagued by doubts, and to follow the truth of the heart and one's integrity as realized and committed to in the Two and Three of Wands. Behind the seven wands is a field of purple indicating the power of intuition and guidance from the spirit world.

When this card appears, it indicates a time of courage and needing to make an act of power to fulfill our destiny or soul purpose. This is the moment to take action even if it feels crazy or rash. This card indicates that you should pay attention to your dreams, omens, and intuition in following your path and not what others are thinking and saying around you. This card may also indicate bickering or negative attacks on your person, yet knowing your truth amidst this kind of situation, and is a card of success, as you rise above the situation and take the high road.

Standing in your center is important when you are learning to courageously stand your ground and follow your truth even when it is in opposition of others. Finding a place of neutrality and centeredness helps to keep yourself strong and clear. Many earth-based cultures use a sacred circle to find a point of reference to personal power at various times and places on life's journey. Intentionally creating a sacred space and center for yourself will keep you balanced and centered even as you move into uncharted territory.

Exercise: An Act of Courage

For several years, I taught at a shamanic conference and had the opportunity to do fire walking. This ceremony was a powerful way to connect directly to fire in a fully embodied form. The ritual was held by professional fire walking facilitators to create a sacred space of embers that, once coated lightly with ash, are safe to walk on with focus, intention, and purpose. If you have the opportunity to fire walk, I highly recommend this as a way to both honor the fire and the living fiery spirit that resides within. This act requires a leap of faith and element of courage to practice.

If you cannot do this for any number of reasons, think of another way where you feel an edge about something creatively, actively, or spiritually. Take a bold action or do something you have always dreamed about but have not felt confident enough to do. This requires listening and following the heart which has its own language and ideas about how the path can unfold to honor your soul's wisdom and yearning to grow and experience life fully. We often do not take leaps of faith in fear of failing, losing something, or heeding social expectations. In my full life of leaping time and time again, I have found that fear and doubt will be there regardless of the leap. Choosing to leap even with your fears is part of the courage; however, it puts fear in the backseat and allows you the freedom to experience something of growth and change.

Eight of Wands: Vivid Crystallization

We now enter the energy of the wands in high dynamic motion. Following the courage and boldness of the Seven of Wands, the path unfolds and there is no stopping it. The Eight of Wands is like the moment when a fire that has been stoked for some time at last catches full flame and begins to burn steadily without hesitation. This is the energy of action, full manifestation, brilliant insights, and wisdom activity. This is similar to the energy of the Chariot; renewed and alight with the courage, power, and dynamism of the previous wands, the Eight of Wands is aglow.

In the Waite-Smith deck we see one of the few cards without any human figures, only the image of eight wands moving forward in the air, singing across a blue sky. Sprouting over fields of green the wands move swiftly across the sky over green abundant lands and a blue river symbolizing wealth, fertility, abundance, manifestation, and grace. This card often indicates the arrival of a message or news. This may be a past relation or family member, a message about a business development, or news that can be even be life-changing.

In the Crowley deck, we see a large crystal with dynamic and fiery arrows, like thunderbolts moving outward that electrify the air and illuminate the path. Arching over the crystal is a rainbow symbolizing harmonious communication, beauty, and connection between the worlds. Often the rainbow is viewed as a bridge between spirit or soul and our earthly human existence. This card encourages movement forward on the journey and supports taking actions to continue a relationship with clarity and truth, or developing a business or creative project.

As this dynamic movement races forward, the fire grows steadily within and without, as if the path clears with each footstep. This card indicates renewed and obvious clarity arising in a situation. Things that didn't make sense before now do as obstacles and doubts fall away. This card indicates positive affirmations for a decision around a business, relationship, or your health. It may indicate a journey or travel, an advance in money or career, or even an expedition or adventure unfolding. Thoughts quickly become realities and sprout into pure energized manifestation.

Exercise: Physical Activity

Because the energy is moving much more quickly in support of a situation, this is a good time to do embodied movement. Choose a form of physical exercise to enact out an intention such as going on a long walk or hike through a beautiful place in nature, dancing, doing tai chi, or some other form of physical movement. Allow the sounds of nature or music to accompany you. Before walking, hiking, dancing, or moving, set an intention and stay open to fresh guidance from your surroundings or movements as you embody the Eight of Wands' dynamic energy.

Nine of Wands: Resilience

Following the radiant dynamism of the Eight of Wands, we have grown spiritually and dynamically and are aware of our gifts on the path. Here we face the potential of realizing the truth that our spirit-infused projects, creations, manifestations, and energies are firmly rooted in our earthly existence and they must be let go of and released into the greater world to finish their purpose. Spiritual essence, fiery creativity, and dynamic energies can become a burden if they are not properly shared and offered out to others. There is a saying that a poem is not complete until it is shared, and this is the message of the Nine of Wands.

In the Waite-Smith deck, we see a fervent looking figure, wounded and bandaged from working diligently with the forms of fire and spiritual creation. They seem to be afraid of what is ahead and nervously look back at a stand of eight wands as if guarding the way between opportunity and fear of failure. This card symbolizes a final test of courage, faith, and resilience to relinquish any hold on the expression of one's gifts and spiritual powers. This must be done in a way that still honors the original intention or mission of a project, keeping the spiritual essence alive.

In the Crowley imagery, we see a powerful red wand firmly rooted in the grounding force of the moon, topped by the luminous and radiant sun. The picture gives us an overall sense of strength and purpose in overcoming challenges and obstacles. There is a balance achieved of earth and sky, spirit and form. As this balance becomes manifest in our reality, we often feel a sense of humility and grace in our awareness of the preciousness of human existence. This card indicates integration of seemingly opposing forces and a coming together of our shadow self and gifts to a more unified and holistic sense of self.

The sharing of the Nine of Wands comes with the truth of one's purpose, alignment, and creative force. Here the energy has pushed and evolved in a dedicated and pure way and perhaps fighting for the creation to be launched into the world. This may also indicate a time to set clear boundaries about what is needed to complete a project, return health to a relationship, or resolve creative differences. This card may indicate a need to avoid naysayers and those who have a negative view on life in general, or are fighting with life unnecessarily.

Visualization: Earth-Sky

This visualization helps to balance you as a channel between the earth and sky energies, allowing for you to create a safe and clear space that is integrated and connected. As you do this, stay open to messages around projects, spiritual developments, and relational issues that may be arising in your life.

Sit in a comfortable, cross-legged meditative position. Keep the spine straight. Close your eyes and concentrate on your breath for a few moments. Focus on where you are sitting, on your buttocks, with hips and legs pressing into the ground.

After a few moments, imagine a grounding cord of light extending down into the soil and earth below. Allow your cord to grow straight down, through any rooms below and into the soil of the earth. Make sure your grounding cord is a healthy size and color as it moves through the rock, the water, then more rock into the center of the earth. Notice how it feels to be connected with the earth. You are tapping into the rhythm of the earth.

Now allow your energy to move downward while simultaneously allowing earth energy to move upward, as if your grounding cord is a two-way street. Become a channel for earth energy to move up through your grounding cord. Allow the earth energy to rise higher, through your legs and hips, into your spine and back. Take note of any colors, symbols, and/or sensations that you may experience as earth rises through the body and energy field. When the earth energy reaches the heart, allow it to move through the heart, into your shoulders, down your arms, and out of your hands. Notice any sensations as the energy swirls through your hands.

Next, bring your awareness to the space, the sky above your head, to the area above your body. Take a moment to visualize the dark, indigo night sky above you. Imagine the stars sparkling and the moon shimmering as bright, cosmic light moves down into your energy field. Visualize the energy from the stars, the moon, the sun all swirling downward, illuminating your crown, head, and face. Notice any colors, symbols, and/or sensations as the sky energy moves down through your neck, lungs, and into your heart.

Imagine the skylight swirling in your heart, mixing with the earth energy. Notice how this makes you feel. Be thankful to be mixing earth and sky, to become a true channel of the lower and higher energies, to honor spirit as a creature on earth. Allow the sky energy to move through your shoulders, down your arms, and into your hands.

Finally, bring your awareness back to your body. Bring your hands to the ground, roll out your neck and shoulders. When ready, slowly open your eyes. Take note of any sensations, colors, or symbols that you may have experienced.

Ten of Wands: Releasing the Burden

At last we arrive at the final card of the wands, the Ten of Wands. The intensity of fire, spirit, creativity, and expression has reached its limit—there is a sense of burden and oppression here. When fire burns too long, such as the case of wildfires that wreak havoc across forests and decimate homes, there is an imbalance: too much heat and dry energy. This excess of creative will can overwhelm us both in our bodies as well as in our communities.

In the Waite-Smith imagery, a figure holding ten wands walks toward a distant home or buildings. The figure is bent over indicating the burden of too much energy and the need to release or relinquish the wands. Pushing forward toward the distant landscape, the figure is determined to finish what has been started and lay down the wands that have been collected along the way. This indicates the need to honor and own what you have created as well as let go and burn what is no longer working anymore. Taking stock of the oppressive behaviors, attitudes, and thoughts, as well as clearing out old projects and outdated creative thoughts, will help to open the way for fresh new inspirations. This card may also indicate a willingness to take on a burden to push through a creative project to completion.

In the Crowley deck, we see two large wands placed parallel in front of the eight creative energetic wands burning in the background. Although the feeling is oppressive and forced, there is a spirited dynamic quality in the bright orange colors in the background, symbolizing the need to see what the final obstacles are in finishing a creative project, developing a relationship, or bringing a venture to completion before the next stage can begin.

The ten indicates the end of a cycle and beginning of a new one. Here, the energy has become too heavy to carry forward and there is a need to let go of outdated ideas, old creative projects, thought patterns, and perhaps ancestral karma. Often, we hold onto past ideas waiting for the right time and place to make something happen; however, this card indicates that time has come and gone. By releasing the old ideas, we make room for new creative projects, relationships, and ventures.

Ceremony: Releasing a Burden

Often, we carry burdens from our family history, ancestral patterns, and lineages of both our blood families and social imprints. Releasing these to the fire is a way to symbolically let go of the patterns that may be holding us back from developing further on our path. To rid ourselves of burdens or baggage that may be holding us back, we may use the Ancestral Fire ceremony from the Heirophant's chapter.

To release a burden, take a month or a few weeks to create bundles representing the people or societal patterns that have felt like a burden to you. In these bundles place images or symbols that represent the people to offer to the fire. These can by symbolic of gifts you have received from your parents or ancestral lines along with healing herbs such as lavender, rosemary, or tobacco. By offering these to the fire you are both honoring your parents and their lineages, as well as releasing them and opening the way further for your own path. This also acts as a gift to your ancestral lineage by doing the work of healing patterns that have been passed down and amplifying your own gifts on the earth walk.

COURT CARDS

The court cards are considered their own set of wisdom within the desk. While the major arcana represents the defining, destined moments on our path, and the minor arcana are the situational and dynamic expressions, the court cards are the characters in our mythic life story who play out these destinies and situations. Traditionally, the court cards represent people—either aspects of ourselves or others in our life—but they also embody elemental expressions in human form. Court cards point us toward aspects of our personality, our inner elemental psyche, and human relations in our path. This section offers possible interpretations of the court cards both as people and expressive dynamic elements. As we now know, each suit is associated with an element; similarly, each court person is also associated with an element. For example, queens are associated with the water element, and swords are air, so the Queen of Swords is a relational dynamic of air and water we embody on the path or a person in our lives.

Humans are complex and are not limited to being represented by one court card. We may find that someone may manifest as the Princess of Cups in our life one year and then the King of Wands another. Instead of limiting people to a single court card role, it is more helpful instead to notice the expression of the person appearing in your life at a certain time and whatever is being evoked within you. A contemporary problem with the court cards is these more medieval figures' gender and hierarchical associations. When we loosen our view a bit, we may discover that a male-bodied person can show up as the Queen of Swords in our life; a young woman can express as a knight or prince, and kings are not necessarily wiser than pages or princesses. With time and practice, you will come to associate certain people with certain court cards and recognize their energy when they appear in the reading as those people, someone similar, *or* a particular energy that is being called forth in our lives.

In the Waite-Smith deck, the four court cards are page, knight, queen, and king, while in Crowley they are the princesses, princes, queens, and knights. As they are covered, note that I offer alternative archetypes as a way to more creatively understand the nature of the cards. I also invite you to come up with your own versions of the court cards as people in your life, to extend the possibilities of the court cards beyond gender and ascribed roles.

Pages/Princesses

Pages (Waite-Smith) or princesses (Crowley) are often younger people in our lives. Other archetypes of pages/princesses are seed bearer, planter, fool or clown, and youth. They are similar to aces in that they are seedlike potentials of the suit; although not fully expressed, they carry the suit's potentiated wisdom. They are connected to the element of earth which is the embodied energy of the form.

The pages/princesses are often youthful, idealistic, visionary, and expressive. Traditionally, these cards are associated with children or those who are strong but still need assistance in their path and walk. These people carry fresh ideas and thoughts, and have the excitement to share, but not necessarily the resources, wisdom, or patience to carry that energy forward. Pages, like the Fool, are androgynous and not really male nor female; simply, they are the elemental essence of their suit. Although the word "princess" evokes an inherently feminine quality, a princess can be someone who is very strong, dynamic, fierce, and perhaps more akin to the older definition of the word "virgin," a woman unto herself. This quality is pure and wild, like a virginal forest—any type of human can certainly express it.

Page/Princess of Wands

The Page/Princess of Wands is the earthy element of fire in its brilliance, dynamism, energy, and creativity. This person carries the spark of a brand new idea or vision, and yet must be careful lest it burn out. The Page of Wands is often a younger or youthful person in our lives who has creative ideas and visions. This card may also indicate that you have been asked to attend to a particular project in your life. Perhaps you have received an insight, had an "a-ha" moment or creative idea—now is the time to tend to the spark until the opportunity to manifest it comes to pass.

In the Waite-Smith imagery, the page holds the wand with care and reverence while tending to the ideas they are cultivating. Behind the figure is a vast blue sky indicating limitless vision and possibility. The page stands in the fiery desert, signifying the place of warmth, heat, and also visions. People often visit the desert when in need of divine guidance and inspiration. This card may indicate a time for you to embark on a kind of vision quest to deepen your understanding of your purpose in life. The page is cloaked in yellow with a lizard tunic, indicating the power of dreaming and listening. The lizard is symbolic of being between the worlds, a fiery animal that also has the potential to rest in its own heat and warmth.

The Princess of Wands in the Crowley deck is seen riding a wild wave of flame, holding aloft a sun-topped wand. The figure is naked, showing a golden and vulnerable body which is also powerful and awakened. Below her is a sleeping tiger symbolizing the imminent power of her path and the need to tend to our unseen helpers, which may appear in the form of animals or creatures. This is akin to the energy of an ember, an earthy manifestation of fire that has the potential to build into a dynamic vision.

At times, we may have a sense of these helpers who come to us in visions and dreams as well as during liminal states. They assist us in the practice of tending to our creative fires and visions. The pillar of fire is akin to the temple fires attended to by the priestesses of old who kept the flames burning over the course of hundreds of years to assist those on their journey. The princess is aided by her helpers and yet is a figure of solitude and strength.

Ceremony

Contemplate the magnificence of fire creating earth, the power of raw fire turning into earth. Acquire a piece of lava or volcanic glass and hold it in your hand and tune into the energy. This kind of stone has a magnetic or creative quality. State very loudly what you wish to manifest in your reality. When we call out what we are dreaming in we empower our lives more fully.

Page/Princess of Cups

The Page/Princess of Cups is the water as earth when it manifests in the forms of crystallization, such as ice and snow. These qualities are pure and clean, and each snowflake has its own pure signature imprinted by the emotive qualities that water absorbs around it. The Page of Cups is an offer of love, a potential new relationship, or even just the glimmer of an idea, a new creative interaction which may be romantic, or a friendship or a fun new coworker. Often the Page or Princess of Cups indicates a kind of nostalgia, reminding us of someone sweet from our past who evokes certain memories.

In the Waite-Smith deck we see a figure holding a cup with a fish poking its head out, symbolizing the qualities of dreams, romantic notions, and perhaps even superstitious thoughts. This person can at times be naive and possibly even foolish in their daydreaming as symbolized by their fanciful dress and saucy look in their eye as they gaze winsomely at the fish. Although we often discount daydreamers or those we perceive who have their head in the clouds, and although the Page of Cups may be seen as impractical, they often offer us a part of our magical self or soul that we long for. Behind the figure, water rushes past, a symbol of emotional energy and the connection between our hearts and the feeling realms. This card reminds us of the needed time to dream and vision, to sit by the rushing waters of the river or at the ocean's edge, and let the mind settle for a while.

The Crowley imagery shows the Princess in a gown that fans out in a surrounding blue watery background. She is peaceful and emanates a quality of healing and quietness. The Princess holds a turtle which is a symbol of nourishment and our connection to the earth. This card often indicates a younger or youthful person in our lives who we are taking care of, or the dreamer and lover inside us that needs to be better honored and nourished. The lotus is a reminder that out of the heavy muck of life grows the beauty of enlightenment, that suffering and obstacles are the way of transformation. The earthy salt of our tears is found in this card, in the crystals on her gown, our connection to salt water, and the waters of the womb. This Princess, as all the princesses, may indicate a daughter or son we are taking care of, but also reminds us that the earth could be viewed not only as mother who nourishes and feeds us, but potentially as daughter, something to steward and care for.

Ceremony

Fill a glass bowl of with warm water to represent the heart overflowing with love and warmth. Take a few ice cubes and melt them into the bowl while watching the solid ice form melt into the liquid warmth of water. As the ice slowly melts, contemplate aspects of yourself that have hardened over time, such as painful memories or past relationships. Allow these thoughts to be surrounded by compassion and love, giving space for the innocence of healing and pure forgiveness carried by the Page or Princess of Cups.

Page/Princess of Swords

The Page or Princess of Swords card is the air forming into earth, which happens through the intelligence of plants absorbing air and turning it into leaves and plant matter. The wisdom of the air is transformed into thousands of plant and tree species offering their interdependent nature with our carbon dioxide in exchange for their oxygen. This is often a person thinking of a new kind of learning, envisioning going back to school, or who wants to deliberately deconstruct old mental beliefs and outdated thoughts in order to make room for something new. They may be bringing in a new menu idea at a restaurant, downloading new software, or offering a new lesson plan at school.

The Page of Swords in the Waite-Smith deck stands at attention with clouds behind the figure symbolizing thoughts and concerns. This person may have more doubts or concerns and feels the weight of the sword and the strength it takes to hold it aloft to the sky. The Page stands on uneven ground, showing the grit and deliberation it takes to maintain a sense of focus in a more challenging situation. The red boots show a sense of groundedness and yet the windswept hair may indicate being easily distracted. High above, several birds fly symbolizing messages being carried on the wind of information from the past into the future. This person is often a visionary in intellect and ideas, perhaps an engineer, creative business person, or magician. They can be singular in their ideas, and at times even forceful, but often have a very unique perspective.

The Princess of Swords in the Crowley imagery is dressed in brilliant vivid green and slashes the air in front of her. She is vibrant and strong and her movement suggests a clearing away of the old so as to make room for the new. She rises up on a smoky billow of clouds indicating the strength of air, communication, and the power of thought. She is firm in her beliefs and dedicated to her mission at hand. Her appearance indicates a need to clear out an old way of thinking and deliberately make room for new ideas and thought. She also reminds us to clear out our homes of clutter, which holds stagnant thought-forms and sentiments.

Ceremony

Sit with a tree that you like and acknowledge its presence in your life. Spend time reflecting on the interconnectedness between you and the tree, breathing in the oxygen it offers and exhaling your breath as an offering back to the tree. Contemplate the idea that each plant and tree is an idea or thoughtform of the earth, manifest infinite forms and creations all over the planet.

Page/Princess of Pentacles/Disks

The Page/Princess card is the earth in its full manifestation. Here it is the full-ness of a project that usually involves wealth, land, houses, buildings, and other resources that have taken full form. The Page of Pentacles may be a younger person in your life who is connected to the earth, likes to work in the yard or garden, and is strong and fit. They are somewhat grounded yet retain the innocence and openness of the page or princess role.

In the Waite-Smith imagery, the Page of Pentacles stands calmly and offers up a pentacle as a clear and hopeful seed for the future. The land is green and abundant, and a soft blue mountain against a yellow background indicates the energy of creativity and growth. This figure suggests a new idea relating to busi-ness, wealth, and projects infused with the creative energy of fire. The red hat and scarf symbolize vitality and strength, perhaps virile energy that is potent and progressive.

In the Crowley deck, we see the Princess of Disks holding a staff topped with a crystal that is being plunged into the earth below. This symbolizes the seed of an idea being buried to receive the nourishment of earth in creative manifestation. The Princess also holds a shield, symbolizing protection and potentially the need to set clear boundaries in a situation. Her belly is slightly extended, which may signify actual pregnancy, the wish for a child, or the spark of a new creation in one's life.

Ceremony

Collect stones and reflect on the passage of time in relation to the earth and its wealth of interdependent species. Find seeds and observe their differences and uniqueness. Notice the varied ways in which plants and trees propagate in the cycle of life.

Knights/Princes

Knights (Waite-Smith) or princes (Crowley) are people who act as messengers in our lives. They carry information, ideas, and thoughts. Other archetypes of knights/princes may be messengers, lovers, cowboys(girls), drivers, and young adults. Associated with the element of air, knights move across the land, the world, through relationships and jobs, and bring with them opportunity, change, and creation. Taking the fiery sparks, flames, and coals of the pages, knights blow these alive with wind and breath bringing ideas to life.

Knights are shown riding a horses, garbed in protective armor in the Waite-Smith deck and, as Princes in the Crowley deck, riding other creatures to symbolize their mobility and movement in the world. They are usually strong, vigorous, excited, and clear with their work; at times, it can seem as though they are assisted by unseen or almost magical forces. Often Knights are associated with traveling, communication, messages, and ideas. They can be so focused on a project or idea they may fail to see the bigger picture. This can indicate times in our lives when we need the drive and focus to push forward or the strength and courage needed to meet adversity or obstacles.

Knight/Prince of Wands

This is the element of fire on wind, like sparks moving quickly through the night or lightning flashing through the sky. Here, the seed of fire as found in its forms of pages/princesses is activated by the wind and movement. The Knight or Prince of Wands appears in our life to bring the message of creativity, illumination, and energy. There is a strong desire to move a project or idea into fully expressed creativity at this point regardless of doubts or obstacles. This person may show up as a project manager, marketing strategist, adventurer, generous friend, or a bold and fearsome lover. They may have good intentions yet are prone to rash and reckless behavior. They often have incredible and creative ideas but may struggle with putting them fully into form. As a visionary on your team, they can push forward any idea but may need help with financial or practical support. In extreme cases, they may be aggressive, edgy, pushy, and uncomfortable to be around.

In the Waite-Smith imagery, the Knight of Wands rides a fiery red horse blazing across the heat of the desert with focus and intention. The figure holds aloft a wand, firmly and intentionally bringing a creative vision from idea to manifestation. The background is clear blue skies, excellent for riding. The peaks in the desert suggest the pyramids of ancient times, indicating a spiritual aspect to the knight. The figure wears a golden cape of lizards over the armor which symbolizes active dreaming or the ability to take the vision from the quest during the Page of Wands out into the world. This card may indicate a time to travel, adventure, or see new and different sites that inspire your creativity and sense of purpose.

The Crowley card shows a figure atop a flaming chariot being pulled by a fierce and focused lion. The lion is clearly a symbol of strength, courage, adventure, and energy. The prince expresses creative, fiery visions through communication, clear ideas, and bold insights. Positioned over the figure's chest at the heart center is a round golden disk, symbolizing the energy of initiation and will of the heart to create spiritually through loving force. This person is often warm and generous, willing to give energy to a situation. The prince wears an eleven-rayed crown, a symbol of the solar energy of magic. These spiked crowns are found on powerful solar gods such as Horus of Egyptian mythology. They symbolize the powerful intentions of fiery spirit aloft on the currents of winds, creating and dreaming our world into being.

Ceremony

Acquire a paper lantern, the kind that are illuminated and set aloft into the sky. Write your creative intentions for what you are calling into your life on the lantern. At dusk, go to a high place where you live, or to the water's edge, and release the lantern into the time of the vespers when the air is darkening. Envision your wishes coming true as you watch the illuminated lantern rise up into the sky, fire on the winds.

Knight/Prince of Cups

The Knight or Prince of Cups is the messenger or carrier of watery love and wisdom. This is the soft, gentle rain and mists that blow along on warm airs brushing against our skin and reminding us of the beauty of our temporary bodies. When illuminated by the sun, the mists create a rainbow, a classic symbol of affection and beauty embodied by the gentle nature of this person.

The Knight/Prince of Cups is usually romantic and somewhat idealistic, carrying a message of love and connection. This may be someone who asks you out on a date, proposes deepening a friendship into romance, or a relationship into marriage. This may also be a community offer to work with a group of people on something that you love to do, a generous gift from a family member, or an opportunity to visit a beautiful place. This card often evokes a sense of longing, romance, connection, beauty, and divine grace. Sometimes idealistic, this person may overly romanticize a situation or be unable to see the whole picture. They may not see the flaws or downside and end up abandoning ideas or projects if they become overwhelmed or unsure. In a more negative light, this person may also be secretive or moody, hiding behind their emotions with a tendency for melancholy and distrust.

In the Waite-Smith deck, a figure gently rides a quiet gray horse over a relaxed and calm landscape. The armor is soft and cloaked with a cloth covered in fish, evoking a dreamy countenance. He offers a cup in romantic or graceful hopefulness as a gesture of love and openness. The knight is about to cross over a stream, perhaps an indication that someone will soon be offering you a gesture of love that could change the way you think about them or relate to them. This card also indicates the importance of extending one's loving feelings and thoughts, even at the risk of rejection. When we express ourselves fully, our hearts are able to grow in delight and beauty, allowing us to connect us to our souls' divine aspects, indicated here by the knight's winged helmet.

In the Crowley deck, the figure also wears a winged helmet, a symbol of divine grace and a sense of being in alignment with one's hearted and true purpose. The prince carries a vessel positioned at the heart center from which a snake rises out of, indicating not only transformation and growth but also the depths of emotions that can be beautiful and joyous as well as dark and mysterious. Watery winds blow out from behind the prince, symbolizing communication through love and affection. The prince encourages us to express our love or be open to receiving love from others. A dove pulls the prince forward, a symbol of air over water, the communication of emotions, and a new event that affects our heart.

Ceremony

Acquire an essential oil mister or atomizer and play around with different scents. Aromatherapy is a healing tool that can help to energize or relax the nervous system. As the mists diffuse into the room, inhale the soft scents and invite their qualities to be more fully expressed in your life.

Knight/Prince of Swords

This card is the full of expression of air with air, the winds of movement and change blowing fiercely into your reading. Carrying with it the qualities of communication through sound, voice, letters, and contracts, this card indicates the need to be clear in one's expression—particularly with other people. Swords carry the capacity to cut what is unneeded but always carry the ability to wound and pierce as well. This card may indicate the presence of legislators, lawyers, and editors. They can also be fighters—if possible, it's better to have them on your side. They may be vengeful, ferocious, and prone to attacking others verbally if they feel wronged or provoked. In a reading, they strongly indicate the need to push forward without hesitation and follow intuition regarding toxic or negative situations. They may be someone younger who can assist with editing a document, drafting a contract, or carrying a message. They often show us our own shadow selves in their harsh or critical view, and it is best to note the reflections and see what is helpful and what is not.

The Waite-Smith imagery shows a figure in full armor riding fiercely on a gray horse over the land. Jagged clouds and bent trees indicate a powerful wind, symbolizing clear change, intensity, focus, and determination. This may indicate advancing in a job or career, or learning at school. This is the mind in its rawest form—here it has the capacity to discern situations and make use of powerful levels of intellect. In some readings, this knight may also symbolize aggression, ferocity, and anger in a situation. There could be a need to honor and set boundaries and be clear, or it may be a person who is hostile toward you who needs to be avoided. Either way, this card suggests awareness of a situation that is somewhat dire; don't stay in denial any longer.

In the Crowley deck, the figure wears green armor, a symbol of protection and also vitality. The prince slashes away vigorously with a sword indicating the power to create and shape ideas through mental thoughtforms. In the other hand is a sickle, a symbol of death and the cutting away of what is no longer needed to make room for new ideas. Below the prince are smaller versions of himself pulling the chariot, indicating new thoughts coming into form—a manifestation that is energized by the golden spheres of luminescence and creativity.

Ceremony

On a breezy day, go outside and spend time watching the wind move through the trees. Contemplate the passing and changing shape of clouds and the mystery of being unable to see air or wind except through its connection to form. Practice making sounds out of words or singing a song to a tree, then listen to the wind again. Find your own way of communicating with the unseen forces around you and envisioning yourself as a divine instrument attuned to the natural forces on earth.

Knight/Prince of Pentacles/Disks

This card is the communication and message of earth. The rocks and stones around us bear the marks of wind moving across them over time. Unlike the other knights and princes, this card is much slower, deliberate, careful, and conscientious in its expression. The Knight or Prince of Pentacles or Disks brings news of earthy manifestations such as a new job, information about land or resources, or a contract regarding money or other material goods. Often this card represents a person who tends to land and projects in a slow and dependable manner who may also be somewhat stubborn or unyielding in their approach. The person may resist the advice of others at first but then slowly open if they see someone else set a good example. This person has good ideas about finance, budgeting, how to allocate resources, and building things and projects over long periods of time.

In the Waite-Smith deck, an armored knight stands at attention on a solid, earthy black horse. The figure offers a pentacle or disk symbolizing the offer of wealth and resources. The landscape is red and green and the sky yellow, indicating abundance, production, and well-thought-out plans. The armor and horse are sturdy and immobile symbolizing clear boundaries and perhaps an unwillingness to budge from a particular idea around the focus.

In the Crowley deck, the prince rides a chariot pulled by a bull, symbolizing the earth and being firmly rooted on the land. The figure holds a sphere, which has the potential to communicate earthly visions by way of thoughts but with the intention to firmly manifest and create wealth and abundance. The background is adorned with flowers and spheres symbolizing the different flora and fauna of the world and all its creations. The figure is looking down, indicating a focused sense of self which is less open to receiving the ideas and opinions of others.

Ceremony

Find a stone and hold it in your palm. Connect yourself to the story of the stone and where on earth it came from. What other stones did it live with? Try to find out how the stone formed whether through wind, fire, erosion, mudslide, or all of the above. Many cultures view stones as our ancestors, a kind of people who were here long before us and will continue to be on earth long after us. Blow a wish or intention into your stone and place it back on the ground.

Queens

Queens are the mature, creative, and emotive energies in our lives. Other archetypes of queens may be protector, guardian, healer, transformer, wisdom keeper, leader, priest(ess), adult, and parent. They are protectors of natural places on earth and the wisdom of our emotional bodies. Associated with water, queens offer the power of deep listening, the qualities of receiving or reception, and creating something new with the infusion of emotion, beauty, love, and joy. Although each court card certainly has their mastery, the Queens may very well hold the full potential in their level of wisdom combined with perfect clarity and heartedness. The queens are similar to the bodhisattvas of Tibetan iconography, spiritual warriors who have vowed to refrain from reaching enlightenment until all beings have reached enlightenment. We are comprised of mostly water, as is our planet; with the waters as their guide, the queens truly understand the limitless power of compassion.

Our emotions are often denied as important or relevant, but the queens remind us of the untapped power of our grief, deep love, joy, sorrow, shame, and even anger that teach us about our relation to our path. Emotions are our personal ecological climate and are reflected in turn by the elemental expressions in our weather and climate on earth. Queens are the patient people who nurture us in our lives—they are mentors, guides, and healers. They are also wise protectors of the vision set forth by the pages and communicated by the knights. They bring needed joy, expansion, and ferocity to convey ideas to other people. By nature, queens are relational and work with both humans and the natural world. Queens can emerge in any person—male, female, trans, and nonbinary—they go beyond the feminine and evoke the majesty of the waters.

Queen of Wands

This card is the embodiment of fiery water, the sunlight sparkling on the water's surface. When the sun sets on the ocean, we are enchanted by the fiery pathway that glows from the water's edge to the horizon. The Queen of Wands is like this—a vast body of water that also reflects the perfection of light and beauty. She is deep and unperturbed in her mastery of the fiery emotions. She has the ability to transform anger into clarity and fear into courage, having walked the difficult roads of pain and suffering. She has learned to work with her trauma instead of repress it, and she invites us to do the same. The Queen of Wands will show up as a fiery leader in your life, a mentor for creative projects, a spiritual teacher, class leader, or theater director. Though she may not be the easiest person to work with, she will challenge your ideas and help you to grow and transform quickly on your life path, especially in a creative and dynamic way. The Queen of Wands is fearless in her presence and firm in her abilities.

In the Waite-Smith imagery, the Queen wears a golden robe of creative energy and is relaxed; open and strong, her legs rest on the ground. She looks off to the right, symbolizing the future with a sense of clarity and wisdom from hard earned lessons. The queen holds a sunflower, symbolizing the wealth of creative fulfillment, with the seeds of the future ready to be harvested and planted. At her feet is a black cat, symbolic of the magic and mystery of the unknown.

In the Crowley deck, the Queen of Wands looms majestic, adorned with fiery robes and a crown of rays connecting her to the divine solar wisdom. Her right hand rests on a golden jaguar with black spots. Similar to the black cat in the Waite deck, the jaguar symbolizes the mystery of the dark that still walks with the queen even in her radiance. Also shown in the card is the wisdom she has earned from passing through many trials and suffering, the courage she has gained to move into the beauty of fiery compassion. When she appears in a reading, she encourages us to face our trauma and difficulties and learn from them with an open heart instead of denial. The Queen of Wands appears when it is time to share our story in a creative manifestation. She is similar to Pele, the fire goddess of Hawai'i, who is able to make the fire run like a river down the mountainside, continuously creating new land through destruction. She reminds us to create, step into our spiritual majesty, learn from a mentor, and grow our creativity.

Ceremony

Visit a body of water on a sunny day and reflect on the light and how it moves across the water. If you are at the ocean, notice the thousands of points of light on the ocean waves and imagine that each one is one life on the vast sea of infinity. Watch as the lights appear and disappear just as we appear in form, then disappear like a flash into watery mystery.

Queen of Cups

This card is water in its pure essence and all its forms. The human body is mostly water, and this element carries the imprints of our joy and pain, love and suffering. Similarly, the surface of the earth is mostly water in its numerous oceans, rivers, streams, and lakes. Water is a great listener, a carrier of things in the physical realm such as salt, minerals, debris, toxins, pollutants, and it is a medium for our thoughts, emotions, musings, and dreams. The Queen of Cups is the holder and protector of the emotional realms, able to purely reflect our deepest dreams and wishes and transform the emotions of sadness and sorrow into beauty and gratitude. She is the deep drink of remembrance and offers healing and nourishment to our tired bodies and exhausted minds. The Queen of Cups is a needed balm in today's world of so much fire and creativity and production—we instead need more reflection, quiet, receptivity, and healing. We see this need manifested directly in the toxicity of our oceans and rivers. This queen appears in our life as a master healer, storyteller, wisdom keeper, and elder. She may be a lover who embodies the qualities of nourishment and joy, reminding us to be playful and sweet and discover what enchants us.

In the Waite-Smith imagery, the Queen of Cups is dressed in a flowing blue gown that runs down like water over her body into the river at her feet. She gazes downward into a golden goblet, a symbol of the treasures of the past and beauty which the queen beholds with grace and wisdom. She faces left, indicating memory and the healing that is possible for our personal and ancestral traumas. When she appears in a reading, the Queen of Cups reminds us the importance of practicing deep self-love and care; it is only when we love ourselves in this manner that we can offer healing to others from a nourished place. She is the sweetness of the heart and may indicate the appearance of someone who holds healing wisdom, a loving presence, and the reminder to discover beauty and gratitude.

In the Crowley deck, the Queen of Cups is a luminescent, watery figure who blends effortlessly into the background of watery spheres; a pool of water with lotuses is at her feet. Her form is almost impossible to see as it dissolves into the waters all around. This is reminiscent of a story about Quan Yin, where she appeared to assist a struggling midwife trying to reach a birthing mother in the middle of a snowy night. The goddess of mercy appeared and assisted the midwife, offering a light to help her find her way. But when the midwife looked back, she only saw her footsteps. At that moment, she knew that the helper must have been the bodhisattva Quan Yin, helping without care or need for approval or praise.

Ceremony

Water is believed by many earth-based cultures to not only be sacred to all of life, but also a carrier for and listener to all that surrounds us. We can create a flower essence to capture the beauty and sweetness of flowers in the water. Acquire pure, unfiltered water and set it out in a clean crystal or glass bowl where it will be undisturbed. Add a local flower that grows, being sure to pick ones that are less likely to have pollutions or toxins. Allow the essence to capture the sun's rays and flower's signature for an entire day. When night arrives, pour the waters into a bottle and then preserve it with two-thirds alcohol. You can use the flower essence to nourish and support your energetic body on a subtle level.

Queen of Swords

This card is the airy water of clouds and how they move through the sky carrying the wisdom of form, thought, and perception rising and falling away. Each cloud is unique and expressive, just as each of our thoughts is also unique. The clouds form over lakes and rivers, and then blow across the skies as rain, snow, sleet, and hail. People who can read weather learn how to watch the clouds for signs of what kind of weather is moving through. Similarly, the Queen of Swords is someone who has mastered the art of reading the weather, so to speak, or signs in relation to communication, thought, and ideas. She may be a someone involved in legislation or social justice, such as a lawyer or judge. She may be the CEO of a company that works with data, information, or intelligence. She may work in publishing, editing, media, or other communications.

In the Waite-Smith imagery, the queen sits on a gray throne facing the right side of the card, an indication of a clear and directed look toward the future. She holds an upright sword in one hand indicating her power of presence and clear thinking and a raised open hand symbolizing peace and possibility. Clouds billow behind her, symbols of thoughts and mental activities. The Queen of Swords appears to help us grow our intellect, expand our minds, and overcome obstacles through law, rational thought, mental acuity, or awareness. Quick and mercurial by nature, she can assist us in communication, going back to school, developing legal contracts, and in our business and relations.

In the Crowley deck, the Queen of Swords sits calmly on a throne high in the clouds. She is half-naked, revealing her openness and willingness to bare her chest at all costs. A sword is held pointing downward in her right hand and the left hand holds an old man's head, symbolizing her recent ending of the old ways of doing things. Above her is a child's face emerging from a crystalline structure indicating mental agility, new ideas, and the value of truth and clarity. The Queen of Swords is often quick witted, thoughtful, and has an excellent memory. However, she may also be cruel either intentionally or unintentionally and sharp in her methods of communicating.

Ceremony

Lay out in the afternoon when there are clouds and watch them very closely as they drift by. Notice the different shapes they take and say aloud what occurs to you as the move and transform. Allow the clouds to speak to you showing you their patterns and movement as they cross the sky.

Queen of Pentacles/Disks

This card is contained water. Water, like love, will take the form and shape of whatever vessel it enters. In this way, it is formless and yet will directly reflect whatever form it enters. The Queen of Pentacles or Disks is the mature form of water contained and held in quiet contemplation. She is well resourced and manages the watery wisdom with careful deliberation remembering to save what is harvested for the future. The Queen of Pentacles is the owner of a small business, properties, land, or a master gardener. She is able to work well with finances and material resources, and she excels at time management. She appears in a reading when we need a mentor for longer projects that require careful tending to plans; when buying or selling land or property; or when we are in need of a teacher for our arts, crafts, or artisan projects. The Queen of Pentacles is determined and functional but may also be somewhat set in her ways and not always open to new ideas or patterns. She may resist the visionary aspects of other cards and prefer to take well-worn paths. For better or worse, she often uses her past experiences to define and predict her life course.

In the Waite-Smith imagery, the figure holds a large golden pentacle on her lap signifying the fullness of embodiment. Often this card, along with the Page/Princess of Disks/Pentacles and Empress, may signify pregnancy or imminent birth of babies, projects, or ideas. She has been patiently tending to the energy of growth and is ready to release it into the world nourished by the resources that surround her. The landscape is lush and full, showing an abundant of wealth and support and she does not long for anything materially. She may indicate someone who can assist you in creating more resources in your life and also a healer who works with herbs and plants to support ailments in the body. She is very connected to the earth and the medicines of the land.

In the Crowley deck, we see an elegant figure reclining in her golden full-ness surrounded by protective leaves that symbolize the Queen of Disks' inner strength. She holds a sphere of potentiality, indicating the full embodiment of power and vitality while gazing upon a barren desert. She recognizes the diffi-cult pathways of the past and reminds us that the hardships we have endured in life are often our greatest teachers. Although earthy and grounded, the Queen wears a headdress with enormous spiraling horns that connect her to divine wisdom and guidance. She appears in a reading as a leader, guide, or teacher who is capable of creating or connecting to a community of wisdom and resources that will help us feel more balanced and secure. She may indicate the need for a kind of support group, recovery mentor, or bodyworker to assist us on our path.

Ceremony

Gather several different types of vessels and pour water into them. Contemplate the wisdom that water is like love and takes the form of whatever vessel it enters. When we enter deeply into this concept, we realize it is impossible to judge another person as they are manifesting the perfection of their form. This does not mean we excuse toxic behavior—instead it reminds us that just as blockages in vessels create a lack of flow of water, so do blocks in humans limit full accessibility to love.

Kings/Knights

Similar to queens, kings are also mature in their development but in external, physical forms. Other archetypes related to the king may be the teacher, leader, owner, business person, ancestor, adult, and elder. Kings are well resourced and put energy into fully realized actions and projects. Associated with the element of fire, they are the spiritual embodiment of ideas, visions, dreams, and relations imagined and created by other court cards. Kings are associated with the essence of creative projects; entrepreneurial visions; and sparking relationships between people and their ideas, projects, land, and gardens. They are the people in our lives who own or look after resources and teach us about using the impassioned spiritual light. With the help of kings, we may use the power of fire to embody the seeds formed within the pages/princesses, create and implement the strategies of the knights, and nurture connections formed by the queens.

Sometimes kings are more stubborn or attached to certain ideas and creations, having done things well many times already in their life. Like elders, they hold incredible wisdom and experience yet require a kind of surrender to the pages/princesses to allow for new realities to take form. Kings may also represent our ancestors (of any gender)—those who have crossed over and now offer a particular kind of guidance for the querent.

King/Knight of Wands

This card is the pure energy of fire, such as the sun in the desert, which holds the expansive energy of possibility. Dreams and visions have fully manifested into reality and are being launched into the world. The King of Wands is highly creative and visionary and may be a film director, manager of a retreat center, or spiritual advisor. This person oversees the connections between many people under a powerful vision that has the capacity to inspire others. The King of Wands may be fierce and unstoppable at times in the passionate focus of making sure a vision happens… even at the expense of others. He may sacrifice what he considers the weakest link in service to a mission or project's greater good. This king may show up in our life as a unrelenting boss, visionary teacher, or well-known creator who, similar to the Queen of Wands, will push us spiritually and creatively to develop our gifts. This energy encourages us to see our life as a grand vision and not hold back our raw creative abilities. The King or Crowley's Knight of Wands is on the precipice of magnificent manifestation in which a vision holds the pure spirited energy of fire.

In the Waite-Smith imagery, the King of Wands looks out over a warm desert backed by a clear, brilliant blue sky. He looks left to the past, fiercely watching the completion and manifestation of his own visions. He holds a large wand effortlessly in his right hand with pure confidence and trust in his creation. His appearance in a reading indicates success and achievement in pursuits and the opportunity to share gifts with a wider audience or community. He wears fiery colored robes symbolizing creativity and dynamic energy, and his throne is decorated with lizards, indicating the power of dreaming one's world into being.

In the Crowley imagery, we see the Knight of Wands decked in black gold armor riding a magnificent black horse. The knight rears up in bravado, courage, and fearless energy. The appearance of this card signifies a powerful creative person who blazes into your life and brings about dynamic change. This may be in the form of a lover, teacher, or creative collaborator. Fiery flames surround the knight, indicating the blazing power of creation and manifestation. He holds a huge red flaming torch ready to ignite those he meets, whether they are open to it or not. This card may also indicate a warning of someone who is overly zealous or passionate without discretion.

Ceremony

Acquire a small red candle and inscribe one word that you wish to evoke more strongly in your life, such as power, love, clarity, peace, truth, etc. Light the candle and sit with it. As your candle burns down, contemplate the energy of your chosen word. Write down thoughts, visions, and ideas as they occur to you. Allow the element of fire to teach you about its ability to transform through light and heat.

King/Knight of Cups

This card is the warm steam of hot water, water infused with fire. It is the nourishing feeling of drinking a hot cup of tea on a cold morning, when sick, or when feeling down or in need of support and love. The King or Crowley's Knight of Cups is connected to emotions and the heart's compassionate wisdom. This king wishes to share his discoveries with others and may be the owner of a gallery, a masterful healer, romantic partner, or patron of the arts. He often appears when we need loving support to bring a vision of beauty and love into form. He can sometimes be fanciful in his ideas or overly enthusiastic about creating a reality that is not fully possible or resourced. His tendency is to be open to new ideas and visions and is often less stubborn or stuck in his ways than the other kings or knights. Often empathic, he is able to feel others' emotions and may at times be overwhelmed by their energy even as he maintains a certain sense of stability. When it comes to making decisions, he can be more suggestible and swayed by other's opinions than the other kings.

In the Waite-Smith imagery, the King of Cups rests calmly and gently on a gray throne surrounded by water, an indication of his connection to emotions and an artistic nature. He looks to his left, indicating romantic views of the future and creative hopes and wishes. He wears a fish around his neck, symbolizing fluidity and movement in thought and creations. In his right hand, he holds a cup as an offering, showing he is ready to be of service to his community. His appearance in a reading may indicate an imminent connection with a group of creative people or healers, or a romantic partnering. In his left hand is a golden scepter, a symbol of control and balance.

In the Crowley deck, the Knight of Cups wears green armor, symbolizing vitality, grace, and growth. He rides a white horse into blue waters. This knight is also adorned with huge wings on his back, indicating divine grace and guidance. This card symbolizes the need to trust in our loving, wise selves. He offers a golden red cup with the crab of Cancer, related to home, love, contentment, and connection with others. His offering can often indicate a time of service in our lives, when we discover personal gifts that can benefit others. It can also symbolize the appearance of a new, loving partner or the romantic offer of marriage or commitment from a current partner.

Ceremony

Fill a crystal glass with ice cubes and light a candle next to the glass. As the flames flicker behind the icy, watery forms, write down a list of things you love about life. Similar to a gratitude list, this ceremony encourages us to find what is beautiful and incredible about our paths no matter how mundane it may seem or how much suffering and pain we may be going through. Focusing on the simple beauty of life reminds us to stay present in love and awareness.

King/Knight of Swords

The King or Knight of Swords is the smoke of the fire, carrying the visions, ideas, and thoughts out into the world. Think of smoke signals used to communicate across distances and this king or knight as the carrier of those ideas. The King of Swords is a regal figure who manifests his thoughts and ideas into forms such as legislation, contracts, and agreements. He is the partner of a law firm, the CEO of systems management, an author, or media producer. The clarity of his ideas affects many people and informs them of directions and ways to move in their lives. At times this person may feel overbearing and authoritarian, often resistant to accepting the ideas of others. However, if approached carefully, he can be judicious—his aim is to be equitable and just. He is often psychic and will use his intuition to carefully choose who is allowed in his life and whom he relates to.

In the Waite-Smith imagery, the King of Swords faces forward, clear, and full of direction. He holds no doubts and knows exactly the moves he wishes to take. This card signifies the support of mental visioning, planning, and careful execution. He wears a light blue robe symbolizing effective communication and clarity of thought in his approach. Behind him, puffy clouds move through the sky, indicating thoughts forming and resting along the horizon as they manifest. The appearance of this card in a reading shows that plans are well formed and supports the production of plans in the making. It may also indicate the need for mediated counsel in a situation that feels unstable.

In the Crowley deck, the Knight of Swords rides a golden horse traveling at light speed through a blue and white streaming landscape. He wears green and golden armor, symbolizing vital growth and maturation through communication such as media, the internet, speech, and writing. The appearance of this card indicates the way forward is strongly supported; movement and dynamic change are encouraged. The Knight has dragonfly wings, which symbolize the energy of light and rapid motion, an energy of flitting from one idea to another but with clarity, vision, and focus. He slices the air in front of him with well-aimed swords that clear his path. Nothing can stop the movement of the Knight of Swords and his ability to consciously create thoughts.

Ceremony

Burn a stick of incense and contemplate the slow curl of the smoke as it leaves the burning stick. Notice the curls and gentle current that the smoke catches as it drifts upward toward the sky. Offer a slow tone or simple song to accompany the smoke, turning into the breath as it moves through your body. Chant the word you inscribed on the candle of the Princess or Page of Wands to bring it alive with the power of sound.

King/Knight of Pentacles/Disks

The King/Knight of Pentacles/Disks is earthy fire, symbolized by warm coals. Once the dynamic fire of ideas and thoughts have burned down, we are left with the nurturing coals that can stay warm and embedded in sand for hours, overnight even. The coals or embers patiently hold and manifest the ideas and develop future visions. Coals can be as small as a tiny pebble and yet contain the potential to create a huge fire. The King of Pentacles is a retreat owner, landlord, retail business owner, or parent. This person is firm in his decisions and very well resourced. He is often stubborn and will not vary in his ideas or opinions in response to others. That said, he may be generous with others and willing to share his resources. He often appears when financial support is needed in our work to take it to the next level of benefitting others. The King of Disks is hiring others to enhance his business, investing in new lands, and harvesting his current resources in preparation for continued growth. He has a deep trust in both himself and the process and yet remains steadfast in his commitment to those close to him. He may indicate a deepening partnership, parenting, or shifting into elderhood with wise guidance.

In the Waite-Smith imagery, the King of Pentacles is draped in a luxurious robe printed with grapes symbolizing the harvest of abundance. He rests comfortably on this throne and holds a scepter in his right hand, indicating steadfast balance. In his left hand is a pentacle, symbolizing his own comfort with his wealth. He looks satisfactorily to the left indicating his trust in the future and a sense of knowing of his own prosperity. In a reading, this card indicates a good time to make investments, share resources, and readily accept help from a wise mentor. Behind him is a large castle, symbolizing the acquisition of land and property. This card could indicate buying or selling real estate, land, or other material wealth.

In the Crowley imagery, the Knight of Disks sits comfortably atop a brown horse who stands solidly in an abundant field of wheat harvest. He looks out over his fields, golden concentric rings indicating the manifestation of his visions and their continued growth. In a relaxed position, he holds a flail in his right hand and a large brass-colored shield in his left. This may symbolize the need to set clear boundaries in life and make firmer plans regarding your budget, resources, and money situation. He may indicate the importance of making a firm plan regarding land or property or wealth. Asking for help from a trusted advisor is recommended.

Ceremony

Allow a fire to burn down to coals and watch the pulsing vibrant energy of the fire in the wood. Feel the warmth of the coals emanating from the ground, and visualize this warmth entering your body and relaxing your nervous system. Take a moment to envision a new idea or project you are wanting to create in your life. Burn some dried cedar on the still warm coals while visualizing the project as it has manifested.

LAYOUTS

There are many variations on card layouts or spreads. Ceremonial Tarot includes several different ways to answer questions. After you have created your space and discovered your question, choose a layout that best suits your question or questions.

Celtic Cross and Variation

The Celtic Cross is one of the most common, traditional tarot card layouts, and it involves a long look at life's bigger questions. This layout is appropriate for looking deeply into relationship or career issues or having a query around longer term problems or life path journeys. This layout looks at two aspects of ourselves: the internal soulscape and the external path unfolding. I include both the classical ten-card layout as well as an eight-card variation. For future outcome cards, I always include the word "possible," as I prefer not to be concrete or heavy on future prediction. We always have a say in the unfolding of our own destiny, and even tarot readings will influence the outcome, as does each and every decision we make.

Ten-Card Layout

Inner Soulscape

- Card 1: Self or querent, the person asking the question.
- Card 2: What is moving through in the current moment.
- Card 3: Conscious mind. The ideas, thoughts, dreams and intentions that the querent is aware of.

- Card 4: Subconscious mind. Ideas, thoughts, dreams that the querent is unaware of, buried beneath the surface. These are possible manifestations in the coming months.
- Card 5: Past and specifically what in the past is affecting the current situation and question at hand.
- Card 6: Action to take to help embody, heal, and transform the situation at hand.

The Path

- Card 7: Querent on the path and how they are relating to their external situation at hand.
- Card 8: External influences.
- Card 9: Hopes and fears that the querent may or may not be aware of. Often that which we are secretly hoping for we are also fearing.
- Card 10: Possible outcome or future card. It can be helpful to pull cards until you get a major arcana card to get a fuller sense of the potential coming future.

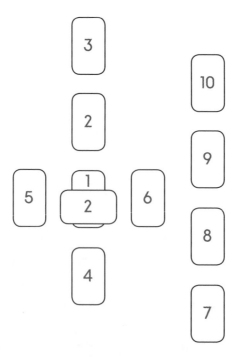

Eight-Card Variation

Inner Soulscape

- Card 1: Self or querent.
- Card 2: Issue at hand.
- Card 3: What is guiding the issue.
- Card 4: What is supporting or grounding the issue.

The Path

- Card 5: What the situation needs or is lacking.
- Card 6: Action to take to creatively grow the issue.
- Card 7: Potential immediate outcome.
- Card 8: Long term outcome.

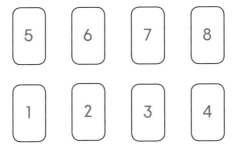

Three-Card Layout (Past, Present, Future)

This layout is a quick look at an issue concerning a relationship or job question. It is helpful when trying to make a decision whether to continue the relationship or the work in question. This layout can also be used to asses a particular arc of a relationship that has a longer history such as a parent, sibling, or long-term partner; the past card is especially relevant in determining the effect on the current issue. It can be useful to separate out and use only the major arcana for this reading to achieve a more powerful and spiritual look at the arc of the issue.

- Card 1: Past energy that is affecting the current issue or problem.
- Card 2: Present issue and what is currently unfolding.
- Card 3: Potential or likely future outcome.

Five-Card Layout

This layout is very helpful for a distinct current or specific issue in a relationship problem, a job or health crisis, or another type of obstacle you are finding hard to solve. This layout helps to hone in on the underlying or root cause of the situation and gives more embodied guidance in the "Action to take" card.

- Card 1: Querent or self.
- Card 2: Issue at hand.
- Card 3: The deeper issue or underlying root cause of the problem that is often unknown to the querent and buried in the subconscious or denial.
- Card 4: Action to take. This card gives a pointed way to work with the issues. Use the ceremonies found in the minor arcana or suggestions of the major arcana to create a supportive way to embody and work with the issue you are struggling with.
- Card 5: Potential outcome.

Relationship Layout

This layout is useful when working on a relationship issue, pattern, or trying to find general guidance on a problem between you and another person. This can be any kind of relationship such as a partner, girlfriend or boyfriend, friend, boss, coworker, parent, child, et cetera. Following is one option to understand the deeper connection between you and someone else. Use the five-card layout for specific issues or obstacles and add one card to signify the other person.

- Card 1: Querent or self.
- Card 2: The other person.
- Card 3: Physical issue or connection of the body, money, resources, and shared spaces.
- Card 4: Mental issue or connection of the mind, thoughts, ideas, and dreams.
- Card 5: Emotional issue or connection of the heart, emotions, health, and relational dynamics.
- Card 6: Spiritual issue or connection of the soul.

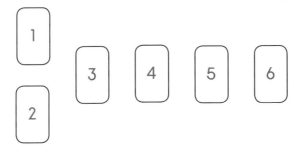

Directional/Elemental Five-Card Layout

This layout is useful when you want to look at the overall essence of a troubling situation or upcoming event, or help to deepen your understanding of a particular relationship in your life. Every card placement is associated with a direction—east, south, west, and north. To assist with your reading, create an altar inspired by your work in the Magician chapter to reflect the directional elements of the tarot.

- Card 1: East, connected to the suit of swords; symbolizes air, breath, mind, beginnings, ideas, thought patterns, conception of the idea/issue/ relationship/business.
- Card 2: South, connected to the suit of wands; symbolizes fire, transformation, alchemy, growth, fullness, innocence, play, spirit, energy, dynamism, and growth of the idea/issue/relationship/business.

- Card 3: West, connected to the suit of cups; symbolizes water, healing, beauty, letting go, death and rebirth, emotions, love, sadness, joy, connections of the idea/issue/relationship/business.

- Card 4: North, connected to the suit of disks/pentacles; symbolizes earth, ancestors, guides, wisdom, clarity, strength, a neutral perspective, overall determination regarding the idea/issue/relationship/business.

- Card 5: Center, connected to the major arcana; symbolizes spirit, guidance, destiny, overall lessons of the idea/issue/relationship/business.

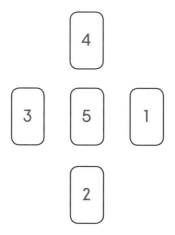

CONCLUSION

Embodying the tarot as a living system is the most powerful way to touch the archetypal forces that affect, transform, and guide the journey of our soul's evolutionary path. There is no doubt that in my twenty-five years of working with tarot that this system has benefitted me immeasurably, becoming a kind of mythic reference to help in navigating the mysteries that the human experience has to offer. Fusing this practice with ceremony will give you the opportunity to orient yourself on the path in relation to the elemental expressions of the minor arcana and open further to the profound teachings of the major arcana.

As your study of tarot deepens, I encourage you to find your own ceremonial, symbolic, and embodied ways to work with the cards and their teachings. Just as there are infinite combinations of cards, the tarot system is infinite in its expression through our lives. Using the Crowley deck as my main focus for the last fifteen years has laid the groundwork for a deep understanding of numerology, symbolic patterning, and astrological elements to bring forth the even more mysterious connection of the tarot to the Kabbalah, or Tree of Life system. You may find in your own working of the tarot similar connections to other systems and modes of studies.

Tarot is a powerful tool; once you gain some confidence and understanding, it can also be an invaluable aid to your friends, family, and eventually clients. I encourage you to practice reading with people close to you. Using cards is a wonderful way to learn the art of active listening, to gain endless valuable truths and insights about the human journey; at the very least, it is always a conversation starter. Tarot is way to dissolve boundaries between people and build a relational bridge between hearts and into the unseen mysteries. I truly hope this book is a benefit to your connections with others.

RESOURCES

The following list contains tarot books, decks, and resources referenced in my tarot journey over the years. The list also includes helpful resources for reversals, connecting the tarot to the Kabbalah, and alternative views on the tarot. These will complement your study and offer further explorations of the spiritual aspects, mental concepts, symbolism, astrological connections, and more.

Becker, PhD, Catherine Kalama. Illustrated by Doya Nardin. *Mana Cards: The Power of Hawaiian Wisdom*. Hilo, HI. Radiance Network Inc., 1998.

Crowley, Aleister, and Lady Frieda Harris. *Crowley Thoth Tarot Deck*. Stamford, CT: U.S. Games Systems, 1969. Originally published 1969 by the Ordo Templi Orientis, Belgium.

Dean, Liz. *The Ultimate Guide to Tarot: A Beginner's Guide to the Cards, Spreads, and Revealing the Mystery of Tarot*. Beverly, MA: Fair Winds Press, 2015.

Douglas, Nik, and Penny Slinger. *The Tantric Dakini Oracle*. Rochester, VT: Destiny Books, 1979.

Duquette, Lon Milo. *Understanding Aleister Crowley's Thoth Tarot*. York Beach, ME: Red Wheel/Weiser, 2003.

Eads, James R. *The Prisma Visions Tarot Deck*. Los Angeles: James R. Eads Studio. https://www.jamesreadsmerch.com.

Greer, Mary K. *The Complete Book of Tarot Reversals*. St. Paul, MN: Llewellyn Worldwide, 2002.

Gruhl, Jason, Jonathan Saiz, and Andi Todaro. *The Fountain Tarot: Illustrated Deck and Guidebook*. Boulder, CO: Roost Books, 2017.

Haich, Elisabeth. *Wisdom of the Tarot*. Santa Fe: Aurora Press, 1984.

Heimpel, Noel Arthur. *The Numinous Tarot*. Seattle: Noel Arthur Heimpel, 2018.

Koda, Katalin. "Ceremonial Tarot with Katalin Koda." Biddy Tarot Podcast, episode 125, 2017. https://www.biddytarot.com/btp125-ceremonial-tarot-katalin-koda/

Krans, Kim. *The Wild Unknown Archetypes Deck and Guidebook*. San Francisco: HarperOne, 2019.

———. *The Wild Unknown Tarot Deck and Guidebook*. San Francisco: HarperOne, 2016.

Place, Robert M. *The Fool's Journey: The History, Art, and Symbolism of the Tarot*. Saugerties, NY: Talarius Publications, 2010.

Pollack, Rachel. *Seventy-Eight Degrees of Wisdom: A Book of Tarot*. San Francisco: HarperCollins, 1997.

Sharman-Burke, Juliet. *The Complete Book of Tarot: A Step-by-Step Guide to Help You Become a Better Reader of the Cards*. New York: St. Martin's Press, 1985.

Snow, Cassandra. *Queering the Tarot*. York Beach, ME: Red Wheel/Weiser Books, 2019.

Taylor, PhD. Jill Bolte. *My Stroke of Insight: A Brain Scientist's Personal Journey*. New York: Penguin Books, 2008.

Waite, Arthur Edward, and Pamela Colman Smith. *The Rider-Waite-Smith Tarot Deck*. Stamford, CT: U.S. Games Systems, 1996. Originally published in 1910, by the Rider Company, London.

Wang, Robert. *The Qabalistic Tarot Book: A Textbook of Mystical Philosophy*. Stamford, CT: U.S. Games Systems, 2019.

Ziegler, Gerd. *Tarot: Mirror of the Soul: Handbook for the Aleister Crowley Tarot*. York Beach, ME: Weiser, 1988.

Ceremonial Resources

These resources provided further support for students who wish to deepen their study of ceremony and spirituality. Each book contains ceremonial teachings, practices, and reclaiming myths which helped to inspire many of the practices available in this book.

Chödrön, Pema. *Tonglen: The Path of Transformation*. Halifax, Nova Scotia, Canada: Vajradhatu Publications, 2001.

Jim, Harry Uhane. *Wise Secrets of Aloha: Learn and Live the Sacred Art of Lomilomi*. San Francisco: Weiser Books, 2007.

Koda, Katalin. "Fire of the Goddess: A Ceremony of Self Marriage." Kalapana, HI: From the Void, 2013. https://vimeo.com/65011452.

———. *Fire of the Goddess: Nine Paths to Ignite the Sacred Feminine*. Woodbury, MN: Llewellyn Worldwide, 2011.

Perera, Sylvia Brinton. *Descent to the Goddess: A Way of Initiation for Women*. Toronto: Inner City Books, 1981.

Prechtel, Martín. *The Smell of Rain on Dust: Grief and Praise*. Berkeley, CA: North Atlantic Books, 2015.

Wesselman, Hank. *The Bowl of Light: Ancestral Wisdom from a Hawaiian Shaman*. Boulder, CO: Sounds True, 2011.